WAR IN SHANGRI-LA

To Beth

WAR IN SHANGRI-LA

A Memoir of Civil War in Laos

Mervyn Brown

Foreword by
The Rt Hon The Lord Carrington, KG, CH

The Radcliffe Press
London · New York

Published in 2001 by The Radcliffe Press
6 Salem Road, London W2 4BU

In the United States and in Canada
distributed by St Martin's Press
175 Fifth Avenue, New York NY 10010

ISBN 1–86064–735–9

A full CIP record for this book is available from the British Library
A full CIP record for this book is available from the Library of Congress

Library of Congress Catalog card: available

Typeset in Sabon by Oxford Publishing Services, Oxford
Printed and bound in Great Britain by MPG Books Ltd, Bodmin

Contents

List of Maps and Illustrations

Maps

Illustrations

Acronyms and Abbreviations

CDNI	Committee for the Defence of National Interests
CIA	Central Intelligence Agency
DSO	(Companion of the) Distinguished Service Order
ECOSOC	Economic and Social Council
FE	Far East
FO	Foreign Office
ICC	International Control Commission
LPF	Lao Patriotic Front
LPRP	Lao People's Revolutionary Party
MIC	*Manufactures Indo-Chine*
NLHS	Neo Lao Hak Sat (Lao Patriotic Front)
PA	personal assistant
PAP	People's Action Party
PEO	Programs Evaluation Office
RLA	Royal Lao Army
SEATO	Southeast Asia Treaty Organization
STOL	short takeoff and landing
USAID	United States Agency for International Development
USIS	United States Information Services
USMAAG	United States Military Aid Advisory Group
USOM	United States Operations Mission
VSO	Voluntary Service Overseas

Note on Orthography and Pronunciation

Transliterating Lao script into the Western alphabet inevitably involves some compromises and there are various ways of dealing with the problem. I have chosen to reproduce Lao proper names in the forms established by the French and still in general use in the early 1960s, rather than in more modern phonetic versions favoured by linguists. Thus I spell the Prince of Champassac as Boun Oum, rather than the phonetically more correct Bunum; and I prefer Vientiane to Viang Chan. Although Souvannaphouma is more correctly written as one word I have written it as Souvanna Phouma because that is how his name was always written at the time and also because it enables me to use the abbreviated form 'Souvanna', which is how we usually referred to him.

Similarly in referring to the two main minority groups who play an important role in the story I have used the names that were in general use at the time, though they are now considered politically incorrect. The people of the southern hills whom we called the Kha, meaning 'slaves', are now properly referred to as the Lao Thoeng or Lao of the mountain slopes; and the people living in the northern mountains whom we called the Meo, meaning 'savages', are now correctly called the Hmong, an ethnic group within a wider category known as the Lao Sung or 'Lao of the mountain tops'. But to avoid confusing readers who knew Laos in earlier times I have retained 'Kha' and

'Meo', which were the names invariably used in speech and documents in my time and also in most of the books written about the period.

As a general rule the Lao names are pronounced as in French, for example 'ou' is pronounced 'oo' as in 'moon'. The main problem is with 'ph' and 'th', which are *not* pronounced as in 'phone' or 'thing' but as strong aspirated 'p' and 't', to distinguish them from the unaspirated 'p' and 't' which sound almost like 'b' and 'd' respectively. Similarly 'kh' is a strongly aspirated 'k' while the non-aspirated 'k' sounds almost like 'g'. For the few Lao phrases that appear in the text I have used my own transliteration to give Anglophone readers an idea of what the Lao phrases sound like.

Foreword by Lord Carrington

In his introduction to this book, Mervyn Brown suggests that it may correct the impression that a diplomat's life is a very easy one. There is, indeed, a belief that diplomats live on champagne and cocktail parties and enjoy a life of endless leisure and pleasure. Those who read this book will realize how wrong they are. They will also realize that foreign postings can be quite exciting, as well as involving decisions which can affect, not just the countries to which diplomats are accredited, but large regions of the world.

It has to be said that Mervyn Brown and his wife are singularly well equipped to live in and deal with unusual situations. I stayed with him once in Dar es Salaam, marooned by an air strike. It was not a country fraught with the problems that bedevilled Laos, but it had its difficulties. What was remarkable about my host and his wife was their wide interest in everything that was happening: people, politics and culture. They brought with them, wherever they went, a talent for and love of music. They took part in all activities of the Embassy and the life of Tanzania and, wherever they went, will doubtless be remembered for their tennis. They were a formidable pair.

It's not surprising therefore that, as a comparatively young man, Sir Mervyn found his posting in Laos exhilarating. Having been in Singapore before going to Laos, he was clearly not as starry eyed as one former Ambassador, who brought his Continental Bentley to

Vientiane and was rather taken aback by the road system — or rather lack of it!

Laos was, as he says, Shangri-La with political problems. The highlight of his book is his kidnapping by the Pathet Lao, a month's experience which he recounts vividly, but with restraint. It must have been, to say the least of it, a disagreeable, if exciting experience, not knowing what was in store, what was likely to happen, or how long he would be held. It is typical of bureaucracy that, on his release he received a letter from the Foreign Office suggesting that he should not claim subsistence allowance for food during his captivity since, during that time, he was still receiving his foreign allowance, less, of course, 15 per cent for absence from your post!

It is, however, the political situation in Laos which dominates the book. The tortuous machinations and intrigues of the various factions, the interplay between the Americans and the Europeans, the fears of the Thais and the support given by the Soviet Union to the Pathet Lao are recounted with clarity and an impending sense of doom. He is both critical and fair-minded about American policy.

With hindsight it is, of course, very easy to criticize, for we know now what happened. The disaster of the Vietnam war and the humiliation of America is recent history. At the time of the Laotian crisis, the Cold War was at its height. There was real anxiety about the expansion of the Soviet Union and we already had abundant evidence of what they were doing in Europe and elsewhere. It is easy to forget the genuine fears based on what we then knew.

We were not then aware of the fatal weakness of the communist system and, as it seems now, its inevitable collapse. The domino theory seemed, at that time, to be a likely outcome of a communist advance in Southeast Asia, with all that that entailed. Nevertheless, there is no doubt that, had there been more support for the neutralists and Souvanna Phouma, there would have been a different outcome, as indeed there might have been in Vietnam, had the Geneva Agreement been implemented.

Mervyn Brown retails the unfolding tragedy with great sympathy and skill. His colleagues in the small diplomatic corps in Vientiane are treated, frailties and all, with understanding and humour, and it is typical of him that he has kept in touch with so many of those in the

British Embassy over the years. His affection for the Laotian people is evident through the whole book and I suspect that many people, after they have read this fascinating book, knowing that they are unlikely to be kidnapped, will want to visit Shangri-La.

Peter Carrington
February 2001

Introduction

For some time friends and colleagues have been urging me to write about my experiences in Laos, especially my period of capture by Pathet Lao guerrillas, which briefly made headlines in 1962. There was never any question of my doing so while I was still in the Diplomatic Service, as I would have been considerably inhibited in my comments on events and personalities and also subject to Foreign Office censorship. I retired 20 years after leaving Laos but then thought it would be worth waiting another ten years until the diplomatic correspondence of the period was opened for inspection in the Public Records Office. This would not only ensure that there was no risk of breaching security regulations but also enable me to refresh my memory.

This book does not claim to be a serious history of the Laotian crisis of 1960 to 1963, but simply a personal memoir of what it was like to be a middle-ranking diplomat in a remote country caught up in a civil war that threatened at one time to provoke a wider conflict. I have therefore, with one exception, deliberately avoided consulting other accounts of the period and have relied mainly on my personal recollections. However, as I have also consulted the Public Records Office archives in detail to confirm or correct my memory of what happened, this account may be of some interest to future historians. I hope that it might also do something to correct the impression fostered by the media that a diplomat's life abroad is one of flesh-pots and luxury in sophisticated capitals such as Paris, Brussels and Rome. Such an impression might have had some justification in the early part of the last century, but is totally outmoded today. Nowadays most British diplomats are likely to spend at least a substantial part of their career in smaller and less comfortable posts in sub-Saharan Africa, Latin America, the Middle East, Southeast Asia or former Soviet Central Asia. These have their own rewards, but in many of them political instability and civil war have added local security risks to the global threat of terrorism which affects all our diplomatic posts even, or perhaps especially, the glamorous ones.

The one other work I consulted while writing the book was *Laos: Buffer State or Battleground* by my former colleague Hugh Toye. Based on his first-hand experience of Laos during the crucial years 1960 and 1961 and subsequent research while holding a fellowship at Nuffield College Oxford, it was considered the best history of Laos when it appeared in 1968 and had no serious rival for nearly thirty years. I have drawn on it extensively for my summary of previous history in my Chapter 2 and for some of the background of the later chapters. It was only after I had completed my first 11 chapters that I became aware of Martin Stuart-Fox's *A History of Laos*, published in 1997. This admirable and well-researched account brings the story up to the 1990s. I found it particularly useful in writing my penultimate chapter and I have also drawn on it for some details and corrections in the earlier chapters.

I am also grateful to Hugh Toye, David and Philippa Campbell and other former colleagues for much helpful advice and comments. The opinions are of course my own and are the same as those I expressed at the time, without benefit of hindsight.

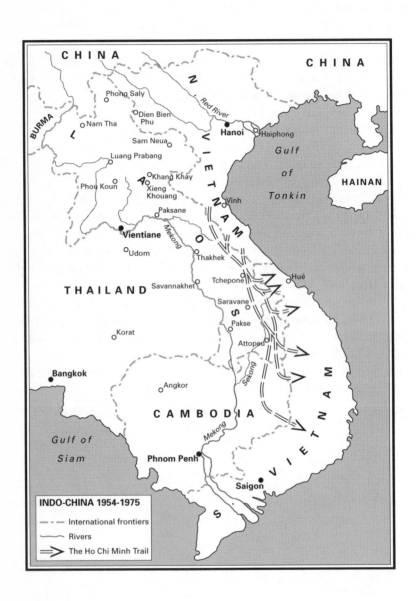

CHINA

CHINA

BURMA

L A O S

VIETNAM

Phong Saly

Nam Tha

Dien Bien Phu

Red River

Hanoi

Haiphong

Gulf

of

Tonkin

HAINAN

Sam Neua

Luang Prabang

Khang Khay

Xieng Khouang

Phou Koun

Vinh

Paksane

Mekong

Vientiane

Udom

Thakhek

THAILAND

Savannakhet

Tchepone

Hué

Saravane

Pakse

Korat

Attopeu

Sekong

VIETNAM

Bangkok

Angkor

CAMBODIA

Gulf of
Siam

Mekong

Phnom Penh

S

Saigon

INDO-CHINA 1954-1975

International frontiers

Rivers

The Ho Chi Minh Trail

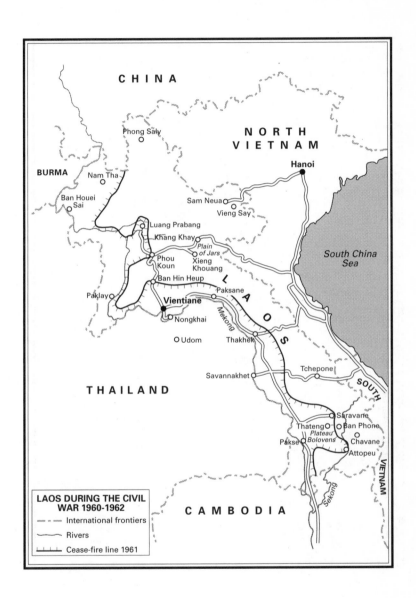

LAOS DURING THE CIVIL WAR 1960-1962

~~~~~~ ~ ~ International frontiers

~~~~ Rivers

⊢⊣⊣⊣⊣ Cease-fire line 1961

CHINA

NORTH
VIETNAM

Hanoi

BURMA

Phong Saly

Nam Tha

Ban Houei
Sai

Sam Neua

Vieng Say

Luang Prabang

Khang Khay

Plain
of Jars

Phou
Koun

Xieng
Khouang

Ban Hin Heup

Paklay

Paksane

Vientiane

Nongkhai

Udom

Thakhek

Mekong

South China
Sea

L A O S

SOUTH

Savannakhet

Tchepone

THAILAND

Saravane

Thateng

Ban Phone

Plateau
Bolovens

Pakse

Chavane

Attopeu

VIETNAM

CAMBODIA

Sekong

xvii

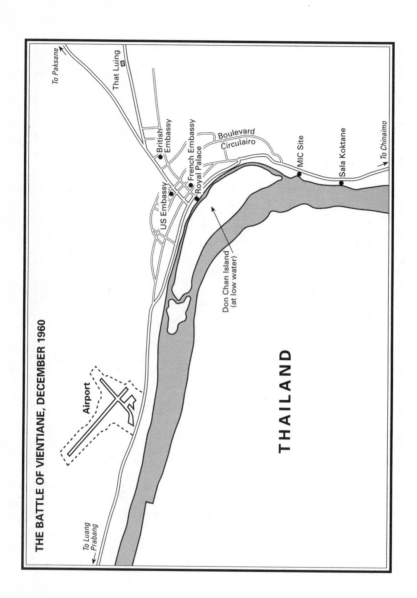

THE BATTLE OF VIENTIANE, DECEMBER 1960

To Paksane

That Luing

British Embassy

French Embassy

Boulevard
Circulairo

Royal Palace

US Embassy

MIC Site

Sala Koktane

To Chinaimo

Don Chan Island
(at low water)

Airport

To Luang
Prabang

THAILAND

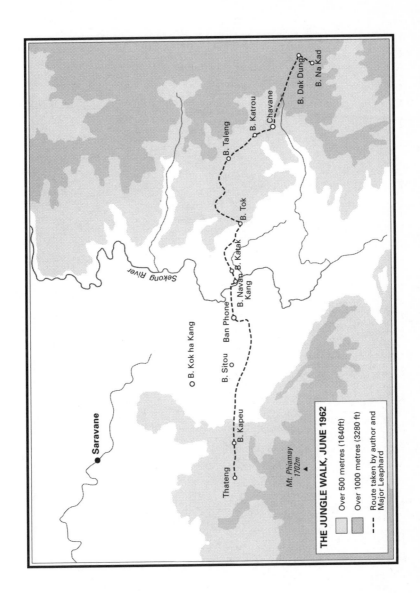

THE JUNGLE WALK, JUNE 1962

Over 500 metres (1640ft)
Over 1000 metres (3280 ft)
Route taken by author and Major Leaphard

Saravane

Sekong River

B. Dak Dung
B. Na Kad
Chavane
B. Katrou
B. Taleng
B. Tok
B. Katak
B. Navan
Kang
Ban Phone
B. Kok ha Kang
B. Sitou
B. Kapeu
Thateng
Mt. Phiamay
1702m

xix

1

Life Before Laos

When I joined the Foreign Office in 1949 I had a picture in my mind of tall, craggy-faced, grey-moustached ambassadors with names like Sir Hughe Montgomery Knatchbull-Hugesson negotiating treaties in the chancelleries of Europe when they were not attending glittering receptions in high-ceilinged ballrooms surrounded by glamorous women. Though lacking the height, the craggy features, the moustache and the aristocratic name I hoped that one day I might be enjoying a similar life style. And if one of the glamorous women turned out to be a beautiful spy trying to seduce state secrets out of me, well that would be an interesting challenge.

So what was I doing just over a decade later lying face down on the floor while howitzer shells exploded only 50 metres either side and a tank battle raged in the road outside? Or spending the night in an unbelievably seedy hotel in a remote mountain village being kept awake by rowdy drunken Soviet Russian pilots in the room next door? And especially what was I doing as a prisoner of a guerrilla band, tied up and being led like a dog through even remoter jungle where life had changed little since the Stone Age?

In retrospect it was perhaps not too surprising that these things, and much more, happened to me in Laos during my posting there in the early 1960s. At that time Vientiane was considered, with the possible exception of Djakarta, the least desirable posting in the Foreign Service. This was partly because it was remote and seemingly a backwater far removed from the areas of major British interest; but mainly because living conditions were decidedly primitive and the normal Western amenities and facilities for recreation almost non-existent. When the first British Ambassador — a somewhat eccentric Irish peer Lord Talbot de Malahide — was appointed in 1955, the embassy office was a Nissen hut divided into two rooms by a blanket hung on a rope. The front room housed the archives and the junior officers. Behind the blanket was the Ambassador's office, furnished with a desk, a few chairs and what seemed to be a low square table covered with another blanket which when removed revealed the office safe. There was no plumbing and the first junior Chancery officer Richard Parsons (later our Ambassador to Spain and Sweden) had the unusual task for a diplomat of planning and supervising the digging of earth latrines. By the time we arrived five years later the Ministry of Works had built a small embassy office and several houses so that conditions had much improved. But as often happens the reputation lingered on so that news of my posting was greeted with commiseration from my colleagues.

In fact commiserations were not really appropriate. The Foreign Office view of Laos was too much influenced by the mundane matter of the lack of creature comforts. Other people who got to know Laos well, especially the French who governed it for 60 years, took a different view. For them it was one of the places in the world which came closest to idealistic concepts of 'earthly paradise', 'other Eden' or 'Shangri-La'. In the nineteenth-century scramble for colonies in Africa and elsewhere it might be said that the British, with their command of the sea, were able to secure most of the economically worthwhile countries such as Malaya, South Africa, East Africa and Nigeria, leaving the French mainly with vast areas of the Sahara desert. But the French were able to pick up some of the most idyllic and charming spots on earth, including Tahiti, Madagascar and Laos. The French view of Laos may have been unduly influenced by the experiences of young district officers who, when touring their district, would be offered the pick of a village's nubile young women as companion for the night. But if the beauty and charm of its women were a major attraction, Laos had much more to offer. The landscape of forest-clad mountains and vertical limestone cliffs was often spectacular. The sparse population was mostly scattered in small villages of houses on stilts surrounded by rice fields where, in the absence of modern development, the people continued their tranquil way of life as they had done for centuries. In the few towns the all-pervading Buddhist religion, with its temples, pagodas and orange-robed monks imposed an aura of peace and tranquillity. While the administrative capital Vientiane was not a particularly attractive town, the royal capital of Luang Prabang, as I was to discover later, could have served as the setting for a Hollywood remake of *Lost Horizon*. And the medieval trappings of the ancient Lao monarchy, supported by a full cast of princes and other dignitaries, seemed to belong to a fairy tale rather than the modern world.

What my colleagues and I did not envisage was that within weeks of our arrival the country would be plunged into civil war and be transformed from a backwater into the centre of a major world crisis. It was the contrast between the idyllic, almost fairy-tale, background and the grim political-military situation, threatening at one time to provoke a world war, which gave a special flavour to our work in Laos and made it the most memorable of our postings.

I had only myself to blame for being sent to Laos. Until then my career had followed a fairly standard pattern. After an initial year in the Foreign Office I was sent in 1950 to Buenos Aires for the usual three years. It was a glamorous posting, almost living up to my expectations of what was perhaps already an outdated image of the diplomatic life. Argentina was still a land of plenty, contrasting sharply with the severely rationed Britain I had left behind (I put on 20 pounds extra weight in my first six months); and social life was a round of cocktail parties, dinners and dances given by the Diplomatic Corps and the large and wealthy foreign business community. We had substantial commercial interests in the country, and Argentina was still a major source of our meat supplies, which were the subject of inter-governmental negotiations each year. There was plenty of political interest in observing the Perón regime at its height in the years before the death of the extraordinary Evita in 1952. And in the background was the constantly simmering dispute over the Falkland Islands and the Falkland Islands Dependencies, as the territories in the Antarctic claimed by Britain were called. During my time in Buenos

Aires, Perón, pursuing an expansionist policy in the Antarctic, had the temerity to send Argentine troops to set up a camp on the airstrip of one of the British bases. But he misjudged the temper of the British Prime Minister, one Winston Churchill. The Argentine interlopers were removed as illegal immigrants by policemen from the Falkland Islands, backed by a company of marines and a frigate. This led to an explosion of anti-British feeling and demonstrations against the embassy, but this soon died down and life resumed its agreeable course.

My next posting was to New York where I worked in the British Mission to the United Nations. My responsibilities were social and human rights' questions in the Third Committee of the General Assembly, various specialist Commissions and the Economic and Social Council (ECOSOC). Not wildly exciting, but an excellent training in the skills of diplomacy, since nearly every working day was spent in committees with representatives of other countries negotiating resolutions and agreements and learning a great deal about the interests, policies and attitudes of the governments concerned. And there was all the fun and excitement of living in New York, with the added bonus of six weeks in Geneva every year for the summer meeting of ECOSOC.

It was during my last Geneva ECOSOC meeting in 1956 that Nasser announced his takeover of the Suez Canal, and when I returned to the Foreign Office at the end of August to join the African Department I found myself in the thick of the ensuing crisis. At that time virtually all of Africa south of the Sahara was still under colonial rule and so the direct responsibilities of the African Department were limited to North Africa, the Horn of Africa and the newly independent Sudan. It was in fact to the Sudan desk that I was officially posted. But on my arrival at the Office on my first day I found that, with the Suez crisis raging at full blast, the Suez desk officer had gone on leave prior to a posting abroad. So, despite having no experience of Africa or the Middle East, I was given the Suez desk in addition to Sudan. The first day, when I did not leave the office until 10.00 p.m., set the pattern for the next four months. The crassly misconceived invasion of Egypt took the Department completely by surprise — only a very few senior officers were in on the secret — and unleashed unprecedentedly passionate feelings in the Office. Unlike Munich, when there was a substantial division of opinion, there was virtual unanimity in condemning Eden. I fully shared those feelings, though with regret as Eden had been a boyhood hero from his days as the handsome, debonair, young Foreign Secretary opposing the dictators in the 1930s. This is not the place for a full account of my experiences at this time, culminating in an extraordinary scene when the members of the African Department, whose offices overlooked No. 10 Downing Street, rushed to the window and booed when Eden emerged to the cheers of the crowd. For the moment suffice it to say that after the collapse of Eden's policies and the withdrawal of our troops, I handed over the enormous task of cleaning up the mess to several other pairs of hands and reverted to dealing solely with Sudan. However, over the next two years I was also assigned to dealing at desk level with a series of crises arising from the transition from colonial status to independence in Libya, Tunisia, Algeria and the Horn of Africa.

It was perhaps as a reward for all this hard work that I was posted to Singapore early in 1959. This was regarded as a good posting from the career point of view: my immediate predecessor went on to become Ambassador in Tokyo and another finished up as Ambassador in Paris. Whitehall is of course the great place for making a reputation and impressing your superiors; and Singapore at the time was a kind of mini-Whitehall. The area of Southeast Asia contained an unusual mix of colonies, Commonwealth countries and foreign countries, which were dealt with respectively by three different government departments — the Colonial Office, the Commonwealth Relations Office and the Foreign Office. The government had accordingly appointed a commissioner-general for Southeast Asia, based in Singapore, to coordinate policies in the area. The commissioner-general also acted as chairman of the British Defence Coordination Committee (Far East) consisting of himself and the commanders-in-chief of our naval, military and air forces in the Far East; and as British representative on the Council of the Southeast Asia Treaty Organization (SEATO), which had its headquarters in Bangkok. In his office in Phoenix Park he was supported by a sizeable staff drawn from the armed forces, the intelligence community and various government departments. My job was FO representative on the Joint Intelligence Staff (FE) with a territorial brief covering Indonesia and Malaysia.

The Commissioner-General at the time was a senior FO man, Sir Robert Scott (known as Rob), an outstanding civil servant who on leaving Singapore became Permanent Secretary in the Ministry of Defence, a unique appointment for a diplomat. He also had the rare experience of being able to read his own obituary in *The Times*. In 1941 he had been caught in Singapore when the Japanese invaded Malaya. He managed to get away on the last ship to leave Singapore, but it was sunk by Japanese bombers. He escaped in a small boat which landed in Sumatra but was picked up there by Japanese troops and sent back to the notorious Changi gaol in Singapore. There he was subjected to various tortures, including being led out to be shot only to be reprieved at the last minute. He survived the war but had been posted 'missing believed dead', and an obituary had appeared in *The Times* written by the paper's Far East correspondent Bill Morrison.

When they met after the war Rob thanked Bill for the kind things he had written in the obituary and jokingly offered to return the compliment. Sadly the occasion arose much sooner than anyone expected, when Bill was killed in an air crash. He achieved posthumous fame in the pages of *A Many-Splendoured Thing*, a fictionalized account of his love affair with the author Han Suyin.

Life in Singapore, then in its final years as a British colony, was very agreeable, combining the attractions of the tropics — notably lots of sunshine and the availability of servants — with the amenities of Western civilization including excellent services, security and shopping, not forgetting first-rate tennis at the Tanglin Club. There were also the attractions of Chinese culture. My wife Beth and I took lessons in Mandarin from a charming lady from Beijing, married to a French *vicomte* who was head of the Alliance Française in Singapore. At the time the Chinese capital was generally referred to as Peking, but she taught us that the correct name in Mandarin was Beijing, pronounced 'Bay-tsing'. She also introduced us to Chinese films and once took us to a Chinese play called *The Storm*: a classic melodrama of passion and unknowing incest inside an extended Chinese family taking place during a fierce tropical storm. At the climax the eldest son of the house, having just discovered that his three-months pregnant girlfriend is his half-sister, rushes out into the garden; there is a tremendous clap of thunder and the head servant enters, bows politely and reports 'Sorry. Young master killed by lightning.'

We lived in a comfortable bungalow with a garden and a staff of a cook, an amah/housekeeper, and a gardener. The work promised to be interesting, as all the posts in the area, from Karachi to Beijing, copied their important reports to us. But after a time I began to feel frustrated. However interesting the reports might be, we had no responsibility for taking action on them, beyond summarizing them for intelligence reports. Responsibility for policy rested with Whitehall and the posts in the countries concerned. Hours were nevertheless long, mainly because most of my working days were taken up with time-consuming and inefficient committee drafting sessions, so that it was necessary to stay late and come in at weekends, even sometimes on Sundays, to catch up with reading the great volume of paper that crossed our desks. Eventually I addressed a long minute to my superiors complaining of the inefficiency of the system and suggesting that the committee drafting sessions should be abolished. This caused a bit of a stir, mainly at the idea of a relatively junior officer questionng well-established procedures. In due course some minor modifications were made to the system; and I was shortly afterwards transferred from the intelligence staff to the more interesting Joint Planning Staff (FE), where the work involved attending monthly meetings of SEATO in Bangkok and one annual meeting of the SEATO Council which that year was held in Washington. But my discontent had been noted, and I was the obvious candidate when an unexpected vacancy occurred at our embassy in Laos in the spring of 1960. Given the reputation of Vientiane, I felt that there was an element of punishment in the posting, but it turned out to be the best thing that could have happened to me.

One area of disappointment in Singapore had been the quality of the domestic cooking. Having learnt to appreciate Pekinese, Cantonese, Shanghai and Szechuan food in New York's Chinatown, we had been looking forward to enjoying similar delights in our own home. But we found that all the good Chinese cooks were working in restaurants, where they were better paid than in private houses. Our own cook, a charming man whom we had inherited with the bungalow, came like most private cooks from Hainan, the island off the south-east coast of China where the plain cooking bore the same relation to the mainland food as British cooking in those days did to French *haute cuisine*. On top of this Ah Chow, like the many other Hainanese cooks, had served under various British memsahibs and had been taught good plain English cooking — roast meats, boiled vegetables, suet puddings and custard. This was not really suitable for diplomatic entertaining and so after a time we found him another post and advertised for a replacement. We found an excellent cook, but he did not last long as we soon discovered that he was in the advanced stages of tuberculosis. So we advertised again and we found Danny.

Whereas previous applicants for the post had been interviewed in the kitchen, somehow it seemed right to interview Danny in the sitting room. He was young, slim, handsome and elegantly dressed and moved with a grace later explained by some ballet lessons in his past. Unlike the general run of Chinese servants who spoke only their Chinese dialect and pidgin English, Danny had been educated at an English school and spoke excellent English. He explained that good jobs were scarce in Singapore; he hoped that if he worked for us we would in due course take him back to England where employment prospects were better. He admitted that he had never cooked professionally before but enjoyed cooking for himself and his friends. He mentioned a few enticing dishes such as prawns with pineapple and chilli, and we engaged him on the spot. As he looked down his nose at the cook's living quarters he was installed in our guest bedroom, where the dressing table was soon covered with an array of hair-dressings, after-shave lotions and colognes.

We were not disappointed. Danny produced a variety of interesting dishes in the Malayan Chinese style, with a fondness for chilli, which is alien to the main Chinese tradition. And he impressed our guests. I recall his first cocktail party, when he floated elegantly around offering trays of cocktail eats and saying 'Do try one of these. I made them myself.' But the news of our posting to Laos was a blow to his plans. Very much an urban type, he viewed with dismay the idea of living in what he imagined, rightly, as the primitive conditions of Laos. When we told him that we could still take him back to London at the end of the Laos posting, he reluctantly agreed to come with us on condition that we took along his cousin Billy as second servant. Billy turned out to be in most ways the antithesis of Danny — Chinese-educated with little English, short but solidly built and strong, quiet and hard-working. The idea was that he would do the cleaning and the heavy work, leaving Danny to exercise his artistic talents in the kitchen.

So in June 1960 we set off for Laos. In those days it was still customary to travel between postings by sea, which was cheaper than air travel and had the great advantage that you could take with you your heavy luggage, in our case augmented by an upright piano bought in Singapore — an essential part of our household. As there was no available sailing of a passenger ship we travelled with Danny and Billy on a tiny coastal steamer, with two passenger cabins, which took four days to reach Bangkok. From there we took a daylong train journey north to Nongkhai, the town on the south bank of the Mekong river, which acts as the frontier between Laos and Thailand. Here we were met by Peter Newman, the Administration Officer from the embassy in Vientiane, some 12 miles upstream on the north bank of the Mekong, together with David Wilson, Third Secretary, and Shirley McColl, wife of the Second Secretary Colin McColl. While Peter Newman stayed on to organize the movement of our heavy baggage, the rest of us set off upstream in a motorboat with David at the helm. It was just at the beginning of the rainy season, so the downstream current was not too strong. We chugged past villages clinging to the steep banks on both sides, with wooden houses on stilts, children bathing and women washing clothes in the river, every-one smiling and waving at us. After about an hour we pulled into the bank on the north side to land in the garden of our new home. A delightful way to arrive at a new post but, as we soon discovered, an illegal one, as we had failed to pass through the customs and immi-gration office located on the north bank opposite Nongkhai. But all was amicably resolved and we heard for the first time the phrase that summed up the Lao people's easygoing attitude to life: 'Bo pen nyang' — 'It doesn't matter'.

2

A Short History Lesson

The slow boat to Bangkok gave me a chance to read up on the history of Laos, which was not one of the countries I had dealt with in Singapore. Like all the peoples of Southeast Asia, the Lao had originally come from China (their language, which like Mandarin has four tones, is in effect a Chinese dialect, but written not with characters but with a 46-letter alphabet derived from Sanskrit). They are part of the Thai race consisting of the Siamese (Thai Siam), the Lao (Thai Lao) and various smaller hill tribes of northern Thailand and Laos including the Red Thai (Thai Daeng) and the Black Thai (Thai Dam). The Shan people of north-east Burma are also ethnically Thai. Today the Lao and the Siamese (now known usually as the Thai) are still very similar. There are differences in the languages — Thai is more complex with a larger vocabulary — but they are mutually comprehensible. The main distinguishing features of the Lao are that they build their houses on stilts, eat sticky rice and play the *khène*, a double bank of pipes tuned to a pentatonic scale — do, me, soh, la, do.

The movement of the Thai peoples into their present homelands was spread over a considerable time, but the main migration took place in the thirteenth century following the Mongol conquest of China. The

Siamese came first to occupy the central and southern plains of modern Thailand, followed by the Lao who occupied the Mekong valley and northern Thailand, driving the original inhabitants into the hills. For the next 600 years they were engaged in intermittent conflict with each other and their neighbours the Vietnamese, the Burmese and the Cambodians, with shifting alliances and alternating periods of ascendancy by each power in turn. (The area of modern Vietnam was traditionally divided into the provinces of Tongking in the north, Annam in the centre and Cochin China in the south; the country as a whole was often called Annam and the people Annamites, but to avoid confusion the terms Vietnam and Vietnamese will be used throughout this book.)

At one stage a Lao prince Fa Ngum in exile in Cambodia returned with Cambodian backing to impose himself as King of Laos, bringing with him from Cambodia Theravada Buddhism and the Prabang, a sacred golden Buddha, in honour of which the name of the ancient capital on the upper Mekong was changed to Luang Prabang. In the sixteenth century a famous warrior king, Settathirat, successfully defended the kingdom in a period of Burmese ascendancy and, finding Luang Prabang too close to the Burmese border, moved the capital to Vientiane. The golden age for Laos came in the seventeenth century under King Souligna Vongsa, who ruled a kingdom comprising more or less the area of modern Laos together with northern and north-eastern Thailand and much of the centre as far south as the city of Korat. In fact most of his subjects were ethnically Lao, as are most of the inhabitants of northern and north-eastern Thailand today.

Souligna Vongsa had no son to succeed him and after his death his empire began to decline and fall apart. One weakness of the Lao kingdom was that it was in effect a confederation of several Thai-Lao states and royal families — Luang Prabang in the north, Xieng Khouang in the north-east, Vientiane in the middle Mekong valley and Bassac to the east of the lower Mekong — any of which might break away or ally itself with one of the neighbouring countries. With the decline of Laos and Cambodia in the eighteenth and nineteenth centuries and the occupation of Burma by the British, Siam and Vietnam became the dominant powers in the area. The Siamese conquered most of the Lao territories south of the Mekong, occupied

Vientiane and exacted tribute from Luang Prabang. Later they reinstated a Lao king in Vientiane, but in 1827 he rashly invaded Siam and was heavily defeated. The Siamese again occupied Vientiane and this time burned and looted it. They also compelled the people of several Lao towns north of the Mekong to move to the south bank, leaving the north bank largely depopulated. About the same time Vietnam annexed the kingdom of Xieng Khouang, but after Siam had encouraged a rebellion the kingdom was restored, paying tribute to both Vietnam and Siam. Similarly a Siamese attempt to annex Cambodia, where the Vietnamese were strongly entrenched, ended with the installation of a Cambodian king (Ang Duong, great-great-grandfather of King Sihanouk) who paid tribute to both of his powerful neighbours.

Thus, before the French intervention, Vietnam and Siam had achieved some kind of equilibrium in the area, with Xieng Khouang and Cambodia acting as buffer states. In Laos the north side of the Mekong remained depopulated. The Annamite chain of mountains separating the Thai peoples from the Vietnamese was occupied mainly by minority peoples, reinforced by a continuing flow of recent immigrants from China, such as the Meo and the Yao. The southern highlands were still peopled by the aborigines pushed into the mountains by the successive waves of Siamese and Lao immigrations, and known as the Kha on the Lao side and Moi on the Vietnamese side of the watershed.

This uneasy balance was upset by the arrival of the French. Starting in 1858 they gradually took over Vietnam and then, inheriting Vietnam's historic expansionist role, occupied Cambodia and the area of modern Laos, compelling Siam to surrender all its fiefdoms on the left bank of the Mekong plus Sayaboury province in the north-west on the right bank of the river. The French had ambitions to control both sides of the Mekong and to extend their dominion into Siam, but were prevented from advancing further by the British, who had important commercial interests in Siam. By assuming the role of buffer state between British and French imperialism Siam was able to survive the colonial era as an independent kingdom.

The French acquisition of Lao territory was completed in 1907, when Siam accepted the new frontiers. But even the French were never able to subdue the aboriginal Kha people in the southern highlands. Starting in 1895, various revolts in the Plateau Bolovens area were not finally subdued until 1910. Even after that date one of the Kha leaders Kommadom was able to hold out and evade capture in the mountainous jungle east of the Sekong river until, betrayed by one of his own people, he was ambushed and killed in 1936. His eldest son Sithone Kommadom was wounded and captured at the same time, along with two other sons, and sentenced to life imprisonment in the remote exile of Phong Saly, 800 kilometres away in the north of Laos. But even after 1936 the French were not able to establish an effective administration in the Kha area.

Control of the northern hill tribes was also difficult, and a major uprising in 1918 took three years to subdue. Throughout the country, even in the Mekong valley where most of the Lao people displaced by the Siamese had returned, the French presence remained relatively light. French interests were concentrated in Vietnam and they set up a unified Indo-Chinese empire with its capital in Hanoi. Laos and Cambodia were treated as up-country regions of the empire, backward but picturesque and highly agreeable postings for the less ambitious members of the French colonial service. Vientiane became the administrative capital of the region of Laos, but the heads of the royal houses of Luang Prabang and Champassac (as Bassac came to be called) were respected as titular rulers of their kingdoms in the north and south respectively. The Vietnamese, more numerous, more dynamic and harder working than their easygoing inland neighbours, provided most of the lower-ranking officials and technicians of the regional administrations, as well as much of the small-scale commercial enterprise. By 1940 there were an estimated 50,000 Vietnamese living in Laos; they constituted a majority of the population in Vientiane and other towns, and their children filled more than half the places in the few schools that existed.

This covert occupation of Laos by the Vietnamese worried the Siamese, especially after the collapse of France in 1940, when they sought to recover at least some of their former territories in Laos and Cambodia. The Japanese, by now the dominant power in the area, allowed Vichy France to continue to administer Indo-China, in return for making its economic resources available to Japan. The Siamese, who had recently renamed their country Thailand to emphasize long-term ambitions to incorporate all branches of the Thai race, also avoided Japanese occupation by collaborating with Japan, to the point of declaring war on Britain and USA in 1942. They were rewarded when, after a clash between Siamese and French soldiers, Japan compelled France to hand over to Thailand the Lao provinces of Bassac and Sayaboury. The reappearance of the Siamese on the right bank of the Mekong opposite Luang Prabang alarmed the royal family there, but in compensation the French agreed that the kingdom of Luang Prabang should be extended to include the provinces of Xieng Khouang, Vientiane and Nam Tha, to cover the whole of northern Laos. With the rival kingdom of Bassac incorporated into Siam, Luang Prabang became the leading royal house in the country. The king at the time was the long-reigning Sisavang Vong, who succeeded to the throne in 1905. His role was mainly symbolic and religious. Administrative matters were left to the Maha Uparaja or Viceroy Prince Phetsarath, eldest surviving son of an earlier viceroy Boun Khong whose numerous progeny was destined to play a major role in Laotian history over the next half-century.

The collapse of Vichy France in 1944 created a power vacuum in Indo-China. The Vichy commander Admiral Decoux assumed full powers, but it was obviously only a matter of time before the loyalty of the French military and the civilian administration would switch to General de Gaulle. To forestall this the Japanese sent in strong forces to take control in March 1945. They announced that the colonial regime in Indo-China was at an end and that Vietnam, Cambodia and Laos had become independent states within Japan's New Order. In Vietnam the nationalist Viet Minh movement led by Ho Chi Minh seized the opportunity to take control. Cambodian leaders also accepted independence. But in Luang Prabang lack of confidence in the ability of an independent Laos to resist Vietnamese expansion led the Crown Prince Savang Vatthana to proclaim, in the name of his father, continued loyalty to France and to call for a general uprising against the Japanese. Within weeks the Japanese occupied Luang Prabang and compelled the king to declare independence. (They also released a number of Laotians imprisoned by the French, including Sithone Kommadom and his two brothers.) The viceroy Phetsarath, realizing that with the French ousted the Japanese were the only protection against the Vietnamese, prudently decided to cooperate with them. But in the south, French and Laotian troops taking refuge in the jungle formed the nucleus of an effective partisan force during the remaining months of Japanese power. Prince Boun Oum, the young head of the ruling family of Champassac, distinguished himself as a courageous guerrilla leader and survived several hair's breadth escapes from Japanese troops, thanks apparently to his ability to make himself invisible.

The suddenness of the Japanese surrender in August 1945 caused chaos throughout Southeast Asia. The Viet Minh, with American encouragement and support, extended their control over the whole of Vietnam, hoping to face the Allied forces with a *fait accompli* and to prevent a return of the French. In Luang Prabang, Phetsarath had set up an independence movement the Lao Issara (Free Laos), which included his brother Prince Souvanna Phouma and his half-brother Prince Souphanouvong; he now declared independence for the whole of Laos. But he was opposed by Prince Boun Oum, who had invited French troops to return to southern Laos, and by King Sisavang Vong who in October dismissed Phetsarath as viceroy and prime minister. The Lao Issara set up a provisional national assembly and a provisional government and invited the king to become a constitutional monarch. When he refused, the national assembly voted to depose him. However, as French troops began to return to Indo-China in force, Phetsarath repeated the invitation to the King, who this time reluctantly accepted it. Shortly afterwards, in April–May 1946, the French reoccupied Laos, and Phetsarath and most of the Lao Issara fled to Bangkok.

The French accepted the unity of Laos, and Thailand was compelled to return the provinces of Bassac and Sayaboury. A new constitution was drawn up and in May 1947 Laos was proclaimed an autonomous constitutional monarchy within the French Union, with France retaining control of foreign affairs and defence. Prince Boun Oum accepted subordination to Luang Prabang in return for the title of Inspector General of the Kingdom, with precedence after the King. Following a general election a new government was formed under Prince Souvannarath, another brother of Phetsarath, early in 1948.

These political advances caused a split among the Lao Issara leaders in exile in Bangkok. The moderates, led by Prince Souvanna Phouma and the movement's chief spokesman Katay Don Sasorith, thought that sufficient progress had been made to justify their return to Laos. But Prince Souphanouvong, who had established close relations with the Viet Minh, was not prepared to accept anything less than full independence. As Commander-in-Chief in Phetsarath's provisional government he had fought alongside the Viet Minh in trying to resist the return of the French to Laos in March 1946. In 1947, after fighting had broken out between the French and the Viet Minh, he returned to Laos to try to organize an uprising against the French. He had little success but established useful contact with Sithone Kommadom, who had returned to the south to assume leadership of the Kha, and an anti-French Meo chief Faydang. Faydang's adherence to the Pathet Lao was to cause a deep split among the Meos between Faydang's followers and those of his nephew and rival Touby Lyfung who later were recruited by the French to fight against the hated Vietnamese.

Souphanouvong's chief of staff, one Phoumi Nosavan, visited Vietnam to discuss with Viet Minh leaders a common offensive against the French. Souphanouvong returned to Bangkok where he proposed that the Lao Issara should unite with the Viet Minh under Ho Chi Minh to win independence by force. This proposal was predictably rejected by the other Lao Issara leaders, who regarded the Viet Minh as the greatest long-term threat to the separate identity of Laos, so Souphanouvong broke away from the movement and went off to pursue his own plans with the Viet Minh. In due course, towards the end of 1949, most of the Lao Issara leaders voted to dissolve the movement and returned to Laos, abandoning Phetsarath to continued exile in Bangkok. He would have liked to return, but his role in dethroning the King made reconciliation difficult. He did not return home until 1957, when the King reinstated him as honorary Viceroy but without any official functions. As head of a major branch of the royal family and founder of the Lao Issara he still commanded considerable influence and respect, but he died two years later.

The happy mood of reconciliation in Laos did not last long, as the country became increasingly involved in the war in Vietnam and through this in the global Cold War between the communist countries and the Western powers led by the USA. In the spring of 1953 the Viet Minh invaded northern Laos and advanced on Luang Prabang and Xieng Khouang. The aged King refused to leave Luang Prabang and a famous blind monk soothsayer accurately forecast that the Viet Minh would stop short of the capital. With the onset of the rains in the summer, most of the Viet Minh returned across the frontier. But Souphanouvong, who had entered Laos with them, stayed on in Sam Neua in the extreme north of the country with the nucleus of the Pathet Lao (Lao nation) movement, which he had formed from his splinter group of the Lao Issara. He himself was not a communist, but a nationalist who wanted an independent Laos for the Laotians. But his movement included a number of Laotian members of the Indo-Chinese Communist Party, including Kaysone Phomvihan, Nouhak Phomsavan and Phoumi Vongvichit. The latter (not to be confused with the already-mentioned Phoumi Nosavan, later to play a major role as General Phoumi and leader of the right wing) was a relative moderate, a member of the ruling class and a former governor of Xieng Khouang province; but Kaysone and Nouhak were hardline communists dedicated to the communist takeover of the whole of Indo-China. And Souphanouvong's total dependence on the Viet Minh meant that he would be in no position to impede Vietnamese designs on his country. For the time being he set up a resistance government in Sam Neua and, using the well-tried methods of Mao Tse Tung, developed his support in the countryside and especially among the hill tribes who were traditionally resentful of domination by the Lao of the Mekong valley. Recruitment among the hill peoples was helped by the appointment of the Meo and Kha leaders, Faydang and Sithone, as vice-presidents of the Pathet Lao and ministers without portfolio in the resistance government.

The climactic battle of the war took place in Dien Bien Phu on the northern frontier between Laos and Vietnam, in an area considered to be the cradle of the Lao people. In the run-up to the battle the Viet Minh made several diversionary sorties into Laos, one of which reached Thakhek on the Mekong river. The catastrophic French defeat in May 1954 had a profound effect on Laos as well as France. It strengthened Laotian fears of their powerful neighbour and the apparently invincible Viet Minh troops and left the small Laotian army incapable of dealing with the Pathet Lao, which acquired some of the Viet Minh aura and was believed to be reinforced by Viet Minh soldiers even when it was not. In France, the defeat was the final blow that made French withdrawal from Indo-China inevitable. It was agreed that Indo-China should be discussed at the conference in Geneva where the great powers were already assembled to reach a settlement of the Korean War. At Geneva the attitude of the United States was to be of great importance.

During and after the Second World War the Americans, inspired partly by Roosevelt's aversion to colonialism, supported Ho Chi Minh and at first opposed the French return to Indo-China. The communist takeover in China and Senator McCarthy's campaign against communists and fellow travellers in the government caused a profound change. Most of the Far Eastern experts in the State Department, who were held responsible for the collapse of Chiang Kai-Shek, were removed and their successors were strongly anti-communist or had to appear so. Their thinking was dominated by a belief in a world communist conspiracy in which China and the Soviet Union collaborated to subvert democratic governments and install communist regimes in their place; and in the domino theory which stated that if Vietnam went communist then Cambodia, Laos, Thailand and Malaya would inevitably follow. No one held these beliefs more strongly than the Secretary of State John Foster Dulles, who brought an almost religious fervour to his task of saving the Free World from communism. In accordance with the doctrine 'he that is not with me is against me' he disliked neutralism almost as much as communism, and appeared to believe that the only defence against a communist takeover was a strong right-wing government backed by military force. By the time he became Secretary of State in 1953 the policy of support for Ho Chi Minh had been replaced by support for French colonialism as the only effective barrier against communism. Under Dulles, American military advisers were attached to the French forces and American aid was increased to amount to 70 per cent of the cost of the war.

Dulles was therefore bound to be unhappy with the Geneva settlement of July 1954. This provided for the withdrawal of the French from Indo-China and the temporary partition of Vietnam between a communist north and an anti-communist south, divided by the 17th parallel, but with nationwide elections to unify the country due to take place in July 1956. It was generally assumed that the Viet Minh would win these, partly because the north was more populous than the south, but also because Ho Chi Minh, as the liberator and conqueror of the French, was genuinely popular throughout the country. To give the Thais some assurance and protection against a Viet Minh-dominated Vietnam, it was agreed that Laos and Cambodia should form a neutral buffer zone. The two kingdoms agreed that they would not join any military alliance, allow any foreign military bases on their territory or accept any foreign troops or military advisers other than 5000 French defence and training forces in Laos. The Pathet Lao forces were to be integrated into Laotian national life, after being regrouped in the northern provinces of Sam Neua and Phong Saly. As in Vietnam and Cambodia, an International Commission for Supervision and Control (usually abbreviated to International Control Commission — ICC) consisting of India, Canada and Poland was set up in Laos to supervise the withdrawal of foreign troops and the other provisions of the agreement.

With Senator McCarthy still rampaging in Washington, Dulles could not afford to be associated too closely with a settlement that handed over a territory to communism, and he managed to avoid signing the agreement. He acquiesced reluctantly and only on condition that Britain and France joined the USA in a mutual assistance defence treaty with Australia, New Zealand, Pakistan, Thailand and the Philippines, the Southeast Asia Treaty Organization (SEATO), to resist the further spread of communism in the area. By a separate protocol the signatories agreed to recognize armed aggression against Laos, Cambodia or South Vietnam as endangering their own peace and security and to react accordingly (in ways unspecified).

If the 1954 Geneva settlement had been scrupulously implemented by all parties, it might have secured at least a substantial period of peace in the area. If the 1956 elections had been held in Vietnam and resulted as expected in a Viet Minh victory, Ho Chi Minh might well have concentrated on unifying and building up the country. Having achieved his principal aim he would have had little interest in adventures across his western frontiers, which would have risked confrontation with American military power. The Laos–Cambodia buffer zone worked both ways: it also protected Vietnam from Thai influence and American military bases on its doorstep. But the settlement was soon undermined, mainly because of American influence. The anti-communist government in South Vietnam, faced with the near certainty of a Viet Minh electoral victory in 1956, repudiated the agreement to hold nationwide elections, with the full approval and support of the Americans who were already pouring substantial aid into the south. The subsequent Vietnam War, which was to traumatize the United States in the 1960s and 1970s, was thus made inevitable.

Of the two buffer states Cambodia, with a homogeneous population more or less united under the popular leadership of King Sihanouk, and with a moderately prosperous rice-based economy, posed little problem. But Laos, sparsely-populated, with a hopelessly weak economy and deeply divided ethnically and politically, was ill suited to the role of buffer. Roughly the size and shape of Italy, it had an estimated population of only 2.5 million. Little more than a million of these were the dominant Lao people of the Mekong valley, linked closely to Thailand where many more millions of their fellow Lao lived. Many of the more numerous minority hill tribes had close links with similar ethnic groups across the frontier in Vietnam, and were resentful of the Lao who had traditionally treated them with arrogance and contempt (Kha is a Lao word meaning slave). It is not surprising that the Pathet Lao found its recruits mainly among the hill tribes: while the origin of the movement was in anti-French nationalism, much of its motivating force came from anti-Lao tribalism. Even so, if Laos had been an island the integration of the Pathet Lao with the rest of the nation might well have been achieved peacefully and the people could have returned to their traditional happy lotus-eating existence. But its geographical situation on the frontiers of the Cold War made this unlikely and ultimately impossible. Rather than a buffer, Laos acted as a vacuum, sucking in forces from outside which would eventually tear it apart.

The principal outside force was by now the USA which, having taken over the role of France in covering the substantial Lao budgetary deficit, exercised a major influence on the government. This influence was to be exercised to prevent the integration of the Pathet

Lao on any terms other than virtual Pathet Lao surrender. At first the prospects of integration were good. Prince Souvanna Phouma, who had been Prime Minister since 1951, saw clearly that the country's interests were best served by a policy of neutrality abroad and conciliation at home. He believed that he could work with his half-brother Souphanouvong and wean him away from dependence on the Viet Minh. Following initial talks between the two princes, the withdrawal of French and Viet Minh troops and the regrouping of the Pathet Lao troops in the two northern provinces were completed in November 1954; the Pathet Lao had also agreed that their administrations in the two provinces would be subject to the authority of the government in Vientiane. But meanwhile Souvanna's position had been weakened by the assassination in September of his closest supporter the Minister of Defence Kou Voravong. In November Souvanna resigned and was replaced by Katay Don Sasorith, though Souvanna remained in the government as minister of defence.

Katay, who was from southern Laos, had close links with Thailand, and shared Thai suspicions of the Pathet Lao as a front for Vietnamese expansion into the Mekong valley. In return the Pathet Lao withdrew from him the confidence they had shown in Souvanna Phouma. Prolonged and difficult negotiations broke down over the right of the government to take over the administration of the two Pathet Lao provinces before the general elections due in August 1955. Katay decided to go ahead with the elections, postponed until December, in the remaining provinces under government control, and without the Pathet Lao. After the elections, in which votes were divided among four parties, Katay was unable to muster the necessary majority and resigned, leaving it to Souvanna Phouma again to form the government.

Souvanna resumed negotiations with his half-brother and, despite the open disapproval of the Americans, reached an agreement in principle at the end of 1956, under which supplementary elections would be held to give the Pathet Lao the opportunity to obtain seats in the Assembly and meanwhile they would join a coalition government. The idea of a coalition in particular alarmed the Americans. They seemed to attribute almost mystical powers to communists and to believe that whenever they joined a coalition government it would only be a matter of time before they subverted it from inside and took over sole power themselves (as had happened in Czechoslovakia in 1948). The American Ambassador Graham Parsons, a loyal disciple of Dulles, orchestrated a major campaign against the agreement led by Katay, which caused Souvanna to resign in May 1957. But neither Katay nor anyone else was able to form an alternative government. Souvanna returned to power in August, and on 12 November he and Souphanouvong signed a detailed political and military settlement, which became known as the Vientiane Agreements. Souphanouvong handed over control of the two northern provinces, swore allegiance to the King and, together with Phoumi Vongvichit, joined a new government of national unity headed by Souvanna Phouma.

The sky did not fall in, and the agreed arrangements went well. The 1500 Pathet Lao soldiers chosen for integration into the national army were grouped into two battalions, one stationed at the Plain of Jars, a high plain to the north of Xieng Khouang scattered with large prehistoric stone jars, the other at a village between the Plain and Luang Prabang; the remaining Pathet Lao troops were demobilized back to their villages. Souphanouvong, a highly intelligent man and a trained civil engineer, proved to be a notably effective Minister of the Plan. The Pathet Lao leaders, who meanwhile had set up a political party, the Lao Patriotic Front (Neo Lao Hak Sat — NLHS), settled down in Vientiane and the process of integration seemed to be working. What eventually destroyed it was the supplementary elections held in May 1958.

The four traditional parties already represented in the Assembly saw no reason to combine their forces against the Pathet Lao and each put up a candidate for each of the 21 seats being contested (20 new seats and one vacant). The Pathet Lao/NLHS in alliance with a left-wing Peace Party, won 32 per cent of the vote. But with the non-Pathet Lao vote split they won 13 of the 21 seats (their successful candidates included Prince Souphanouvong and the Kha leader Sithone Kommadom). This Pathet Lao 'victory' in partial elections produced a near-panic reaction from the Americans and Thais. The facts that 68 per cent of the population had voted against the Pathet Lao and that the Pathet Lao deputies would constitute only a fifth of the Assembly of 59 members were brushed aside; the result was presented as a stunning communist victory. (One cannot help wondering whether the course of history would have been altered if there had been a system of proportional representation, under which the Pathet Lao and its allies would have won only seven seats.) Ambassador Parsons, who a few months earlier had returned to Washington to become Assistant Under-Secretary of State for the Far East, was especially shaken because, recognizing that virtually no American aid had percolated through to the countryside, he had promoted a crash programme of rural projects, which he was confident would weaken the appeal of the Pathet Lao in the villages. He and the State Department were also apprehensive of a Congressional Committee enquiry into American aid which was likely to be severely critical. Apart from the expansion of the army from 15,000 to 25,000, there was almost literally nothing to show for the substantial sums poured into the country other than the enrichment of a few government officials and foreign businessmen via corruption and the black market. To forestall or divert criticism it was essential to show a firm line against communist penetration. American aid, on which the Laotian budget was now almost totally dependent, was suspended. The excuse was the need for monetary reform, but the real reason was to force Souvanna Phouma out of office.

The Prince deserved better from the Americans. He was not in the least sympathetic to communism: at the time of the Geneva settlement he had skilfully avoided having Chinese and North Vietnamese embassies by arguing that there was no Chinese Nationalist representation in Vientiane and that the South Vietnamese legation was a relic from pre-independence days which did not justify a similar exchange with Hanoi. After the supplementary elections he had united the 36 non-Pathet Lao deputies in the Assembly in a new party, the Rally of the Lao People. He had also encouraged the formation of a non-parliamentary anti-communist organization of officials and army officers, the Committee for the Defence of National Interests (CDNI). But this counted for nothing against American fears of Pathet Lao subversion of the government and the Assembly. They threw their support behind the CDNI and used it to undermine the Prime Minister. When the new expanded Assembly was inaugurated, a sufficient number of deputies (allegedly bribed by the Americans) voted to block the Prime Minister's reappointment and Souvanna

Phouma resigned. Phoui Sananikone, the able head of a leading Vientiane 'bourgeois' family, who had already been prime minister briefly at the beginning of the 1950s, formed a new government in August 1958. It included four members of the CDNI but predictably the two Pathet Lao ministers were excluded. Prince Souphanouvong became leader of the opposition; Prince Souvanna Phouma was appointed Ambassador in Paris.

Phoui immediately abandoned Souvanna's neutralist policies. Officials suspected of pro-communist sympathies were dismissed and Phoui stated that as far 'as peaceful coexistence is concerned ... we shall coexist with the Free World only.' He also exploited an incident in December when a Laotian military patrol, visiting a village in the north which on the map was just inside Laos but had for a long time been administered by Vietnam, was fired on by Vietnamese troops. This was blown up into a Viet Minh incursion into Lao territory, and Phoui also accused the Pathet Lao of planning an insurrection. Because of this alleged threat the Assembly in January 1959 gave Phoui emergency powers for 12 months. Phoui then formed a more right-wing government including three army officers. One of these was Colonel Phoumi Nosavan, a nephew of Marshal Sarit who had recently assumed dictatorial powers in Thailand on the basis of an alleged communist threat. As we have seen Phoumi had been chief of staff of Prince Souphanouvong in the 1940s, but he had since moved sharply to the right and was seen by the Americans as the future strong man of Laos. Around the same time a Nationalist Chinese consulate was opened in Vientiane and the South Vietnamese legation was raised to the rank of embassy, in breach of undertakings given by Souvanna Phouma to China and North Vietnam.

These significant moves away from neutralism led Prince Souphanouvong, strongly supported by China and North Vietnam, to call for the return of the International Control Commission, which had been withdrawn after the completion of the supplementary elections. Phoui Sananikone rejected the demand and in February made a statement, immediately supported by the Americans, that as Laos had fulfilled its obligations under the Geneva Agreement, it was no longer bound by the limitations on military aid set out in that agreement. Shortly afterwards the Americans brought in 80 Filipino technicians to reinforce their Programs Evaluation Office (PEO), an organization staffed by military in civilian clothes to administer US military aid.

The government now decided to press on with the integration of the two Pathet Lao battalions into the national army, and agreed to accept into the army 105 officers named by the Pathet Lao. A minister later admitted that the intention was that once the integration had taken place the commissions of the Pathet Lao officers could be nullified by requiring them to pass examinations which, in view of their lack of formal education, they were bound to fail. However, on the appointed date, 11 May 1959, the two battalions refused integration, citing various reasons, notably the absence of their principal leaders. The real reason was no doubt the government's retreat from neutralism and the consequent sharp deterioration of the political situation from the Pathet Lao point of view. The government responded by placing Prince Souphanouvong and the three other main Pathet Lao leaders under house arrest and surrounding the two battalions by government troops. On 17 May Souphanouvong agreed to order his soldiers to accept the government's terms. One battalion did so (though many individuals later absconded) but the other battalion escaped in the night with all their families, possessions and arms, to a camp near the North Vietnamese border. The Laotian government denounced the escape as an act of open rebellion and stated that only a military solution now seemed possible.

A few weeks later the US Congressional Committee published its report on American aid operations in Laos, highlighting corruption, mismanagement and wastage. Some urgent action was clearly needed to forestall the obvious next step of reducing the aid. On 29 July the Laotian government announced that frontier posts in Sam Neua had been attacked by Pathet Lao troops supported by Viet Minh. Prince Souphanouvong and the other Pathet Lao deputies were put in prison and Laos complained formally to the United Nations of Vietnamese aggression. Further Pathet Lao/Viet Minh attacks were reported over the next six weeks as the affair was blown up into a major crisis. Units of the US Seventh Fleet were sent into the region and there was talk of sending US troops into Laos. It soon transpired that there had been no Viet Minh invasion, which in any case would have been highly unlikely at the height of the rainy season. What had happened was some minor Pathet Lao military activity, causing panic in government outposts which, to justify their flight, sent grossly exaggerated reports of the strength of the attackers and the involvement of the Viet Minh. These reports were accepted by the government and further embroidered to ensure that there would be no more talk of cutting aid. The tactic succeeded beyond expectations. US military aid for 1959 showed an increase of 30 per cent over 1958; the size of the army was increased to 29,000 men; and the PEO received another 100 military advisers in civilian clothes.

The Americans thus compounded their original error of regarding the communist threat as a military problem, to be countered by ever more military aid, rather than as an essentially political problem deriving mainly from the alienation of the Laotian government from the hill tribes and its failure to take any action to improve the primitive conditions in which the tribes lived. The Pathet Lao, most of them from the hill areas, were able to infiltrate successfully using peaceful methods, working alongside the peasants in the fields and helping them build houses and schools. When the government troops tried to re-establish themselves in the disaffected areas they took on the character of a punitive expedition and further alienated the local people. Moreover, however much money was spent on expanding the Laotian army, the chances of achieving a solution by military means were remote, owing to the ordinary Lao soldier's pathological fear of the Viet Minh, which rubbed off on the Pathet Lao.

The crisis fizzled out, and a UN mission reported no evidence of a Viet Minh invasion. (A story current at the time was that, in an attempt to provide evidence to the UN mission, the government recruited some 'hostesses' from the main nightclub in Vientiane, flew them up to Sam Neua, dressed them as peasants and told them what to say to the mission; the manœuvre failed when a member of the UN mission recognized one of the women whose services he had recently employed.) Hammarskjöld himself visited Laos and advised the government to return to a policy of neutrality, but to no avail. Meanwhile the old King Sisavang Vong died on 29 October 1959 and was succeeded by the crown prince Savang Vatthana. At the end of the year a rift developed between the prime minister Phoui Sananikone and the right-wing CDNI led by Colonel Phoumi, whom Phoui blamed for the fiasco of the Viet Minh 'invasion'. The CDNI wanted to maintain the momentum against the Pathet Lao by establishing dictatorial powers and postponing indefinitely the elections due early in 1960. Phoui and his moderate supporters wished to undertake new negotiations with the Pathet Lao before the elections. Faced with CDNI intransigence Phoui formed a new government, excluding the CDNI members. Phoumi, now promoted to brigadier-general, responded with a *coup d'état* to take over power himself. The new King showed where his sympathies lay by formally dismissing Phoui as prime minister on 30 December.

Phoumi's coup may well have been encouraged by the PEO and the Central Intelligence Agency (CIA). However, the State Department was aware of the disadvantages, at least presentationally, of a military regime in Laos and the American Ambassador joined with other Western ambassadors in expressing concern to the King. In response the King named a provisional government responsible to himself and headed by an elder statesman Kou Abhay. But this was merely a façade and the real power remained in the hands of General Phoumi and the military. They now set about organizing, or rather rigging, the elections to ensure a victory for the government. Boundaries were redrawn to break up Pathet Lao centres of influence, educational standards were raised to exclude Pathet Lao candidates who had had no formal schooling, and powerful military forces raided 'insecure areas' to intimidate the local voters. A joint list of candidates from the CDNI and the moderate Rally of the Lao People was set up, ostensibly to avoid splitting the anti-Pathet Lao vote but also to secure Phoumi's control of the new Assembly. When all else failed the counting of votes was adjusted to ensure that no Pathet Lao candidates were elected. In the Assembly a new party formed by General Phoumi held 35 seats to 17 for the Rally party. Prince Souvanna Phouma, who had returned from Paris to stand successfully as candidate for Luang Prabang, was elected President of the Assembly. To preserve a civilian façade his nephew Prince Somsanith was made prime minister of the new government, which took office on 2 June 1960, but the real power remained in Phoumi's hands.

Phoumi had intended that Prince Souphanouvong and other Pathet

Lao leaders should be brought to trial as soon as the new government was formed. But ten days earlier the prince and his fellow Pathet Lao prisoners managed to escape from their Vientiane gaol. Over the next four months he would cover some 500 kilometres on foot rallying support in various parts of the centre and north before finally arriving in Sam Neua. Other escapees dispersed to rally their supporters and Sithone Kommadom made his way back to the southern mountains to resume leadership of the Kha people.

Thus by June 1960 the whole basis of the Laos settlement worked out at Geneva and amplified by the Vientiane Agreements of 1957 had collapsed. The country that was intended to act as a neutral buffer was now in the hands of a right-wing government closely allied to Thailand and firmly committed to the American side in the Cold War. The policy of integration of the Pathet Lao had been abandoned; denied the possibility of taking part in the parliamentary process, they had been driven into opposition which could only be expressed by military means. General Phoumi's government, for their part, appeared to envisage only a military solution imposed by their enlarged army supported by American advice and training and massive financial support. It seemed only a matter of time before civil war would break out.

3

Last Days of Peace

It was to this uneasy situation that we arrived towards the end of June. But there was little sign of tension in Vientiane. The Lao, who seemed at least on the surface to be some of the friendliest and most peaceful people in the world, went smiling about their daily business. While government officials and other office workers wore Western suits, the ordinary Lao men mostly wore shirts and sarongs or trousers. The women, famous for their elegance and shy beauty, wore the same kind of national dress irrespective of rank: white blouses, long slim skirts of beautifully embroidered local silk, a stole of similar material around their shoulders and their hair brushed back into an asymmetrical chignon decorated with a flower or simple jewellery. For us, having served only in large modern cities, there was a special fascination in finding ourselves in what was little more than an over-grown Asian village or rather a collection of villages, consisting of wooden Lao houses on stilts, a few main streets with shacks of one or two storeys serving as shops owned by Vietnamese and Chinese, some open markets, a scattering of French colonial houses and a fair number of Buddhist temples from which shaven-headed monks in saffron-coloured robes emerged every morning and evening to do their rounds with their begging bowls. The main part of the town of Vientiane straggled for about a kilometre along the left bank, namely the north side, of the Mekong which here runs west to east, and looking across the river to Thailand on the right bank. Most of the streets ran parallel to the river, but from the centre of the town a road ran north a little way to finish at the impressive curved golden obelisk of the That Luang pagoda, surrounded by a large open space reserved for festivals and royal ceremonies.

Two days after our arrival we were able to witness one such ceremony — the funeral of Prince Souvannarath, half-brother of Souvanna Phouma and himself a former prime minister. The richly ornamented gilt coffin was placed on the back of a huge painted wooden bird, some four metres high and ten metres long, supported on the chassis of a large truck and pulled along by ropes manned somewhat incongruously by a score or so of boy scouts in shorts and berets. The mourners followed on foot, first the family led by Prince Souvanna Phouma then members of the government and senior officials with their wives. The men wore the Laotian court dress of a white uniform jacket and a silk sarong tucked between their legs to form what looked like loose breeches above black silk stockings and Western-style shoes, the women a more sober but still richly embroidered version of their normal dress. The procession moved slowly up the long road to the That Luang temple where after appropriate religious ceremonies the coffin was placed on an enormous funeral pyre. This was lit at dark to cast a bright glow on scenes of festivity in which most of the population of Vientiane seemed to join.

Our own house was located at what was known as the 'MIC site', some distance along the road that ran by the Mekong to the east of the town, at the point where the river began to turn south. It was the former site of a large verandaed bungalow on stilts belonging to the manager of *Manufactures Indo-Chine* (MIC), a French company engaged mainly in making cigarettes. When the British Embassy was first established the British government bought the bungalow to house one of the embassy families. Later the Ministry of Works demolished the bungalow and built three houses, single-storeyed bungalows raised on concrete stilts in a pleasing gesture to the local style. Our house at the eastern end of the property was a simple rectangle: in the centre a square-shaped living/dining room ending in a balcony overlooking the Mekong; at the four corners of the rectangle the kitchen and three bedrooms each with a bathroom. (As in Singapore Danny spurned the servants' quarters, and Billy and he, together with his array of scents and lotions, installed themselves in the third bedroom adjacent to the kitchen.) The house at the other end of the site was occupied by a bachelor First Secretary John Main. The largest house in the middle was divided into two semi-detached units to accommodate the administration officer Peter Newman and one of the wireless officers Ken Rymer and their wives. Beyond John Main's house a small Lao bungalow remaining from the original MIC site was the home of Madeleine Davies, who was to be my secretary.

Most other members of the embassy staff were housed in rented property, sometimes wooden Lao bungalows, sometimes modern bungalows built usually by government ministers for renting to foreign diplomats at a rent that would recover building costs in four years or less. The Ambassador's residence was newly built by the Ministry of Works in the centre of the town. In the same compound they had built a small bungalow for the security officer and a long low building to house the embassy offices. The process of installing air-conditioning in offices and houses in tropical countries had only just begun and had not yet reached Laos. So during the hot season (ten months in the year) the combination of ceiling fans and open windows created a constant risk of secret documents being blown out of the window.

The embassy staff was small and it did not take long to get to know them all. The one I saw most of was naturally my secretary Madeleine Davies, an attractive young lady aged about 21 on her first posting abroad. Having a French mother she was bilingual, which was a great asset. From her Welsh father she inherited a touch of Celtic romanticism, but this was balanced by a typically French bourgeois commonsense, which helped her to cope admirably with the difficulties and dangers that lay ahead. My neighbour John Main, prematurely white-haired, was a charming Scottish intellectual who would soon leave the Service to become a professor of philosophy in a Scottish university. I had already met the Second Secretary Colin McColl in Bangkok where he had been studying the Thai language. He had moved a few months earlier to Vientiane, where he had quickly made the conversion from Thai to Lao, becoming the embassy's Lao-speaking expert. Highly intelligent, with an infectious enthusiasm for everything he did, he was at the beginning of a successful career that would lead to a knighthood. David Wilson, the Third Secretary who had piloted us up the Mekong on our arrival, was an adventurous young man who would have been at home in the Colonial Service of an earlier time in a remote part of Africa. He was always disappearing in a Land Rover, exploring up remote jungle tracks and hoping, we believed, to be captured by the Pathet Lao. He was due to depart soon for a sabbatical leave to join an Antarctic expedition, after which the Foreign Office planned to send him to Tokyo to become a Japanese language expert. Our Ambassador John Addis advised that he would be more suited to the wide-open spaces of China than to the industrialized urban environment of Japan and so David was in due course sent off to Hong Kong to learn Chinese instead. He was to become the leading China expert in the FO, ending up as Governor of Hong Kong and retiring to the House of Lords as Lord Wilson of Tillyorn (yes, he was another Scot).

The recently-arrived military attaché was Lieutenant-Colonel Hugh Toye, one of a breed that is more common than generally supposed, the military intellectual. He had already published one book, an account of Subhas Chandra Bose and the Indian National Army entitled *The Springing Tiger*; and on leaving Laos he won a research fellowship at Nuffield College, Oxford, and acquired a D.Phil. degree, after which he published *Laos: Buffer State or Battleground*, which held its place for many years as the best general history of Laos available. Able and energetic, he was to prove invaluable in obtaining and interpreting information about the complex military situation that was developing. He was well supported by his delightful wife Betty, a member of the Foreign Service before she married Hugh.

The Information Officer Trevor Wilson, who arrived shortly after we did, really deserves a whole book to himself rather than just a paragraph or two. Most unusually, he was five years beyond the compulsory Foreign Service retiring age of 60. But he was not, and never had been, a member of the Foreign Service, being employed as a contract officer. Before the Second World War he was manager of Barclays Bank in Nice in the south of France. Evacuated to England in 1940 he was recruited into the Army Intelligence Corps, where it was thought that his local knowledge of the Côte d'Azur would be useful in planning an eventual invasion by that route. In November 1942 he was submarined into Algeria in advance of the main Allied invasion. Somehow he got hold of some German cyphers left behind in the hasty German withdrawal. Shutting himself in a room for two days he succeeded in breaking the code, so that for the remainder of the North African campaign we could read German military messages. For this major contribution he was awarded the MBE! In 1944 he seems to have been one of the first Allied soldiers to enter Paris. He never mentioned this himself, but years later I read an article in the *New Statesman* by his fellow member of the Intelligence Corps Malcolm Muggeridge, describing how he and Trevor Wilson had entered Paris ahead of the main body of Allied troops, driving a white Rolls-Royce belonging to one of the Rothschilds. Some time around the end of the war Trevor was transferred to Southeast Asia Command and became attached to the newly reopened consulate in Hanoi. The Viet Minh had just taken over control of Vietnam, and he became very friendly with Ho Chi Minh in the period before the French returned. Later he was employed as a contract information officer by the colonial government of Malaya. This ended when Malaya became independent, but in view of his unusually wide experience of Southeast Asia, the Foreign Office was happy to offer him the job in Laos.

Trevor was married, but his wife Mabel was an invalid who had stayed behind at their home in Gloucestershire. ('She's dying, poor thing,' he told some people who travelled out to Laos with him, but in fact she lived on for quite a few more years.) In appearance he was the typical retired bank manager, very much like Arthur Lowe as Captain Mainwaring in the TV series Dad's Army. Alternatively, with his well-cushioned body and his pink, round, bespectacled face, he could be described as Pickwickian. He was a delightful companion with a ready supply of amusing anecdotes and shrewd comment delivered in a slightly hesitant, even bumbling manner, at times more bumbling than at others. But there was no bumbling in his written style, which was clear and incisive. Because of his past career in army intelligence he was, outside the embassy, generally but wrongly thought to be the local representative of the Secret Service. In fact the job of embassy information officer is much more to do with propaganda than intelligence, the supply of information about Britain to the local government and media rather than the acquiring of information. The local media consisted only of the government radio and a Roneoed government newssheet, which included items from the Agence France Presse news agency. But after the crisis broke, Trevor was our main point of contact with the numerous reporters of the world press who flew into Vientiane, and the exchange of information was very much a two-way affair.

Space does not permit pen portraits of all the embassy staff. In addition to the already-mentioned administration officer and wireless officers there was an archivist, a cypher officer, the military attaché's clerk, several secretaries and the security officer (whose wife, a former FO secretary, acted as John Addis's personal assistant); and a Laotian staff consisting of the assistant information officer Mr Pheng, who also served as translator of Lao documents, and various drivers, cleaners and guards. Outside the embassy but linked with it were two doctors, Tony Brown and Dick Herniman, who had arrived in Vientiane about the same time that we did. In the last dying year of national service in Britain, they had chosen, in lieu of military service, to accept medical appointments in Laos under the Colombo Plan technical assistance programme. Accompanying them was a VSO (Voluntary Service Overseas) volunteer Ian Bowley, an apprentice engineer from Rolls-Royce. They were expecting to be sent into some remote area to provide basic medical services, which were entirely lacking outside the few main towns; and Ian's role was to help in building a clinic. But owing to the slow Laotian bureaucracy and later the developing civil war this took a long time to arrange. So they spent their time in Vientiane assisting the French doctors in the small hospital. There was also a British nurse Phyllis Aldridge, but she was working quite separately on a United Nations project, and we did not see so much of her.

The technical assistance programme also included the supply of an expert adviser to Radio Vientiane. He was Tony Beamish, whom we had known slightly when we were in Singapore and he was working with the radio there. A man of wide culture and great charm, he became a good friend and we remained in touch until his sad, early death some 20 years later. When he returned to England he became a producer of television programmes. The most notable of these concerned the uninhabited island of Aldabra in the Indian Ocean, home of a unique wild life, including frigate birds and giant tortoises, which was threatened by Ministry of Defence plans to turn the island into a military training area and firing range. The programme and a book he wrote entitled *Aldabra Alone* helped to ensure the success of a campaign he led to persuade the Ministry to abandon the idea and leave the island in peace.

Apart from the medical team, Tony Beamish and the embassy there were hardly any British people in Vientiane, or indeed elsewhere in Laos. The only one I recall from this period was the local Shell manager Desmond Rice, a first-class man who, we discovered later, was also a novelist, writing under the name Desmond Meiring. After he left Laos the following year he published an excellent account, thinly disguised as fiction, of life and events in Laos during his time under the title of *The Brinkman*.

Presiding over this tiny British community was the Ambassador, John Addis, an English gentleman (though of Scottish origin) of the old school, a confirmed bachelor of the days before this status carried the modern implications of the phrase 'he never married' in an obituary. Joining the diplomatic service in the late 1930s, he was posted after the war to the embassy in Nanking, the capital of Chiang Kai-Shek's government. He became captivated by Chinese culture, learned the language and began a modest but valuable collection of early Ming blue and white porcelain which he eventually left to the British Museum. In the 1950s he went back to China as counsellor in the embassy in Peking, and it was his ambition, which happily he was to realize, to finish his career as ambassador to China. He was accordingly very pleased to be appointed, in his mid-forties, to Laos, which was at least on the periphery of his beloved China. He was physically large and, like most Englishmen of his generation and education (Rugby and Christ Church, Oxford), believed firmly in the benefits of fresh air and exercise. His office window was always wide open, whether in the icy winter winds of northern China or the humid heat of Laos, even after air-conditioning was installed. A creature of habit, at 5.00 p.m. every day, unless we were in the midst of a major crisis, he always either played tennis or took a 'constitutional' walk. He was a man of high principle and moral courage, reinforced per-haps by a comfortable private income — he was the thirteenth child of a father who engaged successfully in Far Eastern trade. His physical courage was also undoubted. Some years later when he was ambassador in the Philippines, he was taking his usual early evening constitutional when he was accosted by a man with a gun demanding his money or his life. 'Don't be silly' said John, 'I'm the British Ambassador,' and walked on at his customary stately pace.

My own rank at the time was First Secretary, and my position had the pleasingly old-fashioned title of Head of Chancery. In the eighteenth and nineteenth centuries, and for some traditionalists right up to my time, the word 'embassy' meant the ambassador's residence, and the embassy office was known as the Chancery. The head of Chancery was accordingly the head of the office, responsible for its smooth running, rather like the adjutant of an army regiment. He was also traditionally the head of the political section, and in a large modern embassy he would report to the ambassador's deputy, usually in the rank of minister, along with the heads of the other sections, commercial, consular and information. However, in a small post like Vientiane I was also deputy to the Ambassador and supervised all aspects of the embassy's work, which included the administration of the modest aid programme. The tiny British community did not justify a separate consular section, but I held the Queen's commission as Consul, and the Ambassador also carried the title of Consul-General. A particular responsibility of the head of Chancery was to supervise the administration — accommodation, accounts, local staff, transport and security — though the administration officer carried out the detailed work. I remember in my early days accompanying John Addis on a tour of the residential accommodation. This was still of very variable quality, since in the early years after independence the demand for good accommodation from newly-established embassies and international organizations greatly exceeded the supply. Single junior officers (and for this reason mainly single officers were appointed) occupied rented wooden Lao houses in the centre of the town that were small, dingy, dimly lit and poorly furnished. Trevor Wilson lived in a reasonably comfortable apartment in a more modern concrete building. When we called there we were greeted by an elegant Vietnamese lady housekeeper; and as we inspected the bedroom I noticed the prim bachelor ambassador taking in, without comment, the two pairs of bedroom slippers beneath the double bed. One or two of the other bachelors or unaccompanied married men had similar domestic arrangements.

During the first month I called on my opposite number in other embassies, and John Addis took me to call on the leading ambassadors (there were not many embassies) and the UN representative. The most important was the American Ambassador Winthrop Brown, who arrived a few weeks after we did. Tall and thin and rather austere-looking with rimless spectacles, his appearance and first name indicated descent from the early Puritans in New England. His deputy John Holt, who had been chargé d'affaires when we arrived, was an experienced diplomat and a most agreeable colleague. I also got to know very well the first secretary in charge of the political section Philip Chadbourn, a sophisticated and charming product of the Ivy League east coast establishment. The most flamboyant member of the embassy staff was Robert Campbell James, a scion of the Campbell soup family, inevitably known as Soupy, who made no attempt to conceal his membership of the CIA. With his florid complexion, aquiline nose and moustache he looked like a slightly decadent Edwardian Englishman, an impression he enhanced by wearing Savile Row suits with, even in the hot season, double-breasted waistcoats and a watch-chain, and carrying a silver-topped cane which, as he was always ready to demonstrate, was hollow and filled with brandy. A certain arrogance of manner completed the impersonation, but he was a colourful asset to the small foreign community and entertained generously with Black Velvet, the mixture of champagne and Guinness I have always thought was a waste of both.

The French, as the former colonial power, still exercised great influence. With close contacts at all levels of the Laotian government, a military mission of 5000 soldiers and a French community scattered around the country, they had unrivalled sources of information. Their Ambassador, Pierre Falaize, had been a journalist before joining the Free French during the war and then occupying various important posts in the government service. He had already been ambassador in Amman and Tripoli and must have been disappointed by his posting to Laos — he told his colleagues at Tripoli that he was being '*discipliné*'. Short, tubby and balding, he did not cut a romantic figure, and when wearing the flat-capped French tropical diplomatic uniform he could have passed for a conductor on the Paris metro. But he was intelligent, shrewd and amusing, with a wicked smile and a fund of mostly salacious stories. During the forthcoming crisis we were to work particularly closely with him and his staff and found them to be excellent colleagues. Particularly good friends were the military attaché Colonel Jean de la Patellière and the Thai/Lao speaking counsellor Michel Cadol with a delightful Thai wife.

The other 'Western' country with a special interest in Laos was Australia. At the time of our arrival they had no resident embassy but their ambassador in Saigon, Bill Forsyth, was also accredited to Laos and visited quite frequently. However, they had already decided to appoint a resident ambassador to Laos at the end of the year, and meanwhile they had just sent a young third secretary Don Kingsmill to act as Chargé d'Affaires. A delightful young man, dark haired and neatly built, rather like a young Ken Rosewall but better looking, he became a most valued colleague and a lifelong friend. The Australians had also appointed a resident military attaché, Lieutenant-Colonel Crosby, inevitably known as Bing, who was a great addition to our small community. He had retired from the Australian army after distinguished service in the Second World War, but when the Korean War broke out he immediately volunteered for active service. He was turned down because of his age, whereupon he re-enlisted as a private under a false name and age. When the press found this out he became something of a national hero, and public outcry compelled the government to restore his commission and reluctantly allow him to serve in Korea. This episode seems to have made him unsackable and he was long past the normal retiring age, probably in his sixties, by the time he was sent to Laos. But he retained his adventurous spirit and often accompanied David Wilson on his trips up jungle tracks looking for the Pathet Lao.

The Indian Ambassador, Perala Ratnam, was of some importance as the representative of the leading neutralist power that had provided the chairman of the International Control Commission. He had come directly from a posting in Moscow and was regarded by the Americans as dangerously left-wing. His vivacious wife was indeed outspokenly pro-communist, but Ratnam himself was much less so and throughout the coming crisis he was a useful and influential voice in support of neutralism. Of the other ambassadors, the Thai obviously enjoyed a close relationship with the government, more so than the South Vietnamese and the Cambodian. There was also an ambassador from Japan, which was just beginning to regain international respectability and overcome memories of its wartime behaviour in the region. The rest of the diplomatic community comprised representatives of the UN specialized agencies providing aid programmes of various kinds, and a special representative of the UN Secretary-General, dating from the time of the Laotian complaint to the Security Council. There was no embassy from the Soviet Union, China, North Vietnam or any other communist country.

John Addis also took me to call on various ministers, notably the Foreign Minister, Khamphan Panya, a senior member of the CDNI, with whom we negotiated and signed an aid agreement at this time. I particularly liked the cheerful, typically round-faced Information Minister, Nouphat Chounramany whom I got to know better on the tennis court. Though Phoui Sananikone was still out of favour, his family was well represented in the government with two of his brothers, Oun and Ngon, holding important ministerial posts. Then there was the Minister of Health Dr Oudom Souvannavong, a member of the other leading *bourgeois* family of Vientiane. He was the only qualified Laotian doctor, and was reputed to have made a fortune by selling in his own pharmacy drugs and medical equipment donated by the World Health Organization; with part of the proceeds he had built a spacious mansion across the road from the MIC site.

The non-official foreign community was almost exclusively French, and we met most of them at the French ambassador's Bastille Day reception a few weeks after our arrival. One Frenchman we got to know well was Jean-Pierre Geoffroy Dechaume, the youngest of nine children of a well-known French painter, all of whom were distinguished as artists or musicians. Jean-Pierre made a modest living by painting portraits and Laotian landscapes in an agreeable representational style. His wife was a delightful French-Lao *métisse* who was known in Laos by her French name Yvonne and in France by her Laotian name Khamsay. In addition to painting, Jean-Pierre played the recorder competently. Our piano had now arrived from Bangkok and we were soon organizing regular sessions of baroque chamber music, usually on a Sunday morning at our house, involving Beth on piano, myself on clarinet, Jean-Pierre on recorder, Colin McColl on flute and, for a short time, an excellent Swiss bassoonist working in one of the UN offices.

Our other main leisure activity was tennis, and it was here in Vientiane that we made our first acquaintance with the rigid hierarchical system that governs French tennis. In a normal French tennis club, players are divided according to their skill into *première série*, *deuxième série* and *non-classé* and play on courts designated for each *série*. At the beginning of the season a *tournoi de classement* is held to allocate players to their appropriate *série* and to rank players in order in each. As soon as the tournament is over players start challenging those ranked above them to improve their position, and especially to escape from the shameful status of *non-classé*. Nearly all the play is singles and the atmosphere is tremendously competitive, which is probably a major reason why France in recent years has produced many more top-class players than Britain. In Vientiane of course the atmosphere was much more relaxed. With only two courts at the club it was not possible to book and doubles games were made up as players arrived. Even so one court was allocated to the *première série* for the better players and the other to the weaker players of the *deuxième série*. Beth and I qualified on merit for the *première série*. But we found that there was a special rule at the Vientiane club: eminent personages such as ministers, princes, ambassadors and generals were made honorary members of the *première série* irrespective of their tennis skill. And so it would be quite usual for me to greet the other members of my doubles four with: '*Bon jour Altesse, bon jour Excellence, bon jour mon général* (usually General Ouane, the Chief of Staff of the army who, I later discovered, was much involved in the illegal opium traffic). The quality of the tennis was, shall we say, variable.

Most evenings would be taken up with official receptions or diplomatic entertaining. At weekends we could explore the numerous Buddhist temples and pagodas and begin to find our way around the ramshackle town. It was a particular pleasure to wander about the spacious open-air market admiring the displays of mangoes, lychees, pineapples, chickens, ducks and buffalo meat and every other sort of local produce while inhaling the fragrance of frangipani and magnolias from the flower stalls; and then to stroll along the river embankment under wide-branched *pepul* and blue gum trees which provided shade for little thatched huts where you could buy bowls of Chinese soup or noodles and various snacks wrapped in banana leaves and washed down with Lao beer, or rice wine. When not engaged in these various activities we could sit on our balcony and gaze at the great river Mekong flowing almost beneath our feet. When we first arrived the river was relatively low and there was a small beach in front of us from which local fishermen waded out to cast elegant nets. But as the monsoon rains got under way the river rose and broadened to its full width of over half a kilometre, and the fast-flowing muddy current would carry on its surface drowned water buffaloes, trees and even small islands of vegetation. Looking westwards over the river towards Thailand we were treated to spectacular lightning flashes illuminating the clouds; and when the sky was clear enough the sunsets were superb.

So the scene is set and the *dramatis personae* have been introduced. Action, unbeknown to any of us, was about to commence.

4

The Little Captain
and the Invisible
King

On the morning of 9 August 1960 a group of us going in to the office from the MIC site noticed unusual activity by military vehicles and red-bereted paratroopers stationed at various strategic points of the town. On arrival we were told that during the night the 2nd Parachute Battalion led by a Captain Kong Lae had seized control of the capital while Phoumi and most of the government were in Luang Prabang. While we had had an uneasy feeling that something was liable to happen at some stage to upset the precariously balanced political situation, the timing and form of the coup were completely unexpected and no one had heard of Kong Lae (also spelt Konglè, the last syllable being the very open Lao 'e', more open than the French 'è' or 'ê', probably best rendered in English as 'lair'). In similar circumstances there is a tendency for some journalists to report rather gleefully that the British Embassy/Foreign Office was taken completely by surprise, with the implication that an efficient, well-informed embassy ought to know when a coup is going to take place. This is of course complete nonsense. I had considerable experience of this sort of thing in Argentina in the early 1950s when Perón was becoming less popular and the embassy reported a coup plot on average once a month. None of these planned coups was ever carried out, for the good reason that if the British Embassy heard about a coup plot it was more than likely that the government would also hear about it and would nip it in the bud. The simple rule is that the coup that succeeds is the one the embassies know nothing about.

In this case there wasn't even a plot that we might have got wind of. The coup was conceived solely in the mind of the small, slightly built 26-year-old Captain Kong Lae. Hugh Toye, doing his job as military attaché, got to know him well and gives a good description of the man and his motives in his book. Kong Lae came from a peasant family of the minority Pou Thai tribe to the east of Savannakhet. As a boy he witnessed the activity of local guerrillas opposing the Japanese, the Viet Minh and the returning French. Joining the army at 17, he was made an officer at 19 and rose quickly to become acting commander of the 2nd Parachute Battalion. His battalion was involved in much of the military action, mostly phoney, of the late 1950s, including the pursuit of the escaping Pathet Lao battalion in May 1959 and the Sam Neua crisis of August. Despite all the talk of Viet Minh invasions he never saw any Viet Minh, and began to realize that Lao were fighting Lao at the behest of foreign interests (the Viet Minh and the Americans) and of corrupt politicians in Vientiane. He decided to take action to restore peace among Laotians. He saw his opportunity when he was ordered to take his battalion through Vientiane northward to carry out anti-guerrilla operations. Passing through the capital in the hours of darkness he was able to seize the radio station, the airfield, the power station and the arsenal without bloodshed. Appealing directly to the people over the heads of their rulers he declared his aims as the ending of the civil war, the removal of foreign troops and the suppression of those who were 'making their harvest on the backs of the people', a traditional Lao phrase for the exactions of corrupt rulers. The only solution was for Laos to pursue a neutral policy as between the two world power blocs.

The Kong Lae coup sparked off a major diplomatic crisis. The trickle of telegrams we normally received every day became a flood, as we reported developments in Laos and received instructions from the

FO and comments from the numerous other posts that were interested. This posed an immediate problem for me as Head of Chancery
because of our primitive means of communication. Our telegrams
were sent, and received, manually by Morse code (20 to 24 words a
minute) via a small radio transmitter to Singapore, which would relay
them via a more powerful transmitter to interested posts in the area
(including Bangkok, Saigon, Phnom Penh, New Delhi, Peking and
Canberra among others) and to the FO, which would itself relay them
to posts such as Paris, Washington, New York and Moscow. The
sheer volume of traffic placed a heavy burden on our two wireless
operators, but they were able to cope by working very long hours
every day. A more serious problem was our ancient cypher system.

Cypher machines had been invented many years before, but for cost
reasons had not yet been issued to small posts like Vientiane, where
we still relied on the time-honoured system of book cypher or the one-
time pad. To encypher a message one looked in the encypher code
book to find groups of four figures corresponding to the words or
phrases in the message. These figures were then written under rows of
randomly-generated figures in a 'one-time pad' (so-called because it
was used only once) and subtracted from them. The resultant figures
were then written on a message pad and handed to the wireless
operator to transmit. At the receiving end the encyphered figures were
written in the appropriate place on an identical one-time pad, and
subtracted to produce the figures with which the sending post had
started. These figures were then looked up in the decypher code book
to find the words and phrases of the original message. This process
was more interesting (and longer) than encyphering since some groups
of figures were usually distorted in transmission, producing what were
known as 'corrupt groups', and much ingenuity of the crossword-
solving kind was needed to fill in the gaps, by a combination of trying
out different combinations of the figures and simply guessing what
would fit into the context. The system worked and because of the
one-time principle was entirely secure, but it was cumbersome and
very slow. An experienced cypher officer working on his own could
encypher not many more than 100 groups (more or less equivalent to
words) in an hour, while two working together might manage 200 or
more groups an hour; decyphering might take longer if there were a

lot of corrupt groups. Thus a long telegram of 1000 words or three or four pages might take four or five hours or more to encypher and at least the same amount of time to decypher.

Normally, the cypher work would be done by the registry staff, of which our establishment was three officers — two archivists and one cypher officer. Even if they had been at full strength they would not have been able to cope unaided with the number of telegrams we had to send and the flood of telegrams coming in from the FO and various other interested posts. But at the time of the crisis one of the archivists had left on transfer and his successor had not yet arrived; and the cypher officer had just been sent home to face a disciplinary charge. He was an efficient officer and a nice man, but in low spirits following the break-up of his marriage; and the poor quality of his living accommodation did nothing to lift his depression. With no radio or television and with the uncertain electricity providing hardly enough light for reading, it was inevitable that he would spend most of his evenings in bars and nightclubs. He was not a heavy drinker but unfortunately he had no head at all for alcohol; and after only one glass of beer he would order drinks all round and sign any chit the barman placed in front of him. The bills mounted rapidly and by the time I arrived he owed the main nightclub, the Vieng Ratray (known to English speakers as the Green Latrine as it was housed in a green wooden building), more than £1000, a huge sum in those days amounting to more than his annual salary. As a cypher officer heavily in debt must rank as a major security risk, I called him in and told him he must stop visiting bars and nightclubs. I arranged for regular deductions from his salary to start paying off his debts and asked other members of the staff to entertain and visit him and generally keep an eye on him. This worked well for a few weeks. Then it became his turn to escort our outgoing diplomatic bag to Bangkok and bring back the incoming bag brought out from London by the Queen's Messenger. Unfortunately on the return journey the air hostess plied him with free drinks with the result that at Vientiane airport he staggered off the plane leaving the diplomatic bags behind. As leaving diplomatic bags unattended was a major offence I had no alternative but to send him home to face a disciplinary court, which recommended that he be transferred to a home government department.

So our cypher staff was reduced to one archivist, who had a full-time job coping with the rapidly-expanding files. I therefore drew up a roster of two-man, or rather two-person, teams involving nearly all the British staff working all day and well into the night. Disregarding strict security rules limiting access to cyphers to established members of the Foreign Service, I brought in Hugh Toye and his clerk and Trevor Wilson, who proved to be a whizz at figures, rattling off the subtractions faster than anyone could write them down. The Ambassador joined in and I even called in Beth and some of the other wives to perform the purely passive role of writing down the figures as they were called out from the code book or the subtractions. An additional problem was the 7.00 p.m. curfew imposed by Kong Lae. On the first evening after the coup I was working late on the cyphers with the archivist Philip Massé and it was well after seven when we finished. Left to myself I would have tried to sneak home to the MIC site via the Boulevard Circulaire, a grandly-named earth road built on an embankment between rice fields round the north-east periphery of the town and lined with dilapidated shacks constructed of corrugated iron and packing cases. But Philip lived in a flat in the centre of town and had no car so I decided to risk driving him to his home. We covered some distance by keeping to quiet side streets but eventually we had to come out onto one of the main streets. Headlamps flashed, whistles blew and we were quickly surrounded by paratroopers brandishing their weapons. We feared that at the very least we would be spending the night in a guardroom or a prison cell. But we were merely ordered to spend the night in the main hotel, the Settha Palace, where we had a good night's sleep after an excellent French dinner and a bottle of Beaujolais. Next day the Ambassador agreed that, as long as the curfew lasted, anyone working late on the cyphers would spend the night in his residence adjacent to the office.

Kong Lae's intention had been to overthrow the government and replace it with a neutralist government headed if possible by Prince Souvanna Phouma, then President of the National Assembly. Unfortunately for this plan, at the time of the coup nearly all the ministers of the government were in the royal capital of Luang Prabang to discuss with the king the vitally important question of the arrangements for the funeral of his father, King Sisavang Vong, who had died nine months earlier but whose body was waiting for the bonzes to decide on a propitious date for its cremation. The government immediately instructed General Phoumi, as Minister of Defence, to put down the rebellion and recapture Vientiane; and he departed for Savannakhet, his home town and the main military base in the south. In Vientiane, Souvanna Phouma refused to be party to any unconstitutional move to set up a rival government. However, although the government was temporarily in Luang Prabang, most deputies of the National Assembly, which had the power to endorse and dismiss governments, were in Vientiane. On 13 August, under some pressure from Kong Lae and a hostile crowd of townspeople and left-wing students, the Assembly voted unanimously for a motion of no confidence in the government of Prince Somsanith. When the motion was conveyed to Luang Prabang next day Somsanith, a decent man who wished to avoid bloodshed, insisted on resigning. The King accepted his resignation and the Assembly's recommendation that Souvanna Phouma be asked to form a government. He did so on 16 August, appointing as Minister of the Interior the left-wing leader of the Peace Party Quinim Pholsena, who had acted as a channel of communication between Kong Lae and Souvanna Phouma. In accordance with tradition, his ministers were sworn in at the Wat Sisaket temple in Vientiane. Kong Lae formally handed over to the new prime minister the powers that he had seized, accepted the authority of General Ouane as Commander-in-Chief and declared that the coup was at an end.

However, formal investiture by the King was needed to complete the legitimization of the new government, and Phoumi was able to prevent this. On 15 August he had set up, with the commanders of four of the five military regions, a 'Committee against the *coup d'état*' and declared martial law. On the excuse that martial law suspended government activity, the investiture documents were withheld from the King when they were taken to Luang Prabang on 17 August.

Meanwhile, there had been intense diplomatic activity in Vientiane. John Addis had immediately realized that the Kong Lae coup and the formation of the Souvanna Phouma government provided probably the last chance of avoiding civil war and restoring Laos to the neutral status envisaged in the 1954 Indo-China settlement. He urged the FO to throw its full weight behind Souvanna Phouma and formally recognize his government as soon as it was formed. Despite warning noises from our Ambassador in Washington about the inadvisability of acting against the Americans in an area where their interests were much more important than ours, the FO accepted his arguments and we became the first country to recognize the new government. John Addis told me at the time that he would have resigned if his advice had not been accepted. Fortunately he received first-class support from the home team in the Foreign Office led by Fred Warner, head of the Southeast Asia Department, who was to become ambassador in Laos later in the 1960s and to finish up as ambassador in Tokyo.

Other embassies, notably the French and the Indian, followed the Addis line and the UN Special Representative Zellweger, with the full approval of the Secretary-General Hammarskjöld, gave active support. When we heard that Souvanna Phouma's emissary had been unable to present the investiture documents to the King, it was agreed that Zellweger should fly up to Luang Prabang and seek an audience with the King to find out what was happening and try to persuade him of the need to proceed with the investiture of the government. It was assumed, wrongly as it turned out, that the King could not refuse to receive the representative of the UN Secretary-General. His arrival in Luang Prabang threw the palace staff into confusion, and one courtier went off to seek instructions. He returned with the memorable message: *'Le roi n'est pas visible et ne le sera pas.'* An English-speaker would no doubt have said something boring like: 'You can't see the King, now or at any time.' But the image, or rather the idea, of an invisible King brightened our lives for some time, fitting in as it did so well with the fairy-tale atmosphere of princes, palaces, temples and costumed ceremonies which overlay the grim political realities of the situation.

Down in Savannakhet, Phoumi was mobilizing his forces with some assistance from the Americans, who supplied a transmitter to broadcast his propaganda against Kong Lae and an adviser to help plan the recapture of Vientiane. For the time being civil war was averted when Souvanna Phouma flew to Savannakhet and persuaded Phoumi to agree to a meeting of the Assembly in Luang Prabang, away from the pressures of Vientiane, with a view to the formation of a national coalition government. The Assembly duly met in Luang Prabang and on 31 August unanimously approved a new government led by Souvanna Phouma, this time with General Phoumi as Minister of the Interior; and Phoumi announced the dissolution of his Committee against the *coup d'état*. But the optimism generated by these developments was short lived. On the next day Phoumi was about to board a plane that would take him and the other ministers down to Vientiane when he was handed a message warning him of a plot to assassinate him during the formal installation of the government in Vientiane. He therefore boarded another plane, which took him to Savannakhet where three days later he revived his Committee against the *coup d'état*. The message about the assassination plot came through American channels, and it was thought at the time that it might have been invented by CIA or PEO officers who were unhappy about Phoumi joining Souvanna Phouma's government and wanted him to revert to leading a military rebellion against it.

If it was a CIA/PEO manoeuvre it succeeded in its aim of reopening the rift between the neutralists and the right wing. On 10 September, after some more exaggerated or mythical reports of Pathet Lao/Viet Minh activity in the north, Phoumi announced from Savannakhet that a Revolutionary Group had seized power and abrogated the constitution on the grounds that Souvanna Phouma's government, which had negotiated a cease-fire with the Pathet Lao, was responsible for the alleged deterioration of the military situation. The Group was obviously directed by Phoumi, but its titular head was the respected Inspector-General of the Kingdom, Prince Boun Oum, ruler of Champassac. His adherence added considerable weight (in every sense of the word — he was solidly built) to the right-wing cause. It also emphasized at the dynastic level the regional north–south division that was developing in the country.

A rift was also developing between the Americans and their Western allies. Many elements in the CIA, the Pentagon and the State Department (where Graham Parsons was now Assistant Secretary of State for Far Eastern Affairs) assumed that Kong Lae, variously described as unstable and unsound and 'an extremely sinister figure', was a communist or a tool of the communists. This was completely misguided. Kong Lae was politically naive and knew little about com-

munism except that it was a bad thing. (When Trevor Wilson warned
him to be cautious in his dealings with China he replied 'Why? The
Chinese aren't communist, are they?') To accusations that his action
had opened the door to communism he replied that communism could
not take hold in Laos, as it was contrary to the national character and
the Buddhist religion. But irrespective of their view of Kong Lae those
Americans, deeply imbued with the Dulles doctrine, were hostile to
the neutralist solution. However, at first their ambassador Winthrop
Brown went along with his British and French colleagues, without
going so far as recognizing the Souvanna Phouma government. An
intelligent, experienced diplomat, he appeared to accept intellectually
that neutralism was the only long-term solution for Laos and was able
to persuade a reluctant State Department to support Souvanna
Phouma, although they attached a condition — 'provided that the
Pathet Lao are not included in his government' — which would of
course negate Souvanna's policy of peace and conciliation. As late as
10 September when the Boun Oum Revolutionary Group was set up,
the Americans declared that they would not support it. But already,
possibly without the Ambassador's full knowledge, the American military and the CIA were working actively to build up Phoumi's military
and political strength.

In Vientiane it became apparent that the CIA and the PEO were
slanting the intelligence they were feeding to the Ambassador in order
to justify a policy of support for Phoumi, most obviously by lending
credence to and possibly instigating Phoumi's exaggerations and lies
about Viet Minh invasions. During August, when the Mekong flood
waters were at their height, a report by a hydrological expert was
deliberately altered to indicate an imminent danger of serious flooding
in Vientiane which would have cut off American families from food
and other supplies. Winthrop Brown was persuaded to evacuate all
American wives and children, which the intelligence experts no doubt
hoped would lower morale in Vientiane and indicate lack of confidence in Souvanna Phouma's government. In fact, apart from a few
puddles on the roads, Vientiane remained dry and there was never any
serious risk of flooding.

In Thailand Marshal Sarit had denounced the Kong Lae coup and
shown his disapproval of the neutralist government by imposing a

blockade of the frontier opposite Vientiane; he also permitted Captain Siho, a half-Vietnamese intelligence officer loyal to Phoumi, to mount sabotage raids on Vientiane from the Thai side of the Mekong. But he left the frontier with Savannakhet open, and from mid-September American military supplies poured into Savannakhet from Bangkok. Aircraft of Air America, an ostensibly civilian charter company under contract to the US government, which freighted those supplies to Savannakhet, also distributed some of them to outlying garrisons loyal to Phoumi.

While all this was going on, we in the embassy were fully occupied reporting events to London and holding almost daily meetings with the American, French and other embassies. Cooperation with the French and Americans was close, and the ambassadors used to show each other their telegrams, Falaize with obvious pride in his elegant and witty style. There was a clear difference of style between the British and American telegrams. Ours, always written in the first person singular as from the ambassador, irrespective of who drafted and authorized them, were necessarily concise but always written in normal grammatical English. The Americans, with a much larger staff and machine cyphers, sent many more and longer telegrams and used telegraphese and abbreviations. Thus the three Western ambassadors would be referred to as USAM, BRITAM AND FRAM. When John Addis mentioned this to his staff, we mistakenly conflated the last two and seized delightedly on BRAM. Henceforward, whereas in most British embassies the ambassador is nearly always referred to as 'HE', John Addis was known invariably as 'BRAM'.

Despite the long hours of work, social life gradually resumed after Kong Lae's curfew was lifted on 16 August. Danny and Billy had settled in quite well, making friends in the Chinese community in the town, and it was time to try out Danny's culinary skills on the members of the Vientiane cocktail circuit. However, Danny was never fond of hard work, and preparing food for a large party was much more work than cooking for a private household. On the day before our first sizeable reception, he approached Beth with a swollen thumb, probably caused by a splinter, and said that it was too painful for him to work in the kitchen. Beth gave him first aid and short shrift and sent him back to the kitchen where in due course he produced some very acceptable food. The party was a success and next day I congratulated Danny. 'Yes, it did seem to go well', he replied, 'but I do think that Mrs Brown was *flippant* about my thumb.'

Among the guests we entertained was a newly arrived couple from the British Council. Owen Gwyn Thomas, a handsome black-bearded Welshman, invariably known from his initials as Og or Oggy, had been sent to open up a British Council office library and cultural centre in Vientiane; and also to train students at a 'new university' at Dong Dok, seven kilometres away, to teach rudimentary English. His vivacious wife Sally was from south London and they had met at Cambridge, where a common love of music had brought them together. At the end of our party they sang an unaccompanied duet with consummate musicianship and professional timing; and thus began a lifelong friendship with us. Their posting to Laos was the first step in a lifetime devoted to good works on behalf of the poor in the Third World, while bringing up an international family consisting of their own two daughters and a son, an Indian girl abandoned as a baby in Dar es Salaam and a boy given up for adoption by Jamaican parents in England. Og was to spend much of his life working for Oxfam at a salary that was a tiny fraction of what his talents and qualifications could have commanded in the professional world. Their way of life may have been short on material rewards but it was full of joy and laughter, which their many friends were fortunate to share.

The Thai blockade began to cause shortages, as most food and other supplies for Vientiane came across the Mekong from Thailand. Fortunately we were allowed access to the French commissary and, for a time, the American commissary, which were regularly restocked by air supplies, as the airport remained open and flights from Bangkok were not interrupted. However, as the MIC site was right on the Mekong we were in the front line for the raids mounted by Captain Siho. On the night of 18 September we heard automatic fire and a series of explosions coming from a small island just off the Lao side of the Mekong, a hundred yards or so to the north of us. It seems that Siho's raiders were directing machine-gun and mortar fire on the town, surprisingly with no casualties, though several mortar bombs fell close to houses occupied by colleagues in the embassy. Four nights later Beth and I were sitting on our mosquito-netted balcony overlooking the Mekong when the house was shaken by a loud explosion, apparently in a nearby petrol dump. Shortly afterwards there was a rapid series of three or four explosions in the garden almost under our feet. With instinct reinforced by memories of military training I dived for cover behind the nearest sofa, leaving Beth seated on the balcony. Fortunately neither of us was hurt and there was no damage. We deduced that the explosions were from rifle grenades fired by the retreating saboteurs, rather than from mortar shells, which would have made more noise and probably done us more harm.

In September we met Prince Souvanna Phouma socially for the first time at a dinner given by the French Ambassador Falaize. Shortly afterwards he accepted a dinner invitation from John Addis. After dinner he made a little speech, beginning: 'Gentlemen I have some terrible news to tell you. Today I am 60 years old.' Although short and stocky like most Lao, he had a natural dignity and the self-confidence of a grand seigneur. Educated in France, where he quailfied as a civil engineer and acquired a French wife (albeit with a Laotian mother), he was a cultured man of the world, with a fondness for good company, good food and wine, and a good cigar with his brandy. But he remained very much a prince of Laos, and a patriot who served his country to the best of his ability over many years. Unlike his half-brother Souphanouvong he was not an intellectual and was not greatly concerned with detail. But he was shrewd and intelligent and had a broad statesmanlike vision of where his country's true interests lay.

At this moment, however, his hopes of uniting the country and averting civil war were fading rapidly, thanks largely to the growing hostility of the Americans and the consistently unhelpful attitude of his distant cousin King Savang Vatthana. The King's preference for the right-wing group may have been due partly to jealousy of Souvanna Phouma — there was a complex history of rivalry between the two branches of the royal family. But his overriding motive was probably an atavistic fear of the Vietnamese, whom he invariably referred to as 'les Annamites' and therefore of the Pathet Lao whom he saw as the agents of Viet Minh penetration into Laos. Souvanna Phouma's task of trying to bring the Pathet Lao and the Phoumis together into a durable coalition government would have been difficult enough even with the support of the Americans and the King. In the face of their active opposition his efforts were doomed to failure and civil war became inevitable.

In mid-September more reports of Pathet Lao movements in the north lowered the morale of the government garrison at Sam Neua. Its commander, who was loyal to Souvanna Phouma, flew to Vientiane to ask for reinforcements and military supplies. At the urging of Winthrop Brown, Souvanna Phouma agreed to send arms and ammunition, but owing to a typically Laotian administrative muddle it was 48 hours before they were ready for dispatch. By then it was too late. Phoumi, with his characteristic energy, had himself sent reinforcements and supplies to Sam Neua, with a general who took over the town in his name. At the time the incident was seen to be decisive in ending Winthrop Brown's attempt to pursue a policy of support for Souvanna Phouma, who was now labelled as weak and ineffective. It soon became obvious that the immediate aim of American diplomacy was the ousting of Souvanna Phouma from the premiership and his replacement by Phoumi, the strong man who they believed was the only one who could save Laos from the Pathet Lao/communists.

The error of this judgement was shown only ten days later. Kong Lae had been dropping small teams of parachutists in different areas to rally the people to Souvanna Phouma's government. On 28 September he dropped a party near Sam Neua. The sight of the parachutes floating down induced panic in the nervous garrison of 1500 soldiers, and they all fled from the town and surrendered to the nearest Pathet Lao troops they could find. The Pathet Lao took possession of Sam Neua, emphasizing that they did so in the name of Souvanna Phouma, and awaited the arrival of their leader Souphanouvong who was approaching the end of his marathon four-month's walk from his prison in Vientiane.

Meanwhile there had been a further demonstration of the reluctance of Phoumi's soldiers to die for him. On 19 September, Phoumi had ordered his two battalions located at Paksane, 150 kilometres to the east of Vientiane, to advance on the capital. Kong Lae met them west of the river Nam Ka Dinh with only two companies of paratroops. Though they were heavily outnumbered their morale, boosted by a belief in the invulnerability of their young commander and his bodyguard, was high, and on 21 September they easily routed Phoumi's men. One battalion fled almost without firing a shot; the other, commanded by a Japanese mercenary, put up some resistance and suffered about a hundred casualties before it also fled across the Nam Ka Dinh.

The possibility of a military collapse in the south was averted by the King summoning a military conference of generals and regional commanders with the aim of restoring the unity of the army. Souvanna Phouma, though Minister of Defence, was pointedly excluded, but Boun Oum was allowed to attend. The outcome was, no doubt deliberately, unhelpful to Souvanna Phouma. A cease-fire was agreed between Vientiane and Savannakhet, thereby preventing Kong Lae from exploiting his victory at Nam Ka Dinh; and at the King's express wish the generals agreed on a common front to fight the Pathet Lao, thereby undermining Souvanna Phouma's policy of negotiating with the Pathet Lao.

However, he still kept trying and, at the beginning of October, responding to an approach from Souphanouvong, announced the opening of talks with the Pathet Lao on 11 October and the establishment of diplomatic relations with the Soviet Union. The American response was to suspend financial aid to Laos and, on 12 October, Graham Parsons arrived in Vientiane. He threatened that US aid would be terminated unless Souvanna Phouma broke off the talks with the Pathet Lao. Souvanna Phouma refused, and his position was strengthened by the arrival of the Soviet Ambassador with an offer of aid. (Kong Lae did not help his reputation with the Americans by organizing a parachute drop display to welcome the Ambassador.) Parsons returned to Washington more determined than ever that Souvanna Phouma must go.

5

The Battle of Vientiane

Around this time I started to feel distinctly unwell. The first symptoms were sharp pains in the lungs whenever I coughed, sneezed, laughed or even took a deep breath. Then I started to vomit every time I had something to eat or drink, even a glass of water. Most alarming of all to those who knew my healthy appetite, I lost the desire to eat. During my many years in the tropics I have had my share of digestive upsets, but on other occasions my usual response to a bout of vomiting was to eat another meal to replace the food lost. But now I did not want to eat anything. The two British doctors Tony Brown and Dick Herniman and the doctor attached to the American Embassy were baffled and so they arranged for me to be evacuated to a private nursing home in Bangkok that was used by the British Embassy there. At Bangkok airport I was met by John Patterson, a Third Secretary with whom I had worked on SEATO matters, and an ambulance whose crew insisted on putting me on a stretcher. We charged away with the siren screaming. From my supine position I could not see out of the ambulance. But I was aware, from the lurching of the vehicle, the screaming of the tyres and above all from the blanched face and staring eyes of John as he peered over the driver's shoulder, that the journey was at least as life-threatening as my illness might prove to be.

On arrival Dr Gotteschlick, the German in charge of the nursing home, examined me and took X-rays and blood and other samples. I heard the formidable but jolly and attractive Australian matron Elsa Craig say to him: 'Do you think it might be Loeffler's syndrome, doctor?', but he brushed the suggestion aside and prescribed a whole range of pills to treat my symptoms. However, when the test results came in he announced that I was indeed suffering from Loeffler's syndrome, mentioning proudly that he had been a pupil of Dr Loeffler who had identified the condition. It was apparently caused by a tiny tropical worm that attacked the lungs; the main symptoms were shadows on the lungs showing up on the X-rays and an alarming increase in the number of white corpuscles in the blood, from a normal 4 per cent to, in my case, 28 per cent. The treatment was rest for several weeks and drugs to kill off the worms and to build up my red corpuscles to their normal 96 per cent. My private room was air-conditioned and comfortable, looking onto a sunlit, tropical garden, and my recovery was helped by the ministrations of some very pretty Thai and Chinese nurses. My appetite returned, I was told there were no restrictions on what I could eat and asked what was my favourite food. I replied: 'vanilla ice cream with chocolate sauce', and so for the remainder of my five-week stay in the nursing home I had vanilla ice cream and chocolate sauce with lunch and dinner every day.

It was an agreeable enough existence, but I was impatient to get back to the excitement of Vientiane. With the help of frequent visits by the Bangkok embassy staff and weekly calls by staff from Vientiane bringing the diplomatic bag I kept myself informed of developments in Laos. Following Parsons's visit and the suspension of aid, the Americans offered to resume cash payments if Souvanna Phouma would permit deliveries of American military supplies direct to Phoumi, on the specific understanding that these would be used only against the Pathet Lao and not against the government. The dangers were obvious, but Souvanna Phouma agreed, presumably because he thought that he had little choice. With a 90 per cent deficit on both the budget and the balance of payments, Laos was quite literally bankrupt, and without American money the government would not be able to pay its officials or the troops which remained loyal to it.

The result was to legitimize the support that the Americans had been providing to Phoumi and which was now further increased. Military supplies that should have gone to Vientiane, where the frontier was still closed, were diverted to Savannakhet, where the frontier remained open. Some 200 Laotian paratroopers whom the Americans had been training in Thailand were handed over to Phoumi in breach of a specific promise to Souvanna Phouma. All this evidence that the Americans were on Phoumi's side helped him to persuade more and more of the government's supporters to defect to Savannakhet. The defection to Phoumi of the garrison at Luang Prabang on 11 November was a particular blow to Souvanna Phouma.

With the end of the rainy season the road north from Savannakhet became more practicable for military movement, and Phoumi was ready to launch his campaign. A first attack on two companies of Kong Lae's paratroops on 23 November was defeated. Five days later Phoumi's troops resumed their advance, this time accompanied by tanks and the sole artillery battalion of the Laotian army, equipped with 105-millimetre howitzers and mortars. The guns proved decisive as the paratroops had never experienced artillery fire and were demoralized by the shells exploding around them. After suffering over a hundred casualties they withdrew to Paksane, badly shaken but with their morale sustained by the survival intact of Kong Lae's 'invulnerable' bodyguard. In Vientiane news of the battle further weakened Souvanna Phouma's position. As more of his moderate supporters defected, students and other left-wing groups, secretly encouraged by Quinim Pholsena, engaged in noisy demonstrations and gave the impression that the government was losing control.

Early in December I was discharged from the nursing home, apparently cured of Loeffler's syndrome, but still feeling weak and needing a period of convalescence. I returned to Vientiane (where first my successor in Singapore, Philip Mansfield, and then another colleague from Singapore, Kelvin White, had been holding the fort during my absence) and reported to John Addis, who agreed that I should stay at home for a week or so until I felt strong enough to return to work. During this time Beth and I went on regular walks, each day a little longer, into the countryside on the outskirts of the capital. Crossing the main road immediately outside the MIC site, within 50 metres we were in the peaceful timeless world of the Lao peasant. With the rains over and the short cool season just beginning, the weather was perfect. We walked along narrow causeways separating fields of rice stubble or under trees along footpaths connecting small villages. From time to time we met village people who greeted us with enchanting smiles, the joined hands *wai* salutation and '*sabai di bo*?' ('are you well?'). Otherwise, apart from our soft footfalls on the earthen track, occasional bird calls and the snorting of water buffaloes, all was silent. It was difficult to believe that only a few hundred yards away a major crisis was being acted out. But as soon as we returned to the MIC site the frequent passage of military vehicles at high speed in both directions indicated that events were approaching a climax.

At this time a key role was played by Colonel Kouprasith Abhay, the commander of the Vientiane military region (and son of the former Prime Minister Kou Abhay). Though ostensibly loyal to Souvanna Phouma, he was in touch with Phoumi, who ordered him to carry out a *coup d'état* in Vientiane on the grounds that left-wing pressure had made government impossible. The coup was to be supported by paratroops from Savannakhet, for which control of the airfield at Paksane was necessary. On 6 December Kouprasith ordered Kong Lae's paratroops at Paksane to withdraw 'to facilitate peace negotiations'. The greatly relieved paratroops happily complied and Paksane was immediately occupied by Phoumi's forces. On 7 December the President of the National Assembly, Prince Somsanith, using the excuse of the left-wing demonstrations, took refuge with 18 deputies in Kouprasith's camp at Chinaimo, three kilometres downstream from the MIC site. Later they proceeded to Savannakhet to join some 20 deputies who had already defected to Phoumi, encouraged by substantial bribes from the American Embassy.

The coup was set to take place on 8 December. But in the early hours of that morning Souvanna Phouma got wind of what was happening. He summoned Kouprasith, who assured him that the coup was intended to support the government against left-wing influences; his troops were wearing white ribbons, white being the colour of true neutrality. Souvanna Phouma accepted this concept, and some of Kong Lae's officers were happy to go along with it. However, the sight of some of Phoumi's paratroops dropping at Chinaimo in the afternoon, clearly visible in Vientiane, cast doubts on the 'neutrality' of the coup, and in the evening Kong Lae peacefully resumed control of Vientiane. On 9 December the main body of Phoumi's troops with their artillery, who had been brought across Thailand from Savan-nakhet, began to cross the river from Nongkhai. With overwhelming military strength on his side, Phoumi no doubt hoped to take over Vientiane without a fight. The confusion caused by Kouprasith's actions had indeed fatally weakened the defences of Vientiane. Many of the soldiers on the government side who had worn Kouprasith's white ribbons in the belief that his coup would bring peace now stayed with him. But Kong Lae's paratroops were determined to put up a fight. To distinguish themselves from the 'white' troops they wore pieces of red cloth torn from the red neckerchiefs that were part of their combat uniform.

With a battle now inevitable Prince Souvanna Phouma, who had worked so hard to avoid civil war, realized that he could do nothing more, and in the evening of 9 December he flew to Cambodia with most of his ministers. The minister of information Quinim Pholsena stayed behind, and on the next day he flew to Hanoi to ask for artillery. The response was immediate: on 11 and 12 December Russian aircraft arrived in Vientiane with three French 105-millimetre howitzers and three Chinese heavy mortars with ammunition. Mean-while on 11 December the 38 deputies in Savannakhet, constituting a majority of the National Assembly, voted a motion of no confidence in Souvanna Phouma. On this occasion the King in Luang Prabang did not delay or prevaricate, but on 12 December signed a royal decree dismissing Souvanna Phouma's government and giving power provisionally to the Savannakhet Revolutionary Group. A further ordinance followed appointing a provisional government headed by Prince Boun Oum, which was immediately recognized by the USA and Thailand.

A couple of days earlier I had returned to full-time duty at the embassy. I found that there had been several staff changes during my absence. David Wilson had gone off on his Antarctic expedition and been replaced by David Campbell (yet another Scot), a young man of similar adventurous disposition who had served briefly in Nigeria before transferring from the Colonial Service to the Foreign Service when Nigeria became independent. Peter Newman had left and been replaced as administration officer by Fred Kempson, who was accompanied by his wife Betty and two children, a girl of nine and a boy of four. Despite the imminent threat of a battle, everyone was in good spirits. I recall the considerable hilarity when Mr Pheng, our translator, relayed the news from the radio that the King had dismissed Souvanna Phouma. Mistranslating the French '*démissioner*' he announced that the King had 'diminished' Souvanna Phouma. Henceforward the verb 'to diminish' was used in our private language with the special meaning of to get rid of or to best someone in a contest. Thus you would 'diminish' your opponent on the tennis court; and the phrase 'BRAM diminished Boun Oum' meant that John Addis had got the better of an argument with the new Prime Minister.

One of my first duties was to make preparations to safeguard embassy staff as far as possible during the forthcoming battle. All staff, as well as the two doctors, were issued with Union Jacks to display on their cars (a privilege normally reserved for the Ambassador) in the hope that this would dissuade troops of either side from firing on us. It was agreed that all children with their mothers, together with one pregnant wife (Sally Thomas) should be evacuated to Bangkok. (We would have preferred all wives, even those without children, to leave, but to a woman they insisted on staying with their husbands.) Staff living near the embassy would move into the Ambassador's residence, where the ambassadorial flag would presumably deter any marauding soldiers. Remaining staff and wives would move into the MIC site, which was at least protected by a high fence running along the main road. In retrospect this latter decision may have been unwise, as the front-line roadblock defended by Kong Lae's paratroops was located at the Sala Koktane, a boating club/restaurant only 200 metres downstream from the MIC site. Phoumi's advance troops were at a roadblock only a few hundred metres further downstream. Hugh Toye visited the two sides and found that a degree of fraternization was taking place; and agreement had been reached that if an attack was ordered the troops of both sides would fire in the air.

The concentration of staff at the residence and the MIC site was carried out in the evening of 12 December. At the MIC site we created our own mini-version of the ball in Brussels on the eve of Waterloo. We invited all present to a champagne supper, played our complete recording of *Die Fledermaus* on the hi-fi system and waltzed to the small hours. Next morning all seemed quiet. Around midday the air attaché Group Captain Joe Holmes, based in Bangkok, arrived in his aircraft at Vientiane airport, on the far side of town, to lift the first group of evacuees, consisting of Oggy Thomas with Sally, now in the last week of her pregnancy, Shirley McColl and a Frenchwoman, each with a baby only a few weeks old. Despite the protests of Shirley, most unhappy at leaving Colin and missing all the 'fun', they departed successfully shortly after one o'oclock for Udorn airfield in north Thailand to the south of Nongkhai. At Udorn Oggy, arriving with three 'wives', two with small babies and one heavily pregnant, was treated with envious respect by the airport staff. Joe Holmes returned at 1400 hours to find that the second batch of evacuees had not arrived. Soon the airfield came under shelling and machine-gun fire, but Joe waited until 1600 hours when the firing became more severe and he took off for Udorn, whence he took the first lot of evacuees down to Bangkok. On the next day Sally gave birth to a baby girl, Katey, and Oggy made history by being the first father in Thailand to insist on being present at the birth.

Back at the MIC site the second group of evacuees, consisting of Fred Kempson and his family, had been descending the steps of their house in order to leave for the airport at about ten past one when heavy firing broke out from the direction of the Sala Koktane. The Kempsons returned to their house. The other occupants of the MIC site, including Beth and me and some servants, took refuge in the garage underneath our house. With concrete walls on three sides and the open side facing away from the direction of the firing, it seemed the safest place to be. Before retreating there we closed and locked the two gates giving access to the site from the main road. This proved to be a waste of time as the troops came not along the road but along the river shore and through our garden, so we had to rush out and unlock the gates to enable them to continue their retreat along the road.

The first soldiers, retreating Kong Lae troops with their distinguishing red scarves, appeared in the garden about ten minutes after the firing started. They gave the impression that they had been ordered to withdraw. Although one soldier discarded his pack and several got rid of their red scarves there was no sign of panic. Most of them were cheerful and smiling. Some looked very young and may have been students who had been given uniforms and weapons in the previous few days; they seemed to regard the whole business as something of a game. One or two attempted to set up their machine guns in the garden in order to return fire, but we had little difficulty in persuading them to join their comrades in retreat. Altogether something like 80 'red' soldiers passed through the site. At one stage two 'red' armoured cars retreated at full speed down the road with their crews looking apprehensively backwards.

At about 1.40 p.m. the first Phoumi troops appeared in the garden wearing white scarves or armbands. They too were cheerful and smiling and seemed very confident. One of them was carrying a bazooka, and an officer swaggering about with a cane directed two rounds to be fired in the direction of the island just north of the site. The blast completely shattered the windows of the servants' quarters under one of the houses, showering a terrified woman servant with broken glass. There seemed to be no obvious target for the bazooka — there were certainly no Kong Lae troops on the island — and we had the impression that the main purpose was to make a lot of noise to frighten the enemy. (A well-established tradition in Laos, originating in China and no doubt designed to minimize casualties, awarded victory in battle to the side that made the most noise.) Our impression was borne out by the volume of the supporting fire given by armoured cars and tanks which stopped from time to time to loose off all their armament down the road in the direction of the retreating 'reds'. There was very little return fire and it is doubtful whether the armoured vehicles had any specific target, but they certainly made a shattering din. Several windows in our houses were broken at this time by small arms fire. Fortunately, apart from the servant who was cut by flying glass, no one was hurt. Madeleine Davies, who had been resting on her bed in her small bungalow before joining us when the battle started, later found a bullet hole in the headboard of the bed precisely where her head had been resting on the pillow.

Perhaps a hundred 'white' troops passed through the MIC site garden, keeping pace with the armoured cars and tanks on the road. They were followed after a short interval by more troops coming along the road, mainly on trucks but some walking, and also by more armoured cars and tanks. On several of these were perched light-skinned, fair-haired soldiers who were obviously American 'advisers'; and we subsequently learned that the attacking troops also included a number of Thai 'volunteers'. In the midst of all this at about 2.30 p.m. Ken Rymer, the wireless operator who lived at the MIC site, suddenly turned up in his Land Rover. He had had the alarming experience of driving through both front lines. Driving from the embassy he had come upon a temporary defence line of the 'red' troops who had made no difficulty about letting him through. Some 200 metres further along the road he encountered the advancing column of the 'white' troops led by an officer on foot and supported by armoured cars and tanks. The officer waved to him to stop but let him through when he explained who he was.

All the noise of battle must have been very frightening for the Kempson children, but worse was to follow. Shortly after 3.00 p.m. four gunboats flying the Laotian national flag and a white flag indicating that they were Phoumist chugged up the river from the south towards Vientiane. They circled around about half a kilometre upstream from the MIC site and appeared to be firing (mainly machine guns but also some small cannon) on the island and also on the south-eastern part of the town, which was then still occupied by 'red' troops. The naval attack continued for nearly two hours during which only scattered bursts of small-arms fire were returned. But around 5.00 p.m. shells, coming presumably from the howitzers brought by the Russians, which had been deployed at the airfield to the west of the town, started dropping in the river in the general area of the gunboats, causing them to retreat hastily downstream. Shellfire pursued them down the river until shells were falling opposite the MIC site. It then seemed that the gunners, while maintaining the same range, gradually altered their angle of fire so that the shells, now at greater intervals, fell closer to the eastern shore, then on the island and then on the river bank directly opposite the MIC houses and less than 100 metres away.

By then darkness was falling and the perimeter lights blazing along the MIC site fence offered an obvious aiming point for the Kong Lae/ Russian gunners. Failing to find the switches, we had to break into the generator to turn it off, thus extinguishing all lights on the site. All of us, men, women and children, then concentrated in the Kempson home in the central house, and I advised everyone to lie face down on the floor. During the next hour a number of shells fell near the MIC site, sometimes as close as 50 metres on either side. As a former artillery officer I was familiar with the principle of bracketing, and waited, not so much in fear as in a spirit of calm resignation and fatalism, for the next shell to explode on top of us. Fortunately the shell with our name on it was never fired. We were lucky to survive unharmed, as the gunners were almost certainly aiming at the road running just by the MIC site, which was the link between the 'white' forward troops and their base at Chinaimo, and along which 'white' vehicles continued to pass with their headlights on. Shellfire continued intermittently throughout the night, some of it close to our houses but most of it passing high overhead, probably in the direction of Chinaimo. During most of this time we remained prone on the floor in total darkness, lit only by the sporadic flashes of exploding shells and the occasional headlights of passing trucks.

Some time about midnight we heard some movement on the road immediately outside the house. A cautious glance out of the window revealed a group of Laotian soldiers in the ditch outside the house, one of them with a bazooka pointed towards Chinaimo. Although it was too dark to see the colour of their scarves it seems likely that they were 'reds'. After a few minutes very heavy firing broke out. Armoured cars and tanks appeared on the scene, blasting away with all their armament, and unlike the previous afternoon a good deal of fire seemed to be returned. The noise of this minor military engagement, on the road only five or ten metres from where we were lying, was quite deafening. It must have been terrifying to the two children but, comforted by their mother and the other ladies, they behaved admirably and did not utter a whimper. After half an hour the firing ceased and the armoured vehicles withdrew. On the following morning there were four knocked-out vehicles, two trucks and two jeeps, about 150 metres down the road towards Vientiane but facing towards Chinaimo. The likely explanation is that a party of Kong Lae troops had infiltrated across the paddy fields and had lain in wait to ambush Phoumi vehicles. Armoured vehicles were then brought up from Chinaimo to drive them away. The four vehicles could have been knocked out by the Kong Lae troops but could equally have been destroyed by the 'white' armoured vehicles, which seemed to be blazing away indiscriminately in the dark down the road towards Vientiane and could easily have hit some of their own vehicles coming from the opposite direction.

On the next morning, 14 December, with sounds of battle still coming from Vientiane, it was still not safe to leave the MIC site, and we were able to watch the continuation of the naval campaign. We had a grandstand view as, owing to the curve of the river, we could see nearly all of the river front of Vientiane between one and two kilometres away. At about 11.00 a.m. the largest flotilla seen during the battle, consisting of six gunboats and five landing craft (used as gun platforms and not as troop transport) came up the river from the south. The flotilla advanced tentatively until the leading boats were opposite the centre of Vientiane while the others were dispersed at intervals downstream. The leading boats then began firing apparently into the centre of Vientiane. After a short time mortar or howitzer shells began dropping in the river near the gunboats and the whole flotilla, which had clearly been apprehensive of this, immediately turned tail and retreated downstream. As I wrote rather pompously in a report at the time, it was an inept and craven exhibition. It was repeated in the afternoon, but it was a smaller group of four gunboats that fired a few rounds into central and west Vientiane before being driven back by Kong Lae's artillery.

The same story was repeated on the following morning, 15 December, with two further sorties by the Laotian navy, each time with four gunboats. They were now venturing much closer to the Vientiane shore and seemed to be directed with more determination. However, when after a fairly long interval shellfire was returned it again had the effect of driving the gunboats back downstream. Then in the afternoon four gunboats and four landing craft appeared on the river. This time there was no return shellfire and they moved in much closer to the Vientiane shore, firing for about two hours in the direction of the airfield and west Vientiane where there appeared to be a few Kong Lae pockets of resistance. Observing through a power-ful naval telescope belonging to John Main (a former naval officer) we could see mortars mounted on the decks of the landing craft. The gunners did not appear to be aiming at specific targets. They simply pointed the mortars roughly in the direction of the town and dropped shells casually into the mortar tubes while laughing and chatting to each other. Some of the ammunition they were firing appeared to be incendiary. A fire was started on the river front and subsequently columns of thick smoke arose from further into town.

The absence of return shellfire indicated that Kong Lae had with-drawn his artillery and presumably most of his troops beyond the airfield and that the three-day battle of Vientiane was almost over. We had already established contact with the embassy via the Boulevard Circulaire and found the staff there in good spirits. They had had a less exciting time than we had at the MIC site, and had seen very few soldiers; but a number of shells had fallen in the area, probably coming from both sides, and a two-inch mortar bomb had exploded outside John Addis's open office window, causing him to sit up and exclaim 'Good God, what was that?' The first shells fired apparently at random by Kong Lae's gunners landed in the compound of the French Military Mission, which immediately dispatched an officer to the airfield with the request that the fire be directed elsewhere. Some had fallen in the nearby Thai Embassy compound and also in the compound of USOM, the American aid mission; and the main building of the American Embassy had burnt down, having caught fire from an adjacent building. It is possible that this damage to the property of Phoumi's two main allies was deliberate; but it is doubtful if Kong Lae's gunners had the technique to direct their fire so accurately. Colin McColl, who was one of those included in the embassy party, had taken his flute along, and John Addis had an old Broadwood upright piano, which he took with him everywhere. At the height of the battle, with a number of shells bursting in the area, a member of the French Embassy carrying a message from his Ambas-sador to John Addis, was astonished to hear the strains of a Bach flute sonata floating from the residence. Greatly impressed, he rushed away to tell his colleagues, exclaiming: '*Quel flegme, quel sang-froid britannique!*'

It had been a strange kind of battle. Troops of both sides kept a respectable distance from each other, and if they did meet by accident they would aim high. The reason was only partly the instinct of self-preservation but mainly the Buddhism which is deeply embedded in the Lao mind and which prohibits the killing of any living creature. It was thus psychologically almost impossible for a Lao soldier to point his rifle at another human being and pull the trigger. (The hill tribes who made up the bulk of the Pathet Lao did not have this problem as they were animists, and this may help to explain their psychological dominance over Lao government troops.) But in pursuit of victory to those who make the most noise many thousands of rounds — small arms, mortar and artillery — were fired into the air; and what goes up must come down. Spent rifle and machine-gun bullets falling from the air were not a serious threat, but mortar and artillery shells exploding on the ground were another matter. Military casualties were light: 22 of Kong Lae's soldiers dead and 14 of Phoumi's. But hundreds of civilians were killed, and more hundreds injured, by the random shelling and mortaring of the town. Nearly all the Lao inhabitants had fled from the town into the surrounding fields and jungle or across the river when the battle started, so the casualties were mainly among Vietnamese and Chinese traders who had stayed on, presumably because they had more to lose from potential looting.

The hundreds of wounded created an immediate medical problem. There was only one small colonial hospital, poorly equipped and with only a few score beds. The only qualified Lao doctor, the ex-minister of health Oudom Souvannavong, had fled the capital before the battle (his fine house opposite the MIC site had received a bazooka shell, which blew a hole in the exterior wall of the dining room; we suspected, but could not be certain, that this was a politically-motivated attack). There remained only a few French doctors attached to the hospital, together with the two British doctors Tony Brown and Dick Herniman, who as the battle receded scoured the town in their Land Rover picking up the wounded. They reported to the embassy that the hospital was seriously short of essential drugs, plasma and other medical supplies. Our telegram to the Commissioner-General's Office in Singapore asking if they could help was timed at 1505 hours on 15 December, but owing to the pile-up of other telegrams it was not received at Phoenix Park until 2330 hours. Diplomatic, army and air force staff worked through the night to collect the supplies from army medical stores, lay on an aircraft and obtain flight clearance, and by 0700 hours next morning the supplies were airborne. Vientiane airport was still closed, but after staging through Bangkok the aircraft arrived at Udorn airfield at 1400 hours. The supplies then had to be taken by road to Nongkhai, across the ferry and then to Vientiane, where they arrived in the early hours of 17 December, only 30 hours or so after our request reached Singapore — a brilliant piece of military organization.

All the Lao nurses (male) had also fled the town so that there was no nursing care. A few Frenchwomen with nursing experience came to the rescue; and Beth, with no nursing training but a serious interest in medicine, took over the care of a whole ward. As the town water supply had been cut off she filled large containers with water from the taps at the MIC site, boiled it and took it to the hospital (as in many hospitals in Third World countries, food was brought by the victims' families). She changed sheets and wound dressings, emptied bedpans and even scrubbed floors. She also assisted the doctors with operations (Dick was a surgeon and Tony an anaesthetist) — a gruesome business as many of the injuries were to the eyes. The reason for this was that the victims, instead of lying prone, tended to be squatting on the floor when the shells burst almost literally in their faces. However, Beth's interest in the intricacies of eye surgery soon overcame any repugnance to the sight of blood and mutilated flesh. (This experience revived her interest in medicine: she would have liked to become a doctor, but at her school girls did not 'do' science apart from biology, and so she lacked the physics and chemistry which were additionally necessary as the basis of medical studies. On our return to a London posting, she acted as an unpaid assistant collating and analysing material for a major medical research project. Later she studied privately for A-levels in the three science subjects, then took a joint honours B.Sc. in biochemistry and physiology, followed by a Ph.D. in biochemistry which qualified her for medical research.)

With the battle over we were faced with an immediate need to evacuate more staff, not for safety reasons but because with supplies from outside cut off we were running out of food. Beth and I had

built up a fair stock of tinned food before the battle, but this disappeared with alarming speed as we had to feed all the staff concentrated at the MIC site. The new evacuees included some members
of the embassy deemed less essential and most of the remaining wives,
but not including Beth who was doing essential work at the hospital
(in any case it would have required considerable physical force to get
her on the plane). They also included Danny and Billy who had had
enough excitement. During the first night of the battle, when shells
were dropping all around and a minor battle was taking place ten
metres away, Danny and Billy had been caught outside the house and
took shelter under an open staircase, too scared to move anywhere
else. Next day they asked if they could return to Singapore. I naturally
agreed, the more willingly as I knew that John Main was leaving
shortly and his excellent Vietnamese cook would become available.
On the day of their departure for Bangkok Danny formed up with a
carefully prepared *envoi*: 'Well goodbye Mr Brown. Take good care
of yourself. As Shakespeare says, parting is such sweet sorrow.' When
they arrived in Bangkok the Ambassador kindly invited all the Vientiane refugees to the embassy Christmas party. As their names were
on the list of evacuees, Danny and Billy also received invitations,
which they readily accepted. There was some consternation when it
was realized that they were Chinese servants (albeit with British pass-
ports from Singapore), but it was decided that it would be too
embarrassing to withdraw the invitations. In the event Billy said little
but behaved impeccably, while Danny enchanted the other guests with
his urbane conversation and his graphic account of the horrors of the
battle. In the end Danny achieved his ambition of coming to England.
On returning to Singapore he got a job as valet to a senior French
diplomat who was then posted to London. After the diplomat left
London Danny worked for a while for the French consul-general in
Liverpool. Subsequently I lost touch with him, but wherever he is I
wish him well.

The embassy staff had been fortunate to avoid any injury, especially
those of us at the MIC site where for a time we had been in the thick
of the battle. Unlike some other foreigners we had not suffered any
looting of the houses that had been left empty when the staff were
concentrated at the embassy and the MIC site. The Americans were

less lucky; one couple living near the British Embassy reported the loss of several items of furniture including a fine electric organ. Our exemption from looting may have had a political reason — we were known to be sympathetic to Souvanna Phouma and the neutralists — or may have been due to the loyalty of some night watchmen who stayed on when most Laotians fled the capital. At our embassy most of the Laotian staff disappeared when the battle started, but three stayed on, two drivers and a night watchman named Ba. The latter, a cheerful chap though somewhat villainous looking with a wispy goatee beard reminiscent of Ho Chi Minh's, was given the keys and kept vigilant watch over the embassy building throughout the battle. When it was over we wanted to reward the three loyal Laotians with a special *ex gratia* payment, but Treasury rules did not permit anything like that. So we calculated some generous overtime and organized a little ceremony at which John Addis praised them for their loyalty and handed over envelopes containing the overtime payments.

The Ministry of Works architects who designed the embassy office building had provided a garage but insufficient storage space for various embassy stores and consignments of imported foodstuffs awaiting distribution. So inevitably the garage became the storeroom and embassy vehicles were parked outside in the compound. Some weeks after the battle Fred Kempson needed to get at some stores and asked Ba for the keys to the garage, which he produced with evident reluctance. When Fred opened the door, there was the electric organ together with other items looted from the American family. I was thus faced with a dilemma. Obviously we had to inform the police of the theft, but we did not want to condemn our loyal servant to the squalor of a Laotian prison. So as a compromise we warned Ba that we were calling the police and told him to make himself scarce. He went away expressing gratitude, but the foolish fellow came back shortly afterwards just as the police arrived and so he was carted off to gaol. In the confusion of the next year or so it was difficult to find out what happened to him. We could only hope that in due course he would be released after serving not too long a sentence, but he never reappeared during my remaining two years at the post.

One more story needs to be told at this stage, though I did not hear about it until some years later. Vientiane was the first post at which I held a position of authority, in this case as deputy to the ambassador. This inevitably created a certain distance between me and the rest of the staff, who did not tell me everything that was going on. So it was only years afterwards that I learned from David Campbell that the occasions when Trevor Wilson's speech was more bumbling than usual were the result of opium-smoking, a habit he had picked up in Hanoi. On the last day of the battle David had spent long hours helping our two doctors to ferry wounded to the hospital and was feeling rather weary. Trevor suggested that he should relax with him over a pipe of opium, explaining that anyone hoping to become a real Indo-China hand needed to master this sociable and entirely harmless recreation. (As an example of its usefulness, he mentioned that in Hanoi Marshal de Lattre de Tassigny had given him the whole of the French order of battle over a pipe of opium.) Trevor drove them in his car to a well-known opium den, a little shack in a side street. As the evening wore on David developed toothache, which served as a form of aversion therapy curing him of wanting to smoke opium ever again. At an early stage he remembered that Trevor's car parked outside was still flying the Union Jack. Moreover it was a Humber Hawk, which had been John Addis's official car until a few months earlier when it had been sold to Trevor and replaced by a new one. Wondering what to do about it, Trevor recalled that when an ambassador was not being driven in his official car the ambassadorial flag was furled and contained in a black leather sheath. No such sheath was available, but Trevor managed to improvise a substitute. And so for several hours the British Ambassador's former official car, familiar to nearly everyone in the small town, was parked outside a notorious opium den with its flag furled and encased in the cardboard inner tube of a toilet roll.

6

World Crisis

On 16 December 1960, shortly after the last shells had fallen, Prince Boun Oum and General Phoumi entered Vientiane, exulting in their defeat of 'the communists'. By lumping together the neutralists and the Pathet Lao (who had taken no part in the fighting) they hoped to eliminate the neutralists as a political force and ensure that they would continue to be the sole recipients of American favour and finance. But if they expected a triumphal entry, with a thankful population cheering their liberators, they were disappointed. The Americans were celebrating, and Soupy Campbell James threw a lavish champagne party, but in the streets only a few sullen bystanders watched as the columns rolled in. Immediate steps were taken to suppress any possible dissidence. Civil servants suspected of sympathy for the neutralists were dismissed, and a National Directorate for Coordination, combining civilian, military and political police, was set up under the command of Phoumi's intelligence chief Siho, now a colonel. This Orwellian euphemism for the secret police, referred to simply as the Coordination, carried out a series of assassinations and arrests and instilled an almost palpable atmosphere of fear in Vientiane over the next few years.

John Addis's report on the first meeting of the Diplomatic Corps with the victorious new government was perhaps lacking in the ideal diplomatic quality of detachment. He described some of the ministers 'dressed as stage commandos in American khaki cottons and Texan bootees, with enormous revolvers at the hip and carrying elaborate silver-nobbed batons'. The corpulent Boun Oum was dressed in bright green uniform — 'Falstaff in travesty as Robin Hood'. John's distaste at having to shake hands with 'this evil gang' was reminiscent of Shakespeare's Mark Antony shaking hands with Caesar's assassins — 'Let each man render me his bloody hand.' After two prisoners had been produced and mocked for the delectation of the diplomats, John and the Australian Chargé d'Affaires ostentatiously left the gathering in breach of protocol.

While the victors were celebrating in Vientiane, Kong Lae and his paratroops were retreating northward up the road to Luang Prabang as far as the road junction at Phou Koun, and then eastward to the Plain of Jars in Xieng Khouang province, where there was a substantial garrison of pro-Phoumi troops. They arrived on the edge of the Plain on the last day of 1960. Phoumi chose this moment to announce that no less than seven Viet Minh battalions had crossed the frontier and that two of them were approaching the Plain. The garrison did not wait to find out if the Viet Minh battalions existed or not (they didn't) but fled in panic south to the Mekong, leaving Kong Lae to occupy the Plain peacefully.

The Plain of Jars, named after some prehistoric stone jars located in the area, was a perfect base where Kong Lae could regroup his forces. A high plateau surrounded by jungle-covered mountains and approached only by a single steep, narrow road from the west, it was easy to defend. It had a small military airstrip to receive a Russian airlift from Hanoi, bringing in a steady stream of equipment and supplies. Quinim Pholsena, who had accompanied Kong Lae in his retreat, now established what he maintained was the only legal government in Laos in some old Foreign Legion barracks at Khang Khay on the northeastern edge of the Plain. Souvanna Phouma, still bitter at the American betrayal, stayed on for some time in Phnom Penh, where he rejected American attempts to persuade him to resign as prime minister as a prelude to the formation of a coalition government he would be invited to join. In February he flew to the Plain of Jars to take over as prime minister of his 'government'.

So far the Pathet Lao had kept clear of the fighting and, contrary to Phoumi's propaganda, had given no help to Kong Lae in his resistance to Phoumi's advance. This was partly because their soldiers were not equipped or trained for conventional warfare; but also because it suited them well to stand aside while their two political rivals fought it out. This attitude now changed. Pathet Lao troops emerged from the jungle to appear in force on the Plain. Prince Souphanouvong joined his half-brother at Khang Khay where an alliance was proclaimed. A joint military command was set up with Kong Lae and the Pathet Lao General Singkapo as joint commanders. Phoumi's victory was now looking distinctly hollow.

The more positive Pathet Lao policy was inspired at least partly by the North Vietnamese leaders who had recently decided to step up the rebellion in South Vietnam. They were therefore interested in securing control of eastern Laos either side of the 17th parallel as a channel for supplies and weapons for the rebels — the famous 'Ho Chi Minh Trail'. The Pathet Lao were accordingly formed into regular battalions and trained in conventional warfare by Vietnamese troops flown in by the Russian airlift along with arms and equipment including artillery. Kong Lae's troops were also re-equipped with Russian arms and their numbers expanded from three parachute companies to five battalions, recruited partly from students who had followed Kong Lae from Vientiane and some remnants of the former garrison of the Plain. However, the separate identity of the two forces was jealously maintained, with the Pathet Lao continuing to recruit mainly from the hill tribes while Kong Lae's troops were drawn largely from the Lao population.

In Vientiane life slowly returned to normal and, with the resumption of food supplies, our evacuees returned from Bangkok. Only a week after the end of the battle John Addis held a Christmas party for the British community. This was so small that he was able to invite all of them to dinner — 30 of them seated around a long table stretching from the dining room through double doors into the drawing room. John, who was no great gourmet, had a Chinese cook. When on his own he always ate simple Chinese food and drank Chinese tea, and when entertaining would usually serve acceptable but not outstanding Chinese dishes. But for Christmas he had imported turkey and Christmas puddings. The turkey was quite good but the Christmas puddings were another matter. Clearly the Chinese cook was unfamiliar with the product and, instead of boiling the puddings for several hours and then flaming them with brandy, had simply heated them up in the oven. The result was solid slabs of stodge on which even the most sycophantic of the guests could make little impression. As we left we consoled each other that at least it would be another year before we would have to face the ordeal again. But we were wrong. A week or so later John had occasion to give a dinner party for some diplomatic colleagues, to which senior members of the embassy were invited. After the main course John picked up the menu, which listed the pudding as *Tarte aux prunes* and said brightly: 'We've never had that before. I wonder what it is.' It turned out to be recycled uncooked Christmas pudding placed between slabs of stodgy pastry and served cold. Among the guests was Falaize, the French Ambassador, and the expression of horror and disbelief on his face as he tasted the first mouthful was something that lingered in the mind's eye for a long time.

However, the morale of our small staff, which was at a high level because of the adrenalin released by the excitement of the battle, managed to survive this ordeal by Christmas pudding. It is a paradox of the Diplomatic Service that morale, particularly among the junior staff, often seems to vary in inverse proportion to the size, importance and glamour of the post. One would expect morale at an embassy in somewhere like Paris to be much higher than at a remote, uncomfortable place like Vientiane. But with a large staff scattered in separate accommodation throughout a large city, and senior officers too busy with their own heavy official entertainment responsibilities to spend much time entertaining their juniors, it is not easy to create a feeling of togetherness; and, for the junior staff, life in Paris is not much different from London, where you see little of your colleagues outside office hours. But in a small post like Vientiane we could all get to know each other very well and senior staff would often include the juniors in their entertaining. There was a real sense of belonging to a family, which was enhanced by the shared difficulties, discomforts, excitements and dangers and by the feeling that we were all contributing to the important work of the embassy in the context of a major world crisis.

Not long after the Christmas pudding episode our morale received a

1. *(above)* Scenes of Vientiane – Statue of King Settathirat and the That Luang pagoda.
2. *(below)* The funeral of Prince Souvannarath – awaiting cremation at That Luang.

3. *(above)* The MIC site – our house.
4. *(below)* Temples and pagodas in Vientiane.

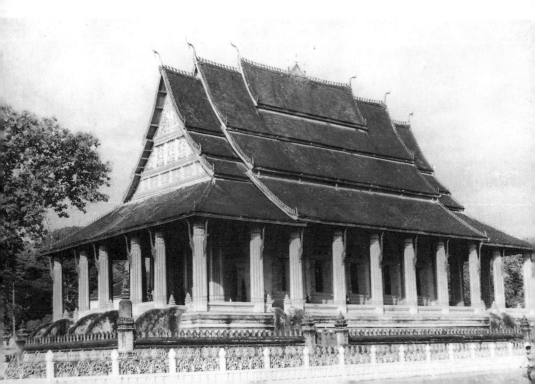

5. *(above)* The Mekong from the MIC site – 'fishermen waded out to cast elegant nets'.
6. *(left)* Captain Kong Lae.

7. *(above)* The Battle of Vientiane.
8. *(below)* Gunboats on the Mekong.

further boost from a most glamorous event — a wedding at the embassy. Our young Third Secretary David Campbell had left a fiancée back in England, 21-year-old Philippa Bunting. The Foreign Office had told David that because of the hardship conditions Vientiane was a bachelor posting, but John Addis had told him that he preferred to have married officers, and so they agreed to marry in January. When lurid details of the battle were reported in the British media, everyone advised Philippa to wait for a while. But as soon as the dust of battle had settled and outside communications were restored she insisted on flying out to marry David. There was of course no British church or registry office in Vientiane, but embassies could register marriages. John Addis could also have exercised the right that ambassadors share with ships' captains at sea and conducted the marriage ceremony himself. Indeed he did this a year or so later when he married a young archivist Harry Kershaw and a charming Lao girl who was working in the Information Section. But on this occasion we imported the Anglican chaplain from Bangkok to conduct the ceremony. John Addis's role was to give the bride away, picking her up from our house where she had been staying. Don Kingsmill of the Australian Embassy was best man and the bridesmaids were Madeleine Davies and young Marilyn Kempson. The main reception room of the residence had been converted into a church interior with an altar brought from Bangkok, and I played appropriate hymns on a borrowed harmonium. I was asked to speak briefly in the place of the absent father of the bride, but my remarks were completely upstaged by the best man Don Kingsmill, whose speech consisted of brilliant parodies of newspaper reports of the wedding in the style of a British tabloid, *Time* magazine and *The Times* of London, the latter commenting snootily on the absence of many of the appurtenances of a fashionable wedding, and concluding 'and the best man was a colonial'. The romance of this lovely young girl flying out and risking the dangers of 'war-torn' Vientiane to marry her fiancé captured the imagination (and did no harm to our reputation for *flegme britannique*). There was a very high 'turn-out,' of the diplomatic corps and David's Lao friends and the reception afterwards was a joyous occasion. It was undoubtedly the social event of the season, indeed of all our time in Laos.

Another new arrival shortly after the battle was Malcolm Morris, the first Australian ambassador appointed to reside in Laos. He was able to settle in quickly by renting the house opposite the MIC site abandoned by the ex-minister of health Oudom Souvannavong, which still had a shell hole in the wall of the dining room. He was far from being a typical Australian. Educated at Geelong College, 'the Eton of Australia', he had gone to Oxford before the 1939 war, during which he served with distinction in the Coldstream Guards. His speech was all you would expect from Oxford and the Guards, without a trace of 'Strine'. His appearance — tall, slim, upright, fair-haired with a small moustache — would have made him first choice for a Hollywood casting director looking for someone to play a British officer and gentleman. (Some time later at Khang Khay Prince Souvanna Phouma asked me to describe a typical English gentleman, and I could do no better than reply 'the Australian Ambassador'.) He was always impeccably dressed, and on occasions when we would wear uniform he would be beautifully turned out in evening dress for an evening function or in grey morning suit and topper for a daytime function. Shortly after Malcolm arrived John Addis asked me late one evening to show him an important telegram which had just come in. I was wearing the slacks and open-necked shirt which was the normal dress in Vientiane outside the office. I found Malcolm at home having dinner alone in the dining room with the shell hole in the wall and wearing a dinner jacket with black bow tie. After all, it was important to maintain standards, even in the most difficult circumstances.

But if Malcolm was not a typical Australian, he was a first-class ambassador for Australia, a highly effective diplomat and a tough and able defender of his country's interests. His embassy office was close to ours, and as we were pursuing the same policy we worked very closely with him. He often, indeed usually, attended our office meetings where he provided insights and information drawn from his own sources which made him a most valuable colleague. In due course he was joined by his delightful family — his English wife Moira and three lovely teenage daughters — who were an adornment to the social scene.

It was around this time that we first got to know a journalist couple who, though covering other countries in the area as well, spent a lot

of time in Laos. Peter Simms, though English, was the local correspondent for *Time* magazine and the Associated Press. His wife Sanda,
a beautiful Cambridge-educated Shan princess from Burma, acted as
correspondent for Reuters. They were a considerable asset as they
both knew Laos very well. Many years later they were to publish a
scholarly history of Laos before the French occupation entitled *The
Kingdoms of Laos* based on a study of royal archives as well as works
by European travellers and historians.

The battle of Vientiane and the prospect of continuing civil war had
aroused major international concern. Before the battle was over the
North Vietnamese called for the reconvening of the Geneva
conference and the reactivation of the International Control Commission, and were supported by China and the USSR. On the day the
battle ended the Indian Prime Minister Pandit Nehru sent a message
to Britain and the USSR, as co-chairmen of the Geneva conference,
proposing the recall of the ICC for Laos. Soon afterwards Prince
Sihanouk invited all interested countries to a conference in Phnom
Penh to reach a new settlement on Laos. The British government
favoured the return of the ICC to supervise a cease-fire, but was
unwilling to commit itself to a conference until it became clearer that
conditions for a successful conference existed. For the time being
international action was blocked by the Americans who opposed the
return of the ICC and even a cease-fire. They still hoped that Phoumi
could improve his situation both politically and militarily and, if not
defeat the Pathet Lao, at least negotiate with them from a position of
greater strength.

Such hopes were rudely shattered by military actions in March
1961. From the beginning of the year Phoumi's troops had been
advancing slowly and nervously up the road to Luang Prabang as far
as the Phou Koun road junction where they joined a force that had
been proceeding even more slowly down the road from the royal
capital. But when the combined force tried to advance eastward
towards the Plain of Jars they were checked by a strong Kong Lae
defensive position. In the first week of March a limited counterattack
by Kong Lae troops sent the demoralized Phoumi soldiers in dis-
orderly retreat far back along the roads to Vientiane and Luang
Prabang.

News of this defeat caused considerable nervousness in Vientiane. One evening shortly afterwards Colin McColl and I were visiting Jean-Pierre Geoffroy Dechaume to rehearse for a musical evening we were planning; the music would have included a lively trio by the English eighteenth-century composer James Hook for three flutes — Jean-Pierre playing the first flute part on his recorder, Colin the second flute and myself transposing the third flute part on the clarinet. We had just finished and were standing outside Jean-Pierre's modest house when the noise of rifle and machine-gun fire broke out all around us. An American military adviser in a jeep drove by at speed shouting at us, 'Get back inside, Kong Lae's all over town.' But as there did not appear to be any immediate danger we ignored this advice. In addition to the small-arms fire we heard the beating of gongs and what sounded like the clashing together of pots and pans. Then we saw a stream of tracer bullets from a machine gun going directly upwards into the sky. Following the tracer line we saw that the moon was in partial eclipse. It was later explained that in Lao mythology an eclipse was caused by a giant frog trying to eat the moon. As the disappearance of the moon would be a great disaster it was necessary to scare off the frog by making as much noise as possible, traditionally with gongs and firecrackers, reinforced in modern times by firearms. Fortunately the efforts were successful and the black shadow soon retreated.

The defeat at Phou Koun was followed by a series of successful Pathet Lao attacks leading to the abandonment of more territory by Phoumi's troops. The idea of a cease-fire, resisted by the Americans as an obstacle to Phoumi's further advance, was now seen as essential to preserve the very existence of the right-wing government. American policy was affected more fundamentally by the change in administration in Washington, where President Kennedy had succeeded Eisenhower at the beginning of the year. At a handover briefing session in January Kennedy was taken aback when Eisenhower stated that Laos was the most important problem facing the United States. Expanding on the domino theory he said (according to Clark Clifford in his book *Serving the President*): 'If we permit Laos to fall, then we will have to write off the entire area. We must not permit a communist takeover. Unilateral intervention would be our last, desperate hope if we cannot get others to go along with us.' Kennedy was impressed and for a time accepted the Eisenhower view. But closer examination of the problem made him sceptical, and he became receptive to arguments in favour of a neutral Laos put to him by Sir David Ormsby-Gore, a close personal friend who had been appointed British Ambassador in Washington after Kennedy took office.

As early as March 1961 Kennedy publicly stated that the United States 'strongly and unreservedly' supported a 'neutral and independent Laos' and called for international negotiations to ensure its genuine neutrality. However, as insurance in case the new policy did not succeed, military support for Phoumi was covertly further increased: units of his army began training in Thailand, and Thai military advisers, posing as Lao, were sent to Laos. At the same time more CIA officers were sent, with the specific task of arming and training the Touby Lyfung wing of the Meos to carry out guerrilla operations against the Faydang group and the Pathet Lao in general. When John Addis heard about this he called on Winthrop Brown to ask for confirmation, to express disapproval and to warn prophetically that any short-term advantage would be outweighed by the long-term cost in human misery.

The reversal of American policy was not easy to bring about. There was a new President and a new Secretary of State (Dean Rusk), but the advisers in the State Department, the CIA and the Pentagon were the same. It is true that Parsons had left the State Department, on appointment as Ambassador in Denmark. But he had been replaced by Alexis Johnson from Bangkok, an even more intransigent hardline anti-communist. At a SEATO Council meeting in Bangkok at the end of March, Dean Rusk appeared to have accepted Johnson's views: Souvanna Phouma was unacceptable as prime minister as he was completely under the influence of the Pathet Lao; Kong Lae was a communist; and military force was the only way of dealing with the Pathet Lao. There was serious talk of military intervention by SEATO or by the Americans, either alone or with British support. The British Foreign Secretary Lord Home argued strongly against Western military intervention, which would have led inevitably to a North Vietnamese and possibly Chinese invasion of Laos. He believed that he had some success in changing Rusk's mind, but commented that 'there is a long way to go before the President can reverse the trigger-happy attitude of their advisers'. While in Bangkok he held a conference of British ambassadors and military commanders in the region and was struck by the unanimity of their criticism of US policy and in particular of Alexis Johnson: 'I would not have believed the widespread contempt which all our missions and the military have for the Americans' handling of this matter.'

Shortly after John Addis returned from the conference in Bangkok I departed with Beth on home leave. I had been in Southeast Asia for more than two years and was overdue for leave. The Treasury was still insisting that we travel by sea as it was cheaper than flying, and so we took a three-day rail journey from Nongkhai down to Singapore to join a ship there. The sea journey took three weeks each way and as I was due 16 weeks' leave (six weeks normal annual leave plus two weeks extra a year for service in tropical countries) we were away for over five months. I regretted having to leave in the middle of the ongoing crisis, but fortunately the Foreign Office takes the view that no one is indispensable, and I suppose I needed a rest after so much intense activity. Murray Simons, a capable young officer with whom I had worked in Singapore, came up to cover during my absence.

One event I was particularly sorry to miss was the funeral of the old King Sisavang Vong in Luang Prabang in late April, some 18 months after his death. There had not been a monarch's funeral for 55 years, so it was an especially important and impressive occasion, attended by the Diplomatic Corps and most of the government (the two opposition princes did not attend). As I was not an eyewitness I shall not attempt a detailed description of the funeral, which I was told was similar to Prince Souvannarath's, but on a much grander scale, with processions, ceremonies, prayers and rituals lasting three days. One innovation was a royal salute by howitzers of the army. Unfortunately the artillery had been formed only very recently, and they had not yet been provided with blank shells for ceremonial use. The assembled diplomats looked on with fascination as the live shells whirred across the valley to explode on the jungle-covered, and hopefully uninhabited, slopes on the other side.

In typical Lao fashion, all military and political activity was suspended during the funeral. But in the world outside, in Washington,

London, Paris, Moscow, Peking, New Delhi, Bangkok and elsewhere there was intense diplomatic activity aimed at preventing the Laotian conflict from escalating into something much more serious. On 18 March Kennedy had begun the reversal of US policy by asking the British government to convey some proposals to the Russians. These were for a cease-fire, the reconvening of the ICC and the resumption of talks to produce a broader-based Laotian government; if there were action on these three points the USA would agree to attend a conference. The Russian response was favourable and over the next few weeks a series of messages between the Russians and ourselves eventually produced agreement. On 24 April the two co-chairmen issued a joint call for a cease-fire, a meeting of the ICC and the convening of a conference in Geneva on 12 May. Within ten days the three Laotian parties had accepted the cease-fire. The ICC, consisting as in 1954 of India, Canada and Poland, flew into Laos and on 11 May confirmed that the cease-fire was generally effective. The Geneva conference was therefore able to reassemble under the chairmanship of Russia (Ambassador Pushkin) and Britain (Malcolm MacDonald), but the auguries for its success were not good.

Throughout April the Pathet Lao had continued to drive back Phoumi outposts, with the obvious intention of seizing as much territory as possible before the cease-fire was declared. They now claimed to control two-thirds of the country, or virtually all of it apart from the Mekong valley. Phoumi sought to excuse his military failure by the announcement of the presence of 60,000 Viet Minh soldiers in the country, and called for increased American aid. The Americans responded by lifting the ban against US military personnel in Laos wearing uniform or participating in operations. On 19 April the American military advisers put on their uniform and openly assumed a tactical advisory role, in clear breach of the 1954 Geneva Agreement; and the euphemistically named Programs Evaluation Office became the more honest United States Military Aid Advisory Group (USMAAG). However, this was also the day of the Bay of Pigs fiasco in Cuba, which weakened the position of the trigger-happy elements in Washington and made it easier for President Kennedy to resist them.

Kennedy had appointed Averill Harriman, Roosevelt's ambassador in Moscow during the Second World War, a former governor of New York State and presidential candidate, as Assistant Secretary of State with special responsibility for Southeast Asia. But it took even this high-powered and forceful representative a long time to resolve the contradictions of US policy. A peaceful settlement of the Laotian question required that the three parties should in the first instance meet to agree on the modalities of an effective cease-fire; and should then form a coalition government, which could send a single delegation to Geneva. From early May a series of tripartite meetings to discuss both military and political matters were held in the village of Ban Namone in 'no man's land' between the two military zones. But interminable wrangling, mainly over procedural questions, prevented any meaningful progress. At this stage some USMAAG elements were encouraging Phoumi to arrange for the cease-fire to break down and thus provide the excuse for SEATO or American military intervention. It was now evident that Phoumi could not defeat the Pathet Lao by military means. Faced with the alternative of a negotiated settlement with Pathet Lao representatives in the government, which they believed would lead quickly to a Pathet Lao takeover of the whole country, some Americans were advising Phoumi to contemplate abandoning the north to the Pathet Lao and establishing a strong position in southern Laos below the 17th parallel, which he could hope to defend with American help.

Progress on a coalition government was impeded by the State Department's insistence on three conditions that were unacceptable to the other two parties: that Souvanna Phouma should not be prime minister; that the Pathet Lao should not be included in the government; and that Phoumi should remain in charge of the armed forces. And so the Geneva conference opened without a united Lao delegation or any early prospect of one. Each of the three parties sent a separate delegation, but for a time the Boun Oum delegation refused to sit with the other two, insisting that as the legal government they were the only delegation entitled to represent Laos. Souvanna Phouma did not help his cause by appointing as his representative Quinim Pholsena, who emphasized his communist leanings by working closely with the Russians and even at times appearing to accept instructions from them.

The change in American policy was helped by Kennedy's meeting with Khrushchev in Vienna in early June where both agreed that Laos was not of vital interest to them and that they could accept a neutral solution. By then, faced with the reality that Prince Souvanna Phouma was the only possible candidate for prime minister who could be acceptable to all parties, the Americans abandoned their opposition to him. In due course and with even greater reluctance they accepted that a government of national unity without the Pathet Lao was a contradiction in terms, though they continued to work to keep Pathet Lao representation in the government to a minimum.

The new policy emerged at a meeting of the three Western foreign ministers in Paris on 7 August, where the Americans agreed that they would support Souvanna Phouma as prime minister on certain conditions. These included satisfactory arrangements for the demobilization of most of the Pathet Lao and Phoumist troops and the merger of the residue into a small neutralist force loyal to the proposed new coalition government; together with full powers for the ICC to supervise the cease-fire, the withdrawal of foreign troops and in due course free elections. As regards the government itself, the three ministers agreed that the key portfolios of Foreign Affairs, Defence and Interior should not be given to the Pathet Lao or left-wing neutralists (such as Quinim), that Phoumi should be given an important civilian position, and that the core of the government should be a large neutralist group with only a few Pathet Lao ministers balanced by an equal number from the right wing.

With the Americans now backing Souvanna Phouma, who was also the candidate of the Pathet Lao and the communist powers, most people thought that it would not be long before Phoumi and Boun Oum would have to fall into line. But this judgement underestimated the resilience and ingenuity of Phoumi and the strength of the forces that were still opposed to a neutralist solution for Laos. The most important of these was Thailand, where Field Marshal Sarit, Phoumi's kinsman, did not believe that a neutral Laos would provide an effective barrier against the traditional Vietnamese enemy. Whereas for the Americans Laos was in the last resort expendable, Thailand was not: it was seen as the main bastion against communist expansion in the area and the keystone of the SEATO alliance. The Americans therefore felt obliged to take seriously threats from Sarit that Thailand might have to come to some accommodation with the communist powers or even leave SEATO if the Americans showed insufficient will to resist the communists in Laos. Thus whenever there was talk of American sanctions to compel Phoumi to accept the agreed solution, rumbling noises from Bangkok would cause alarm in Washington and weaken the will to put the threat of sanctions into effect.

Moreover Phoumi was sustained by the views and advice of the many Americans in Vientiane, in the CIA, in USMAAG and even in the embassy, who openly expressed their disagreement with the new policy and hostility and contempt for President Kennedy and Harriman. This behaviour was astonishing to us in the British Embassy, with our traditions of civil service total loyalty to the government of the day and of Foreign Office primacy in foreign affairs. (My own participation in the booing of Eden in 1956 — a pointless and private gesture, as no one outside the office could hear us — was an isolated and probably unique incident provoked by an outrageous breach of international law and an equally outrageous dishonesty in attempting to justify it.) In Whitehall when the Foreign Office lays down a particular policy it is accepted without question by other departments including the Ministry of Defence. In Laos we saw the Americans behaving in a different tradition. Powerful agencies followed their own agendas and had their own lines of communication with Washington behind the back of the Ambassador; and the hardline military and CIA seemed to think that they had an almost sacred duty to oppose communism, irrespective of the views and wishes of the politicians who happened to be in power at the time. Because of America's failure to coordinate its foreign policy effectively Phoumi, controlling much less than half of an insignificant country, and totally dependent on the USA for money and military supplies, was able to defy the wishes of the world's great powers for the best part of a year.

7

The Plain of Jars

At the end of August 1961 Beth and I returned from leave to find an atmosphere more relaxed than when we left, despite the continuing intense political activity. With the cease-fire more or less effective and the Boun Oum government settled in and accepted by most countries as the legal government of Laos, there was a greater feeling of stability in Vientiane, at least on the surface. Diplomatic entertaining had returned to a normal level and there were fairly frequent official functions and occasional invitations from Lao friends to weddings and other family occasions. At the Lao functions we would of course be served Lao food. This was not always the unalloyed pleasure that we expected after experiencing the delights of Chinese and Thai cuisine. In the more sophisticated houses we might be served very acceptable dishes, delicately spiced in the Thai tradition. But the run-of-the-mill Lao food was, and no doubt still is, a very different matter. The main ingredient is glutinous or sticky rice, a fairly tasteless variety eaten with the fingers after kneading it into a ball, and accompanied by various stews and sauces notably a sauce called *pa dae* made from tomatoes, chillies and pounded sun-dried fish, which often smelt and tasted decidedly rotten. But if the cooking was low in the world league table the Lao themselves, with their good looks, courtesy, smiling charm and attractive culture, more than made up for this, so that an invitation from a Lao family was always gratefully accepted.

Apart from the Asian embassies, which always served their own national food, diplomatic entertaining usually involved high-class French cuisine, with many ingredients flown in from France (morale in the European community received a regular boost when the chalk-written sign '*Arrivage de fromage*' appeared outside one of the leading stores). Our own table was now considered one of the best in town, thanks to Phan Dai, the Vietnamese cook we had inherited from John Main. Though taciturn and of somewhat villainous appearance because of a walleye, he was a superb cook, having worked in Hanoi for Trevor's old friend Marshal de Lattre de Tassigny, the French commander-in-chief in Indo-China in the early 1950s. After the communist victory he took refuge in Vientiane and opened a restaurant, which he continued to run while cooking for John Main and then us. When we were neither entertaining nor being entertained elsewhere he would arrive in mid-morning to cook us a simple lunch and a dinner which he would leave to be warmed up by a young cousin called Dao whom he had introduced as our live-in general servant and who did all the housework and washing and served at table. Phan Dai kept a little black book in which he recorded every day on the left-hand page the cost of the ingredients he had bought at the market and on the right-hand page the menus for lunch and dinner. He had a precise social sense and would carefully grade the menu according to the quality of our guests, from simple but excellent bourgeois cooking for personal friends, lower-ranking diplomats and Lao officials (marked in the little black book simply as *Dîner*) up to superb *haute cuisine* for ambassadors and senior officials (*grand dîner*). Like most Asian cooks he was entirely reliable and resourceful. On one occasion I had ordered a buffet supper for 24 people (*vingt-quatre personnes*). An hour before the guests were due to arrive I saw Dao laying out knives, forks and napkins for four people: it transpired that Phan Dai had not heard the *vingt* in the *vingt-quatre*. Without a word he rode off on his bicycle, and two hours later a superb buffet for 24 people appeared on the table.

A tragic incident, which happened while we were away, was a reminder that Laos was no longer a land of peaceful lotus-eaters and that fears and tensions lay just below the surface of the agreeable social life in Vientiane. A beautiful young French woman called Danielle worked at Radio Laos as a newsreader and announcer. A few years earlier while in London to improve her English she had worked as an *au pair* looking after the children of the Laotian Ambassador Ngon Sananikone, younger brother of Phoui and now a minister in the Boun Oum government. She had been virtually adopted by the family and returned with them to Laos where she invariably wore Laotian dress. She had become engaged to Prince Eckarath, a handsome and charming nephew of Prince Souvanna Phouma and half-brother of Prince Somsanith; he was also a major in the army and an ADC to General Phoumi. Early one morning he was found dead with several bullets in his head in the back seat of his car with an hysterical Lao woman. The official explanation was that it was a *crime passionnel*, possibly the work of a lover of the woman. But there was no arrest or serious investigation, and there was a strong suspicion that it was a political murder carried out on the orders of Colonel Siho. It was a shattering blow to Danielle, and from that day on she never wore Laotian dress again. Some time later she married an American diplomat and, I hope and believe, lived happily ever after.

The diplomatic community now included the Indian, Canadian and Polish delegations of the ICC, each delegation headed by a diplomat, with a senior military officer as his deputy. The Indian chairman was Samar Sen, a highly intelligent and agreeable colleague who was in due course to become Indian Ambassador to the UN. The Canadian commissioner was a French Canadian called Mayrand, of whom I have little recollection; no doubt because I dealt mainly with his First Secretary Howard Singleton, a first-class officer who became a good friend. The military deputy, Brigadier Stewart Cooper, was also outstandingly good. We inevitably saw less of the Poles, whose leader Mr Morski was a political commissar out of a spy novel. But most of his staff were reasonably friendly and co-operative as far as their instructions from the Russians allowed; and it was useful to have them on the spot in Vientiane as, after the battle, the Soviet Ambassador had established himself on the Plain of Jars.

Since the beginning of the year there had been several changes in the embassy staff. John Main had been replaced as First Secretary by John McKibbin, whose attractive wife Pamela was a useful addition to our small tennis-playing community. Hugh Toye had acquired an Assistant Military Attaché Major Clarke Leaphard, unimaginatively but inevitably always known as 'Spots'. He had a French mother and, having lived in France and served in the French army in his younger years, he naturally spoke fluent French. He was very much a fighting soldier rather than a staff officer, having served in the commandos during the war and won a Military Cross during the invasion of Germany. More recently he had spent several years in the jungle in the Malayan campaign. Stockily built and good-looking with a tanned face, fair hair and blue eyes, he was in his late forties but physically very fit and looked much younger. Possessing also a cheerful and open character he soon became very popular, especially with the unattached ladies. Several of these had meanwhile turned up at the embassy. Sally Bull came out as Second Secretary (Information) and Sonia Roberts as Head Archivist to replace Philip Massé. The security officer, whose wife had acted as PA to the Ambassador, had left and John Addis now had a new PA, Patricia Chandler. With a trained soprano voice Patricia became a star soloist at our musical evenings and concerts and a considerable asset to the choir, which Oggy Thomas had formed and which I was allowed to join, my ability to read music marginally outweighing the indifferent quality of my voice. The musical community was also strengthened by the arrival of a violinist and bass singer, young Duncan Mackintosh, as deputy to the Shell representative (now Hugh Morgan who had replaced the novel-writing Desmond Rice). Sadly the excellent Swiss bassoonist had left, so I had brought back from England a bass clarinet to provide the essential bass line for our chamber music sessions.

Another newcomer was an English lady Estelle Holt. Having been recently widowed at a relatively early age, she had embarked on a journey through the Middle East and Southern Asia, which she made the subject of a very good travel book with the somewhat pretentious title *Asia and I*. On reaching Laos she stayed there, partly perhaps because it was the end of the line. As she was personable and good company we and other members of the embassy staff often included her in the cocktail parties, which were the main form of entertainment. However, after a time it became noticed that at the end of the parties when everyone else went home she would hang around, obviously hoping to be invited to stay to dinner. This was considered bad form and the invitations dried up. Then we discovered that the reason for her behaviour was that she was quite literally starving. She had almost run out of money and was living in a seedy Chinese hotel under a brothel and existing on one bowl of Chinese soup a day. Naturally we all then took turns to invite her to dinner and in due course we found her a job as a journalist, acting as a stringer for Reuters. This was quite successful as she was a good writer and got on well with people, although on at least one occasion her inexperience caused me some embarrassment. Once when I was acting as Chargé d'Affaires she came to tell me that the American Embassy had announced at a press conference that Chinese troops had invaded Phong Saly province in the north. Invited to comment I said that we had no such information ourselves and, although I do not recall my exact words, it is likely that I expressed cautious scepticism based on previous Phoumi-inspired reports of large-scale Viet Minh or Chinese incursions that proved to be false. She then went back to the American Embassy and told them that I did not believe their reports, which caused me a *mauvais quart d'heure* with Phil Chadbourn. My scepticism was indeed justified although the report had more substance than usual: the Chinese troops turned out to be labourers building a road from the town of Phong Saly to the Chinese frontier. As for Estelle, despite this lapse and other mistakes resulting perhaps from over-enthusiasm (Trevor Wilson, who as Information Officer had to deal with the press, used to refer to her as 'that dreadful woman') she became a generally well-liked member of our community and was to stay on in Laos for a number of years.

Tennis continued as before, with only a few changes of personnel at the Club. There was perhaps a slight improvement in the average standard of play when the Cambodian Ambassador, probably the worst player of the honorary *première série*, went on leave to Phnom Penh and did not return. Apparently his unusually heavy luggage was opened at Phnom Penh airport and found to contain a substantial quantity of smuggled gold. No doubt he was relying on diplomatic immunity to get away with it, but of course diplomats have no privileges or immunity in their own country, only in the country to which they are accredited. We never heard what happened to him.

By now there were two additional activities to occupy what leisure time we had. The Ministry of Works had constructed an open-air badminton court in the garden of the MIC site, and although neither of us had played the game before we found that tennis skills translated readily to badminton. I was able to beat anyone in the small expatriate community and Beth could beat any of the women and most of the men. This encouraged us to enter the local championships, a decision I quickly came to regret. Badminton is a very popular sport in Southeast Asia as it requires only limited space and fairly cheap equipment; while the warm weather and, outside the monsoon season, lack of wind enable it to be played out of doors. In consequence many of the world's best players come from Indonesia, Thailand and Malaya and even in a small country like Laos the standard of play was relatively high. Most of the players in the tournament were Chinese or Vietnamese students (not many Lao) of an average age of half my own. In the first round my young Chinese opponent ran me all over the place with shots hit with unrelenting accuracy to the sidelines, winning the first game 15–2 and leaving me near total exhaustion and interested only in getting off the court as quickly as possible with a minimum of dignity. In the second game my opponent started making mistakes and I found myself in the lead. I quickly realized that, probably from an oriental feeling of respect for elders, he was trying to let me win the second game in order to recover a little dignity. But I found this charity humiliating and countered with some deliberate mistakes of my own, so that the match was soon over and I was able to return home suitably chastened. As in most third-world countries in those days few women engaged in sport so that competition in the ladies' singles was less fierce. Beth had a fairly easy run through to the final where she met the reigning champion, a young Chinese woman, whom she eventually beat in a long, tough match.

The other activity was language learning. Like most, though by no means all, diplomats we always tried to learn the language of the countries to which we were posted. Starting with good French we had learnt Spanish in Argentina and in Singapore we had begun to learn Chinese (Mandarin dialect). It took us quite a time to grasp the concept of a tonal language, in which a word can have at least four totally different meanings according to the tone (rising, falling, level, falling then rising) in which it is spoken, and in our short time in Singapore we had not got very far, learning only a few hundred characters. In Laos Beth sensibly decided that Chinese would be far more useful in the long run than Lao, and continued to take Chinese lessons, concentrating on the spoken rather than the written language, so that by the end of our time in Laos she could converse easily with members of the Chinese Embassy at cocktail parties. I decided that I needed to learn Lao, and took lessons from our Information Attaché Mr Pheng. Knowing some Chinese already was a big help as spoken Lao is essentially a Chinese dialect, with four tones like Mandarin, but written not in characters but in a 46-letter alphabet derived from Sanskrit, which was much easier to learn. The big problem was the lack of opportunity to speak Lao. Normally one speaks the local language with one's servants, while shopping and in dealing with the local government. But our servants, like most of the shopkeepers, were Vietnamese with whom we spoke French; while the members of the government with whom we dealt all spoke French far better than I could ever have expected to speak Lao. However, I made good progress with writing and reading, and was later to be very glad that I had made the effort.

Learning a language is always worthwhile because of the insights it gives into the culture and way of thinking of the local people. Laotian society was very hierarchical, and this was reflected in the language, where different forms of speech were used, depending on whether the person you were speaking to was of equal, higher or lower rank than yourself. The form of the *wai* greeting also varied in a similar way. When greeting an equal the joined hands would be located just under the chin; for a superior person the hands would be in front of the face, or even above the bowed head if the difference in rank were considerable; while eminent persons such as the Princes Boun Oum or Souvanna Phouma would return a greeting from an inferior by joining fingertips at the level of the waist.

After more than a year the Doctors Brown and Herniman were finally assigned to Paklay, a small town on the Mekong about 100 kilometres upstream from Vientiane, and early in September they set off to their new post by boat along the river. They had a Land Rover, but some of the jungle tracks between villages in their area were too narrow for a vehicle and they had to resort to travel by elephant. Elephants have always been important in Laos, and the traditional name of the kingdom was Lan Xang, meaning a million elephants: the full title was Land of the Million Elephants and the White Parasol, the latter being the symbol of royalty. As there were few roads apart from those connecting the main towns, elephants were the main form of transport for journeys of any length. They were divided into two categories, slow elephants and express elephants, and for a given journey the express elephant was cheaper, presumably because it would take less time and therefore cost less in pay for the mahout and food for the elephant. One wonders why anyone ever chose the more expensive slow elephant — possibly because of the complete absence of time pressure in the leisurely Lao culture and a belief that 'to travel hopefully is a better thing than to arrive'.

Two new young doctors, Tony Bryceson and Colin Prentice (accompanied by his attractive wife Jane, a former actress) had arrived in the summer. Benefiting from the precedent already established, they were quickly assigned to the provincial capital of Saravane in the far south. This was some distance east of the Mekong and not far from the cease-fire line between the government and Pathet Lao forces, but at the time the cease-fire appeared to be holding, at least in the south, and we did not expect any trouble. They based themselves at the provincial hospital in Saravane and, using their Land Rover as a mobile clinic, began to bring simple medical care to the surrounding villages, a number of which were occupied by people belonging to the aboriginal Kha tribes. However, their first report in October 1961 was not encouraging. They wrote that the general atmosphere in Saravane province was one of terror caused by the behaviour of the Royal Laotian Army to the village people, including theft, blackmail and especially the rounding-up of village women for army brothels. All of this was of great political benefit to the Pathet Lao who in contrast usually treated the village people in their areas with respect.

On the broad political scene the stalemate continued. At the Geneva conference the assembled powers were able to agree quite quickly on the framework for a new settlement of Laos. This followed fairly closely the previous agreements of Geneva (1954) and Vientiane (1957) with some necessary updating, for example to accommodate three parties instead of two. Everyone agreed that Laos should be peaceful, neutral, independent, democratic and unified; that there should be a provisional government of national unity in which the three parties would be represented; and that most of the military forces should be demobilized, with small elements of the three separate forces combined in a single national army. They also agreed that in external affairs Laos should follow a policy of peaceful coexistence, not joining any military alliance and not permitting any foreign military base or the use of its territory for military purposes. But no agreement could be finalized without a Lao delegation to accept and sign it, and there could be no Lao delegation until a provisional government of national unity had been formed. This should have been a straightforward matter involving a meeting of the three princes (Boun Oum, Souvanna Phouma and Souphanouvong); agreement that the provisional government should be headed by Souvanna Phouma, the only candidate remotely acceptable to all three parties as well as the Great Powers; and then hard bargaining on the allocation of government posts between the three parties. But Phoumi and Boun Oum used every device — procedural delays, prevarications, reversals of opinion — to delay matters for month after month.

The three princes had met at Zurich in June under the chairmanship of Prince Sihanouk and had agreed on the main principles to be included in a new Geneva settlement. Despite great pressure from all sides it was not until October that Boun Oum and Phoumi were prevailed upon to attend another tripartite meeting, at the 'neutral' village of Ban Hin Heup. Here they finally agreed that Souvanna Phouma's name should be put forward to the King as prime minister of the coalition government. But back in Vientiane they quickly reverted to the line that Souvanna Phouma was totally discredited, in the pockets of the communists and unacceptable as prime minister. And although the agreement at Ban Hin Heup stated that Souvanna Phouma would decide the place of the next Three Princes' meeting, they refused his invitation to a meeting at the Plain of Jars, despite the strongest pressure from the Americans. At one stage Dean Rusk threatened that if Phoumi and Boun Oum did not agree to go to the Plain of Jars the US government 'would have to consider if they had a useful role to play in Laos'. The response to this bluff, as it turned out to be, was a Laotian government statement reaffirming the refusal to go to the Plain of Jars.

And so for many months more a considerable amount of the diplomatic resources of the Great Powers was devoted to the affairs of Laos. In all this activity John Addis played an increasingly prominent role. Nearly every day he would hold meetings with one or more of his ambassadorial colleagues, notably the Americans and the French or with the Commissioners of the ICC. His meetings with Falaize were not always easy to arrange because of the different personal habits of the two men. Falaize, a typical Frenchman from the Midi, enjoyed a substantial lunch followed by a siesta; John Addis, an equally typical Englishman, insisted on his daily exercise, either tennis or a walk, at five o'clock. So Falaize's secretary would telephone to propose a meeting at five. John's secretary would reply that he had a prior engagement at five and would suggest three o'clock, which was of course Falaize's siesta time. They would end up rather crossly agreeing to meet at 6.30, which was convenient to neither of them as it would often conflict with official receptions or cocktail parties.

John Addis also called frequently, with or without instructions, on the leading members of the government, especially Boun Oum, Phoumi, the foreign minister Khamphan Panya or his deputy Sisouk na Champassac, a nephew by marriage of Boun Oum and one of our tennis players. He had fairly regular audiences with the King and also called from time to time on prominent figures such as the ex-prime ministers Phoui Sananikone, Kou Abhay and Prince Somsanith, in the hope that they might influence Phoumi and Boun Oum in a positive direction. But while they were usually unhappy about Phoumi's rejection of a negotiated settlement, they were too scared of Phoumi's secret police to oppose him. In talking to Phoumi, Boun Oum and members of the government John went to the extreme limits of diplomatic courtesy in accusing them of inconsistency, prevarication and downright lying. His favourite method was to ask: 'How can I explain to my government that', for example, 'you agreed at Ban Hin Heup that Souvanna Phouma would appoint the place of your next meeting but now you are refusing to go to the Plain of Jars?' This technique no doubt gave them some uncomfortable moments and added to the psychological pressure on them. But arguments were not likely to move Phoumi so long as he enjoyed the full support of Thailand and believed that his friends in the Pentagon and the CIA would never allow the US government to abandon him. He was also sustained by the support of the King who, apart from his dislike of Souvanna Phouma was (so Phoui Sananikone assured John Addis) jealous of Prince Sihanouk and wanted the Geneva conference to fail because Sihanouk had originally put forward the idea of a new international conference on Laos.

In terms of real influence in Indo-China, Britain was a very minor player and John Addis was punching well above his weight. France as the former colonial power should have been more effective than she was; unfortunately Falaize had shown himself so strongly in favour of Souvanna Phouma that he no longer had much influence with the Vientiane government. The Americans were of course in a dominant position, but Winthrop Brown had limited his usefulness by identifying himself more and more with Phoumi. It was as if, having in October 1960 been persuaded against his better judgement to back Phoumi against Souvanna Phouma, he was desperate to prove that this was the right policy. Harriman complained more than once that when Brown was instructed to bring the strongest pressure to bear on Phoumi he would tone down his instructions so that Phoumi would not take the threat of sanctions seriously. Moreover, as the American ambassador who had deceived Souvanna Phouma in the autumn of 1960 and engineered the downfall of his government, Winthrop Brown was not welcome on the Plain of Jars. So partly by default John Addis became the leading broker between Vientiane and the two rebel princes. He earned the respect of all parties and the confidence of Harriman by his energy and the intellectual force of his arguments. He also exploited to the full his position as local representative of the Western co-chairman of the Geneva conference.

It was in this latter capacity that John Addis first visited the Plain of Jars in September 1961, at the request of Harriman, who needed some specific assurances from Souvanna on the preconditions for American support agreed by the three Western foreign ministers in July. John took Colin McColl with him and they travelled with the Indian, Canadian and Polish commissioners of the ICC in an elderly Dakota the ICC had hired to ferry supplies and personnel to the branch offices they had set up on the Plain. They landed on the airstrip close to the famous jars and were driven across the plain (literally, as the so-called road was impassable) to the small hut in the former Foreign Legion barracks at Khang Khay, which was Souvanna Phouma's temporary home and office. In private talks held in the tiny bedroom Souvanna gave generally satisfactory but not very specific assurances on the points John Addis raised. Regarding the composition of the government, there was general agreement that it should consist of four ministers from Phoumi's group, four from the Pathet Lao and eight from the neutralist group (including Souvanna Phouma). The difficulty was that the Americans insisted that four of the eight from the centre should be 'Vientiane neutralists' — experienced ministers who had served in the present or previous governments but were not members of Phoumi's right-wing group, such as Prince Somsanith and Ngon Sananikone. But Souvanna Phouma insisted that he had to find places for at least six of his loyal supporters who had followed him to Khang Khay, which would leave only one place for a 'Vientiane neutral'. So this point was unresolved. Afterwards they were joined for further talks and lunch by Prince Souphanouvong whom John was meeting for the first time.

Souphanouvong was perhaps the most fascinating of the leading players on the Laotian scene. He was a member of the royal family, but a very junior one, being the son of the youngest of the 11 wives of Boun Khong, the viceroy who had ruled over the turn of the century. He therefore ranked well below Souvanna Phouma who, as the eldest surviving son of Boun Khong's senior wife, was now head of this branch of the family. As a boy Souphanouvong was sent to the French Elycée at Hanoi where his academic brilliance, especially in Latin and Greek, led his teachers to recommend a university course in classics. He preferred instead to follow his half-brother Souvanna and study engineering, which would be of more practical use to his country. At the École des ponts et chaussées in Paris he was again outstanding and passed out at the top of his class. On returning to Indo-China, however, he was given only a very junior post in the railway work-shops of the Trans-Indochinese Railway, where he was paid less than his French colleagues, most of whom were not as well qualified as he was. This experience of racial discrimination, together perhaps with resentment at his lowly status in the family, may have helped to push him in the direction of militant anti-colonialism and collaboration

with the Viet Minh in the liberation struggle. He married an intelligent and forceful Vietnamese woman who was a member of the
Vietnamese Communist Party and undoubtedly had much influence
over him. But there is no evidence that he himself was ever a card-
carrying communist. John Addis judged him rather as the sort of
romantic idealist whom the communists exploit.

John Addis and Colin McColl returned ten days later for further
talks with Souvanna Phouma, when John put forward a significant
proposal to resolve the deadlock on the composition of the central
group in the coalition government. He suggested that Souvanna
Phouma should retain his seven ministers from Khang Khay but that
four 'Vientiane neutralists' should be added, making a central group
of 11 ministers. This turned out to be the final agreed formula, but
many permutations and alternatives were put forward before agreement was reached nine months later. On this occasion John and Colin
travelled in a six-seater Beechcraft leased by the ICC. The pilot was a
plump *métis* from Martinique who used his opportunities to carry out
a little business on the side. Colin McColl's report on this trip ended
as follows: 'At the Plain of Jars there was some delay while, as we sat
in the plane, our Martinique pilot bargained at the door with a crowd
of local soldiers over the price of the opium which he was taking back
with him to Vientiane. When the price had been settled we took off in
a thunderstorm.'

The mountains of northern Laos were and I imagine still are an
important source of the illegal opium which fuels the international
illicit drugs market. Various generals and politicians were involved in
this traffic, and control of the opium trade and of the gold-smuggling
business were important prizes in the struggle for power. Our
Martinique pilot seems to have been much involved. We learned that,
apart from bringing opium down from the Plain of Jars, he provided a
channel for its export. He used to fly his Beechcraft across north-east
Thailand and Cambodia to a rendezvous over the Gulf of Siam where
a ship would be waiting to pick up the waterproofed package he
dropped. Naturally he had no flight clearance but in normal circumstances his small aircraft would escape detection. Unfortunately for
him some time in late 1962 there was a serious dispute between
Cambodia and Thailand and the frontier was in a state of alert.

Returning from an opium-dropping flight, the Thai Air Force intercepted him, forced him to land and accused him of spying for Cambodia. Faced with the possibility of being shot as a spy, he confessed to the lesser charge of drug-smuggling, which earned him a substantial gaol sentence.

My own first encounter with the Martinique pilot was in October 1961 when I was asked to have a further talk with Souvanna Phouma about a month after John Addis's previous visit. I was the only passenger in the Beechcraft as we flew northwards as high as possible over the jungle-covered mountains: Pathet Lao troops had been known to take pot shots at the aircraft if it flew too low. At the Plain of Jars airstrip I was met by Souvanna Phouma's Private Secretary, a good-looking young man called Khamchan Pradith who took me over the plain to Khang Khay in a Russian jeep. We passed groups of Kong Lae paratroops, smartly dressed with red berets, and for the first time I saw some of the Pathet Lao soldiers looking by contrast distinctly shabby in faded khaki uniforms and Chinese-style peaked caps. Pradith told me that relations between the two groups were quite good at the military level but that there was quite a lot of suspicion and hostility at the political level, with the Pathet Lao trying to undermine the Neutralist Party (Lao Pen Kang) which Souvanna Phouma had set up two months earlier.

After about twenty minutes we arrived at Souvanna Phouma's hut in the Khang Khay barracks. As I entered the small living room, six metres by four, with a dining table at one end and four armchairs at the other, Souvanna Phouma emerged from the bedroom and, after shaking my hand dispensed with any further preliminaries to ask: 'Qu'est-ce qu'on dit à Vientiane?' So I told him what was being said in Vientiane. At the time the immediate issue was the place of the next meeting of the three princes. I told him that there was no chance that Boun Oum and Phoumi would come to the Plain of Jars: they would continue to insist on Vientiane or Luang Prabang, and the best hope was to go for a neutral place like Ban Hin Heup. I also had to tell him that Boun Oum and Phoumi had reverted to saying that he was unacceptable as prime minister; and that the Americans would need to be satisfied in detail on their preconditions before they would exert sufficient pressure on Phoumi to bring him into line. At one stage we were joined by Chao (Prince) Sisoumang, one of his nephews, who served as a minister in the Khang Khay 'government'. Then Souphanouvong, whom I recognized from photographs, joined us for lunch.

Souphanouvong was rather shorter and swarthier than his half-brother and wore round glasses, a moustache, long sideburns and a curious Ho Chi Minh-like wispy goatee beard straggling from the end of his chin. He was, however, conventionally dressed in a lounge suit, unlike other Pathet Lao leaders who wore Chinese-style tunics. What struck me most about him was the impression of alertness, with his black eyes darting around and taking everything in. He was undoubtedly clever and in conversation over lunch he enjoyed showing off a wide range of knowledge. But seeing the two princes together it was obvious that those Americans who thought that Souvanna Phouma was under the domination of his brilliant younger brother were mistaken. Equally the reverse was not true. Souphanouvong had his own opinions and was not easily deflected from them: for example he was continuing to insist that Phoumi and Boun Oum must come to the Plain of Jars, whereas Souvanna Phouma was quite ready to contemplate a meeting in one of the 'neutral' villages. But Souvanna Phouma, equally intelligent and immensely experienced, exercised a natural authority as elder brother, head of the family and prime minister designate. It was an equal partnership, but Souvanna Phouma was undoubtedly the senior partner.

This was the first of six visits I paid to the Plain of Jars over the next eight months, half as many as John Addis during the same period while we tried to resolve the difficulties standing in the way of the formation of a coalition government. These frequent trips were a great ordeal for John, who had a real fear of flying. He told me that he could tolerate flying on a commercial airline by imagining he was travelling in a Greyhound bus. But such an illusion was not possible in the tiny Beechcraft as it bucked around in the hot-air currents and it was only too obvious that there was nothing but insubstantial air between us and the mountains below. I never travelled with him but David Campbell, who did on one occasion, told me that it was clear that the flying caused him great physical distress. It was typical of the man that he never allowed this to influence a decision as to whether he should fly or whether he should send someone in his place.

On each of our visits we were entertained to lunch, even though we could see that life at Khang Khay was pretty spartan and that basic foodstuffs, let alone luxuries, were in short supply. So it became our practice to bring with us contributions to the lunch, such as a side of smoked salmon, a tin of ham or cake and a few bottles of burgundy. These gifts were accepted gratefully and with dignity, and in return we were offered such delicacies as could be produced from local resources. Occasionally it might be a game bird, although with so many soldiers around game of any kind was very scarce. Once I was offered ants' nest soup, made by pouring the contents of a nest of red ants into boiling water, the formic acid from the ants providing a chilli-like piquancy. On another occasion I was told on arrival at Khang Khay that I was in luck as a wasps' nest, considered a great culinary treat, had just been found. And so the main dish was sautéed wasps' larvae, accompanied by the inevitable spicy fish sauce. The larvae themselves were fairly tasteless, with a texture rather like brains. But every now and then one's teeth would crunch on a chrysalis containing a fully-formed wasp about to emerge. So a certain amount of diplomatic fortitude was called for, though less I imagine than with the sheep's eye traditionally offered to guests of honour at an Arab banquet.

At these meetings at Khang Khay we would meet other leading neutralists such as Pheng Phongsavan, Souvanna Phouma's right-hand man and candidate for the post of minister of the interior; and occasionally Pathet Lao leaders such as Phoumi Vongvichit, a communist but a relative moderate who represented the Pathet Lao at Geneva, and Nouhak Phomsavan, considered one of the hardline communists. I do not recall ever meeting Kaysone Phomvihan, who was believed to be the real power behind the scene. John Addis was sometimes accompanied by a member of his staff, and scored a notable success when he took Trevor Wilson with him. Trevor obviously fitted in with the Francophone concept of an English eccentric, and John Addis could see Souvanna Phouma almost hugging himself with delight as he took in this elderly, rotund, Pickwickian figure recounting hesitantly tales from his interesting past in excellent French but with a pronounced English accent. He became the centre of attention when he spoke of his time in Hanoi and his friendship with Ho Chi Minh. The normally closed faces of the Pathet Lao present opened up and relaxed into eager smiles as he spoke of their hero. 'And then,' said Trevor, 'sadly I was expelled. ...' Instantly the Pathet Lao faces froze and there was a moment of dead silence. After a perfectly judged pause Trevor completed the sentence, 'by the French'. Shouts of laughter signalled complete success for the raconteur.

Usually one flew up to the Plain of Jars in the morning and returned in the afternoon. But on one occasion I stayed for four nights. There was no guest accommodation at Khang Khay, so for the first two nights I lodged at the nearby village of Phongsavan, where the Russians, Chinese and rather unexpectedly the Czechs had set up embassies accredited to Souvanna Phouma's government; there was also a large hospital equipped and staffed by the North Vietnamese. I myself stayed in an uncomfortable, dirty, noisy and insanitary Chinese hotel above a restaurant run by a bibulous, opium-smoking Belgian called Tewens. The hotel was quite full, mainly with some 20 Russian airmen and mechanics looking after a small fleet of helicopters and aircraft, which maintained an airlift of supplies from North Vietnam. They kept very much to themselves and drank heavily, there being indeed little else for them to do. The partitions between the bedrooms were very flimsy and I was kept awake far into the night by their loud Russian conversation and the clink of bottles. There were also three French airmen, the crew of a Dakota aircraft provided by the French for Souvanna Phouma's use, and a group of North Vietnamese, some of them economists working on an economic plan for the area. We all took our meals in the Belgian restaurant where I was able to appreciate the extreme shortage of provisions in the area. There was no bread, no fish, very little meat, no wine or spirits, not even any soft drinks, but fortunately plenty of beer. And so our meals consisted mainly of rice and vegetables with occasionally eggs or a little chicken.

For the next two nights I went to the regional capital of Xieng Khouang, where the members of the ICC had set up branch offices. I stayed with the Canadians in a reasonably comfortable colonial-type villa and fed rather better on the supplies they brought up from Vientiane. Xieng Khouang was the centre of the area occupied by the

Meo, the minority group that had migrated from the mountains of southern China during the previous century and a half. They were a mountain people who always lived above a height of about a thousand metres and believed that their health would suffer if they ventured lower. Both men and women of all ages dressed in a similar costume of black cloth pyjamas decorated with bright red and blue stripes and wore heavy collars of pure silver and other silver ornaments. They were the principal opium-growers of Laos but, judging by the poverty of the villages I visited, they must have been paid very little for their crop; and perhaps what little they received was invested mainly in their silver ornaments. They were also renowned as warriors and from their mountain-top strongholds they were to play a significant part in the military manoeuvrings of the next few years, and to undergo terrible sufferings in consequence.

The extra time I had on this trip enabled me to talk to more people, mostly officers and soldiers of the neutralist forces. One young Lao paratrooper introduced me to his wife, a pretty French woman carrying their baby son in her arms. They had met at a French university and she had followed him to the Plain of Jars after the battle of Vientiane. Living conditions were obviously very primitive and difficult for her, and though she seemed happy enough she must have known that the future was bleak and highly uncertain. I was able to call on Kong Lae at his headquarters, and though he spoke mainly in French he occasionally spoke, quite well, in the English he had been learning. He told me that he was continuing to work for the formation of a neutral government under Souvanna Phouma but when this was formed he would be quite happy to leave Laos as his presence might hinder the integration of the armed forces. He would really like to be appointed Laotian Military Attaché in London — a happy prospect which alas never materialized.

I did meet one Pathet Lao officer who introduced himself as Pan Norindr, younger brother of La Norindr whom I had known as Private Secretary to Souvanna Phouma in Vientiane and who at the time was in Geneva and Paris working for Souvanna Phouma's interests. There was also a third brother Pheng Norindr who was a prominent member of Phoumi's entourage. This illustrated the fact that the divisions in Laos between right wing, left wing and centre did not arise from conflicting ideologies or any real differences in political beliefs. The three parties rather reflected the divisions in the world outside and were differentiated by the support they received from the United States or the communist powers, with the centre willing to accept aid from both sides. With no strong political views at stake individuals were ready to switch sides to follow what they perceived as their personal advantage at the time. And major families like the Norindr would have representatives in all three groups so that their interests would be preserved whatever happened.

I also had time to look at the famous stone jars, which were located on the edge of the Plain near the airstrip. There were about a hundred, scattered in a small area in front of a cave in a bluff overhung with trees. Shaped like beer barrels they were hewn out of single blocks of what looked like granite, and varied in size from less than one metre to over two metres in height. It is assumed that they were used as burial urns, but nothing is known of the civilization that produced them. Their bases were buried in the ground and they were somewhat reminiscent of the huge stone heads of Easter Island — much smaller, less striking but equally mysterious.

8

Stalemate in Vientiane

The visits to the Plain of Jars were the high points of my diplomatic activities in Laos. It was a rare experience for a relatively junior diplomat to act as an emissary in talks with leading personalities affecting the future of the country and the outcome of a world crisis. But diplomatic work in Vientiane was almost equally exciting because of the ease of access to the leading figures of the government. The diplomatic reception really came into its own as a meeting place and a source of information. There was usually a good turnout of ministers at government or ambassadorial receptions and they would often talk quite frankly to even junior members of the embassy, who could then proudly produce a piece of useful privileged information at the embassy meeting next morning. It was particularly useful when we received urgent instructions after office hours to talk to the government and we were able to track down the minister concerned at a cocktail party and deliver our message.

It was mainly through attending the numerous receptions that I got to know Boun Oum, Phoumi and most of the ministers. The stoutly built Boun Oum, with a handsome face topped by a bristly grey crew cut, was generally affable and approachable. He occasionally liked to play the buffoon, but he was undoubtedly shrewd and intelligent —

John Addis was taken aback when, to illustrate a point he was making, Boun Oum produced a remarkably apt quotation from Racine. Though generally considered as little more than a puppet or figurehead for Phoumi, he had a mind of his own and would not have stayed as prime minister if he had not been in broad agreement with Phoumi's policies. Phoumi was not as physically large as Boun Oum, but distinctly plump, with a round face and small eyes, which almost disappeared when he smiled, which was often, giving the impression of an impassive, smiling Buddha. This impassive countenance added to the aura of power which he radiated and which he enjoyed exploiting. I remember once having to approach him at a reception with an urgent message requiring some action by him. He thought for a moment and, without taking his eyes from my face, raised his right index finger to the level of his waist. Within two seconds an ADC was at his side to receive his instructions.

Throughout the autumn of 1961 Boun Oum and Phoumi resisted American pressure and managed to stall progress on the negotiations by constantly shifting their ground on the main issues — the location of the next Three Princes' meeting, the choice of prime minister and the composition of the coalition government. Their refusal to attend a meeting at the Plain of Jars was eventually countered by a proposal by the two 'rebel' princes that they would come to Vientiane. However, they wished to bring a company-sized military escort each to ensure their security. Boun Oum and Phoumi insisted that they alone would provide security in Vientiane and rejected alternative proposals such as the demilitarization of Vientiane or holding the meeting at the camp of the French military mission. As pressure mounted on them to agree to the escorts, Boun Oum suddenly offered to come to the Plain of Jars without an escort on condition that Souvanna Phouma and Souphanouvong would then come to Vientiane likewise without escort. This was a clever move, as Boun Oum would not be in any danger in the Plain of Jars, whereas Souphanouvong in particular and other Pathet Lao leaders would believe that there was a genuine risk of assassination if they came to Vientiane without a military escort. Only after the strongest American pressure yet — a threat to suspend all contact with the Vientiane government and to deal directly with Souvanna Phouma — did they accept the visit of the two princes to

Vientiane with military escorts. This was on 13 December. But in typical Lao fashion it was announced that, because of a programme of visits by the King and government to the south for important religious ceremonies over the next ten days, the Three Princes' meeting could not take place until after Christmas.

The two princes from the north duly arrived in Vientiane on 27 December with their escorts, and for the first time Pathet Lao soldiers were seen on the streets of Vientiane, along with the red berets of Kong Lae's troops. There were no military incidents, but despite a superficial cordiality there was no progress in the negotiations. Though Boun Oum and Phoumi now seemed to accept that Souvanna Phouma would be prime minister, they reverted to insisting that the key ministries of Defence and Interior should be given to the right-wing group. This was clearly unacceptable and contrary to a previous general understanding that Defence and Interior must go to the neutralist centre. So the two princes returned to the Plain of Jars with nothing achieved.

For the embassy staff, the weeks before Christmas had been clouded by thoughts of the Christmas pudding ordeal to come. However, a week or so before Christmas, Hugh and Betty Toye invited John Addis to a small dinner party 'to try out the Christmas pudding'. When the well-cooked flaming pudding was brought in, Betty explained to John in great detail the lengthy process of preparation required, and henceforth John's Christmas puddings were entirely acceptable.

Christmas 1961 lingers in the memory because of the carol singing by Oggy Thomas's choir. This was composed of some 25 to 30 people, mostly American, French and British in roughly equal numbers, though the British community was very much smaller than the other two. The embassy was well represented — I recall Colin and Shirley McColl, Patricia Chandler, Sonia Roberts and Philippa Campbell as well as myself. As usual with amateur choirs there were plenty of sopranos, led by Patricia, and basses, including three of our instrumentalists, Colin, Jean-Pierre and Duncan Mackintosh, but fewer altos and tenors. Sally Thomas kept the alto line going, helped by 'Big Bertha', a stalwart lady from USIS (United States Information Services). In the absence of anyone else who could read music, my

9. *(above)* The Wedding at the Embassy – David, Philippa, John, Addis and Beth.

10. *(left)* Kong Lae and Phoumi at Ban Hin Heup.

11. *(above)* At the Plain of Jars – General Singkapo and Captain Kong Lae.
12. *(below)* The Plain of Jars – a Meo village near Xieng Khouang.

13. *(above)* The Mekong
Singers at the French
Embassy, welcomed by
Ambassador Falaize.
14. *(left)* Diplomats at
Thakhek Festival – Philip
Chadbourn (US Embassy)
with the author.

15. Tikhi and parachutes at That Luang: *(above)* The teams assemble for the game of tikhi *(below)* A parachutist narrowly misses the pagoda.

feeble baritone was pressed into service to lead the few tenors, helped out by Oggy when things got difficult. In the months before Christmas we prepared a programme of English, French and American carols, which we planned to sing on Christmas Eve at the main Western embassies plus the Canadian ICC delegation. Meeting some friendly members of the Polish delegation on the beach in front of our house I asked if we could also sing for them and suggested that they might in return sing some Polish carols for us. They agreed enthusiastically, but a few days later they came to me rather crestfallen to say that my proposal had caused disagreements within their delegation: 'You know how it is with us' — presumably the hardline communists had objected. I apologized and said that of course we would not come. 'No, no,' they replied, 'we would like you to come and sing but we will not be able to sing in reply.'

On Christmas Eve we were in good voice. Our performances started off well and seemed, to us at least, to get better and better. But we had not calculated on the effect of our appreciative hosts' hospitality. Alcohol flowed freely as a reward for our services: champagne at the French Embassy, Scotch at the British, bourbon at the American, wine at the Australian and rye at the Canadian. By the time we got to the Poles, our last stop, we were feeling no pain at all. I saw that Oggy had put his conductor's score on the stand upside down, but he did not seem to notice and it did not seem to matter. Our performance was less polished but even more enthusiastic than usual. The Poles, already well lubricated with vodka, applauded wildly and, forgetting their undertaking not to respond, launched into some splendid Polish carols, with their rich, deep Slav voices sounding like the Red Army choir in full flow. Over more vodka the Cold War was forgotten and we departed in a state of euphoria, feeling that we had made a small but significant contribution to world peace. Fortunately the Christmas Day holiday next day gave us time to recover.

Another way in which the Laos posting differed from my other postings was the requirement to wear diplomatic uniform. Before 1939 this uniform, the diplomatic version of court dress, was regularly worn at official functions, especially in the European capitals. But in the more democratic days after the Second World War its use steadily declined and by 1960 it was in general use only in monarchies on occasions when the monarch was present. A few years later a short-lived attempt to revive diplomatic uniform was made by the Foreign Office Permanent Under-Secretary Sir Paul Gore-Booth, who was perhaps better known to the outside world as President of the Sherlock Holmes Society and for his fondness for dressing up as the great detective and re-enacting his death struggle with Moriarty above the Reichenbach Falls. He decreed that diplomatic uniform should always be worn by ambassadors when presenting credentials. Accordingly when I was appointed Ambassador to Madagascar in 1967 I acquired a uniform and wore it, once, when I presented my credentials to the President of Madagascar. This was the standard European uniform, dark-blue serge with gold braid and epaulettes, a fore-and-aft hat with ostrich feathers for an ambassador and a ceremonial sword. In Laos we wore the tropical version, a plainer suit of white drill with brass buttons and a rather ridiculous large white colonial-type solar topee surmounted by a brass spike. The ceremonial sword was a bit of an impediment — there was always a risk of tripping over it — but it came in useful on one occasion when we found a snake, bright green and almost certainly poisonous, in our bedroom. No, I did not kill it, but the sword was just the right size and shape to prise the snake out from underneath the furniture or behind pictures and persuade it to leave via the open window.

As Laos was a monarchy we wore uniform at the numerous functions or festivals at which the King was present. One such occasion was the King's Birthday celebrated not as in London with a parade but by an evening reception in the garden of the King's palace in Vientiane, going on until after midnight. Much more important was the That Luang Festival, which took place over three days in November. The That Luang was the chief pagoda in Vientiane, built in the sixteenth century by the great King Settathirath. The festival was in origin a religious occasion but had become the most important national festival attended by the King, at which ministers renewed their oath of allegiance to the King and the Constitution. Being in hospital in Bangkok I had missed the Festival in 1960. For political reasons the King stayed away in Luang Prabang, and Prince Souvanna Phouma presided instead. Apparently it was very much a peasants' festival, a show of popular support for Souvanna Phouma at a time when his position was beginning to crumble under pressure from the Americans, and, in the words of Hugh Toye, a joyous friendly occasion. There were no foreign contributions except from Britain in the form of the RAF Pipe Band and a drill squad from the Sherwood Foresters who were flown up from Singapore and apparently stole the show. Their presence was seen as, and intended by John Addis to be, a gesture of support for Souvanna Phouma at this most difficult time.

In 1961 the atmosphere was more subdued, with tighter organization and security arrangements, but it was still a most enjoyable occasion. In one corner of the large open space in front of the pagoda there was a funfair and numerous exhibition stands mounted by ministries, provinces and foreign embassies, notably the Americans, the French and the Thai. On the central playing field area in front of the royal stand there were various sporting events, including the traditional annual game of *tikhi* between teams representing government officials and the people. The game, rather like shinty in the Scottish Highlands or hurling in Ireland, was very similar to hockey, but with no apparent rules and no limit to the size of the teams, which on this occasion numbered about 80 a side. There was also a veterans' football match between the army and government officials, which the army won 1–0. It should have been a draw as the officials did score a goal but it was promptly disallowed, not surprisingly as the army goalkeeper was the much-feared head of the secret police, Colonel Siho. During the football match a series of horse races took place on a track around the circumference of the football pitch. Unfortunately there was no clear demarcation between the track and the pitch and increasingly the horsemen cut across the corners of the pitch, galloping at full tilt and narrowly avoiding the players.

After the games there was a display of parachute jumping by Lao paratroopers trained by USMAAG. About 50 of them jumped from 1000 feet into the playing field area, which most of them managed to hit, the remainder landing among the crowd or getting their parachute strings entangled among telephone wires. The climax was a jump by two USMAAG instructors from 10,000 feet. As they carried coloured smoke flares we could see them plummeting down until they opened their parachutes at 1000 feet and landed with great precision, one 100 yards and the other 20 yards in front of the King. They were followed by the British contribution, which this year was the band, corps of drums and drill squad of the East Anglian Regiment. Their main performance was to be a stunning display of musical marching and arms drill on the following day. Now they wound up the first day's festivities by Beating the Retreat, concluding with 'Abide with me'. Greatly moved by the beautiful hymn tune the King called John Addis over to congratulate him and to ask 'This music was by Bach or Handel, was it not?' Ever the diplomat, John 'gave an evasive reply'.

On the third day the festival closed with a religious ceremony after dark at the smaller temple of Wat Ongtu. Urn-shaped confections of artificial flowers and coloured paper were carried shoulder-high in procession round and round the temple to the accompaniment of xylophones, cymbals, gongs and drums, with bonzes leading a great concourse of people of all ages and classes, with candles, flowers and incense sticks in their hands. It was touching to see in the thick of the throng of the procession, without guards or any distinction, the Crown Prince, Prince and Princess Boun Oum, Prince Somsanith and other notables. Not for the first time, the thought came to mind that, if only the outside world would leave Laos alone, it could be the happiest and most peaceful country in the world.

Another happy occasion was the Water Festival, which took place in July. Various ceremonies were held to propitiate the river god and to express thanks for the life-giving monsoon rains, but the most spectacular event was a series of pirogue races on the Mekong, now almost at full flood. Under heavy, thundery clouds a number of long, narrow canoes, each manned by up to 40 crew, lined up closely alongside each other. On the starting signal they set off upstream all paddling furiously to generate enough pace to make headway against the strong current; and because of their close proximity there were frequent collisions and capsizals, to the delight of the watching crowds. The races took place in the upstream direction, presumably because with the current behind them the canoes would have shot past too quickly to afford much entertainment. It was a particularly happy time, as the rains were so welcome after the stifling heat of May and early June. During the festival complete strangers would throw water over each other to bring luck; and distinctions of rank, normally so important, were forgotten. On one occasion the Thai

Ambassador had been having a drink with us after playing badminton at the MIC site. As he was leaving, a group of MIC site servants rushed out and hurled a bucket of water over him, shrieking with laughter. He simply smiled, put his hands together in the *wai* greeting and thanked them for the honour they did him.

Most of the festivals took place in Vientiane, but I recall one that was held at Savannakhet on the Mekong some 300 kilometres downstream from Vientiane. As the King was attending, the Diplomatic Corps was invited. John Addis was away at the time at the annual conference of ambassadors in Singapore, so I attended as Chargé d'Affaires, accompanied by Hugh and Betty Toye and Trevor Wilson. I have only a vague recollection of the festival itself, no doubt the usual sequence of parades of various local groups in colourful costumes in front of the King, members of the government and local personalities. What I do remember is our hosts' plans for our sleeping arrangements. The visitors from Vientiane were met at the airport and taken off by various guides to the accommodation where we were to spend the night. Hugh, Betty and I were taken to a small guesthouse and shown into its single bedroom, almost filled by an enormous bed, certainly big enough for three people and possibly more. Our smiling guide looked at us expectantly like a cat bringing a mouse for its owner's inspection and admiration. My diplomatic training led me automatically to consider problems of *placement*; but Hugh, with his more practical military mind, rushed off and quickly found another bedroom for Betty and himself, leaving me to enjoy the splendours of the imperial-size bed alone.

The main festival in the south took place at the ruined temple of Wat Phou, close to Boun Oum's former capital town of Bassac. Wat Phou was the oldest building in Laos, dating from the twelfth century, and was in fact the ruins of a Cambodian temple, a smaller version of the magnificent temples of Angkor. In February 1962 Boun Oum took time off from his prime ministerial duties to preside at his own local festival and invited the Diplomatic Corps to join him. Beth and I represented the British Embassy and flew down with other diplomats to the nearby airport of Pakse. Boun Oum, accompanied by his wife and other members of his family, was a most genial host and we were well entertained with meals of French and Laotian cuisine, while an orchestra of pentatonic xylophones, gongs and *khènes* played in the background. There were the usual processions and sporting activities on a football field close to the temple, but the high spot of the day was an elephant race around the perimeter of the field. The elephants, a dozen or so of them, were reluctant competitors but, prodded by their mahouts, were capable of a remarkable turn of speed, and all made the finishing line apart from one, which, trumpeting furiously in protest, suddenly veered off at right angles and disappeared into the surrounding jungle. Afterwards, while talking to a charming princess, one of Boun Oum's daughters, Beth mentioned that she had never ridden on an elephant before. Hands were clapped, orders were given, howdahs were strapped on elephants and we set off for a jungle promenade with Boun Oum in the lead and an escort of soldiers with rifles walking on either side of us, just in case there might be any Pathet Lao around. There was no question of another race. Progress was slow and stately and we were rocked gently from side to side as the elephants trod carefully over the uneven ground of the jungle. Crossing several shallow ravines posed problems of balance for the huge beasts, and indeed for their riders. At the edge of the ravine one foot would tentatively seek a foothold on the side of the ravine with a sideways lurch to adjust the balance. Slowly each other foot would follow with a corresponding lurch, carefully controlled by the mahout to reduce the risk of the passenger being thrown forward over the elephant's head. Then the same process in reverse as we climbed out of the other side, each of us clinging tightly to the front of the saddle to avoid sliding back over the elephant's rear. But we all managed to stay on board to complete a most enjoyable ride in the cool of the late afternoon. Altogether a memorable visit, though I had a twinge of conscience, as on some other occasions, about accepting Boun Oum's generous hospitality at a time when we were devoting all our diplomatic efforts to unseating him and his government.

A regular feature of the functions we attended was a display of Lao dancing, which was very similar to the better known Thai dancing. On the more formal occasions the dancers/actors would sometimes re-enact a historical legend dressed in glittering traditional costume and wearing hats in the form of pagodas. At other times it would be charming young women in modern formal Lao dress performing the graceful movements of contemporary Laotian dances to the accompaniment of the usual Lao instruments. The movement of the hands, elongated by curved artifical nails attached to the fingers, was particularly striking as the dancers were able to arch their hands backwards almost into a new moon position. All Lao women were able to do this, since from babyhood their mothers would spend a lot of time bending their fingers backwards while the bones and sinews were still supple enough to be affected. Malcolm Morris's eldest daughter Christine learned Lao dancing and occasionally took part in performances with her Lao friends. She could not of course arch her fingers backward in the traditional style, but otherwise she danced most gracefully and, being tall and blonde as well as good-looking she made a striking addition to the normal group of much smaller black-haired Lao dancers.

The turn of the year 1961/2 saw more changes in our small community. Colin McColl had left and been replaced by Barrie Gane, a young bachelor on his first posting abroad as third secretary. Bing Crosby had finally retired and been replaced as Australian defence attaché by Colonel Peach, a large man with an equally imposing wife (Fred Kempson suggested that the Colonel and Sally Bull should exchange surnames). Hugh and Betty Toye left at the beginning of March to be replaced by Colonel John Isaac, a quiet and courteous bachelor, less flamboyant than Hugh but equally effective. The French community was reinforced by the arrival of the strikingly handsome Colonel Laigret with a half-Tahitian wife who embodied the exotic beauty of the South Seas. There tended to be more men than usual on the beach in front of the MIC site when she water-skied on the Mekong with her long black hair streaming behind her. The diplomatic community was also enhanced by the arrival as UN Representative of Jacqueline Granger, a mature but still beautiful French lady with straw-blonde hair, high cheekbones and a tall, slim figure, always impeccably turned out in elegant Parisian clothes, a credit to her nation as well as an effective representative of the international community. And there was now a new chairman of the ICC, Avtar Singh, whom I had known slightly in New York when he was a member of the Indian delegation there. Unlike most Sikhs he was clean-shaven with short hair, what was known in India apparently as a 'mechanized Sikh'. Though quieter in manner than his extrovert predecessor Samar Sen, he was a very capable professional diplomat with whom we were able to work closely.

The New Year 1962 opened with the deadlock in negotiations still unbroken. On 6 January the Geneva co-chairmen invited the three princes to a meeting in Geneva, and the Americans suspended the January aid payment until Boun Oum and Phoumi had accepted. The meeting made some progress in agreeing that the coalition government should consist of ten neutralist ministers and four each from the right wing and the Pathet Lao; but Boun Oum and Phoumi continued to insist that their group should retain the portfolios of Defence and Interior. Meanwhile Phoumi was continuing his second tactic of stirring up the military situation in the hope that if the cease-fire broke down the Americans would have to support him to prevent the Pathet Lao taking over the whole country. In the previous autumn there had been breaches of the cease-fire in Xieng Khouang province where the cease-fire line was particularly unclear and complicated by the existence of pockets of Meo on clumps of high ground on the 'wrong' side of the line. Phoumist troops had shelled pro-Pathet Lao Meos on their side of the line and the Pathet Lao in retaliation had shelled anti-Pathet Lao Meos (supplied and supported by the CIA) inside what they regarded as their territory. In consequence there was a flow of Meo refugees to Vientiane, where they managed to survive the perils of the lower altitude despite the abject poverty of their condition.

In January 1962 more serious breaches of the cease-fire developed in the province of Nam Tha in the north-west, which bordered on China. Phoumist troops, supported and advised by USMAAG officers, attacked a Pathet Lao position at Mahaxay, with US-supplied T6 aircraft firing rockets and dropping bombs. In response the Pathet Lao mortared the airfield at the provincial capital of Nam Tha, with the aim of denying use of the airfield for operations or for bringing in more troops. In order to get the mortars close enough they had to cross the cease-fire line in breach of the cease-fire agreement. This was a risky business, as any significant Pathet Lao advances would alarm the right wing in Washington and cause a reaction in favour of Phoumi. So they refrained from occupying Nam Tha, though they could easily have done so, as the garrison had fled in panic. Phoumi of course exploited the Pathet Lao attacks as a reason for refusing to pursue negotiations until the military situation was restored.

By February exasperation with Phoumi's intransigence led Harriman to propose, and President Kennedy to endorse, a significant shift in US policy. Henceforth, if Phoumi refused to negotiate in good faith, the US government would negotiate directly with Souvanna Phouma and, if satisfied with his intentions, would support him in setting up a government of national unity, with Phoumi if possible but without him if necessary. John Addis immediately expressed doubts about trying to exclude Phoumi, who controlled all the levers of power in Vientiane; and Souvanna Phouma, when informed of the new policy, also said that he wanted to include Phoumi in the government rather than leave him outside as a focus of opposition. So for the time being the policy remained to bring maximum pressure on Phoumi to agree to enter a coalition government under Souvanna Phouma, and US aid was again suspended, this time for a period of months. Phoumi responded by printing the extra money he needed to pay his troops, causing a steep decline in the value of the local currency, the kip, and the development of a flourishing currency black market.

The Western ambassadors were now instructed to discuss with Souvanna Phouma in detail the composition of his proposed government, a remarkable and possibly unique example of outside interference in the domestic political affairs of an allegedly independent country. This included a continuation of the discussions about the balance of the different groups in the coalition. Although various alternatives were discussed, Souvanna Phouma's proposal (originally suggested by John Addis) for four Phoumist ministers, four from the Pathet Lao and eleven neutralists, divided into seven 'Xieng Khouang' neutralists (namely those who had stayed with Souvanna in the Plain of Jars) and four Vientiane neutralists, finally became the agreed formula. But the ambassadors went further, into a discussion of the personalities and political leanings of each individual minister, so that for example it would be agreed that a 'Xieng Khouang' neutralist considered rather left-wing should be balanced by another considered more moderate. I recall at one stage Winthrop Brown arguing that Chao (Prince) Sisoumang should not be included among the neutralists because he was really a communist. '*Mais*', replied Souvanna Phouma disarmingly, spreading his palms, '*c'est mon cousin*' (actually his nephew). And so Sisoumang stayed on the neutralist list.

Another small episode is perhaps worth recording as an example of the informal atmosphere in which great matters of state were discussed. On 22 February Hugh and Betty Toye were giving a party to say farewell and to introduce the new military attaché John Isaac. At the embassy earlier in the day, Hugh heard from John Addis that Souvanna Phouma, who was in town for more talks, was very depressed at the lack of progress. Hugh suggested, and John agreed, that it might cheer Souvanna up if he came to the farewell party; so an invitation was duly conveyed and readily accepted. In due course Souvanna Phouma turned up when the party was at its height and found the American ambassador, Winthrop Brown, already there. Ignoring the other guests, the two of them went over to the sideboard with pencil and paper and, in these unlikely surroundings, made useful progress in drawing up a list of coalition ministers that could be acceptable to Washington. While Phoumi's intransigence prevented any immediate breakthrough, this encounter played its part in strengthening the US government's still fragile support for Souvanna Phouma.

Another unusual and possibly unique feature of our diplomatic activity at this time was our close collaboration with the Russians, especially as we were at the height of the Cold War — the Berlin Wall had been built in the previous summer. Following the Kennedy–Khruschev meeting in Vienna it was accepted that the Soviet government genuinely wanted a peaceful, negotiated outcome to the Laotian crisis and were willing to use their influence with the Pathet Lao to this end. It was of course quite natural for John Addis and the Soviet Ambassador Abramov, as representatives of the co-chairmen of the Geneva conference, to consult together whenever Abramov was in Vientiane (he still spent most of his time in the Plain of Jars). But at times Abramov also attended meetings with the three Western ambassadors (often in fact a group of four to include the Australian Ambassador) to discuss such matters as the composition of the proposed government of national unity. He even had one-to-one

meetings with the American Ambassador, one of which produced a
rare example of Soviet humour. Winthrop Brown was complaining
about the unhelpful attitude of the King, and suggested that if the
King were to impose his authority he could quickly resolve the
differences between the three parties. 'Ah,' said Abramov, 'but he's
not really a card-carrying king, is he?'

Despite the financial sanctions and the diplomatic pressure from the
world's Great Powers, Phoumi refused to budge. He continued to
believe, with the support of his friends in the CIA and USMAAG, that
the US government would never abandon him. He may also have been
encouraged by the manner of Winthrop Brown who, when instructed
to threaten Phoumi with sanctions of various kinds, seemed to do so
in a half-hearted and imprecise way. About this time Abramov, back
in Moscow for a short visit, told the British Ambassador there that
Winthrop Brown had been reported as saying to a friend: 'I represent
the USA and not only President Kennedy; I have to consider its long-
term interests, regardless of the present views of the Kennedy family'
— an attitude no doubt shared by many others in the State
Department and the US Diplomatic Service. But the main prop of
Phoumi's position was the support of his uncle Marshal Sarit of
Thailand. Harriman decided that a major effort must be made to win
over Sarit. This was done by giving him cast-iron assurances, backed
by the stationing of American troops in Thailand, that whatever
happened in Laos the USA would remain committed to the defence of
Thailand. When Sarit was convinced, a meeting was arranged
between him, Phoumi and Harriman in late March at Nongkhai on
the Thai side of the Mekong.

At this meeting Sarit spoke for an hour in support of American
policy and urging Phoumi to accept a negotiated settlement with
Souvanna Phouma as prime minister, followed by Harriman speaking
forcefully on the same lines. Harriman then crossed the Mekong to
Vientiane where he talked with the King, whom he found 'negative
and fatalistic', and then with Boun Oum and Phoumi and the whole
Laotian cabinet. Phil Chadbourn of the US Embassy, who acted as
interpreter for Harriman, told me that at these meetings at Nongkhai
and Vientiane, Harriman spoke with a directness and even brutality
that was beyond anything he had previously experienced in diplo-

macy. But this directness and brutality did not work — indeed it might have been counterproductive with Asians for whom questions of face were important and who would not wish to be seen giving in to such direct pressure. At the meeting with the Cabinet, Phoumi and the rest remained firm in rejecting Souvanna Phouma as prime minister. Over the following weeks Phoumi continued to twist and turn and propose alternative solutions such as the King as prime minister with the three princes as deputy prime ministers, fortunately a non-starter as the King was sensible enough to keep out of the political arena. Harriman had to accept that it would take more time for the change in Sarit's position and the continuing American pressure to put an end to Phoumi's intransigence.

In the Plain of Jars the two 'rebel' princes were becoming increasingly frustrated and impatient. Souvanna Phouma, who became unwell following food poisoning, went off to Paris in early April for medical treatment, and said that he would not return until Phoumi gave a firm undertaking to abide by previous agreements to accept him as prime minister. On his next visit to the Plain on 6 April John Addis proposed that he or a senior member of his staff should make weekly visits in order to maintain liaison while Souvanna Phouma was away. Souphanouvong, who had been very modest in his demands regarding Pathet Lao participation in the coalition government, welcomed the idea. He even suggested that we should open a British consulate at Khang Khay: an attractive idea (especially as I was a likely candidate for the post of Consul) which was reluctantly rejected as it was thought it might give Phoumi an excuse to stop our flights to the Plain of Jars.

On this same visit John Addis raised with Souphanouvong the position of our two doctors working in the south. By now they were working separately, one from the provincial capital of Saravane and the other from the small town of Thateng on the Plateau Bolovens, holding clinics in the surrounding villages close to the area occupied by the Pathet Lao. They had occasionally met small groups of Pathet Lao soldiers, who had been quite friendly when they explained what they were doing. However, we feared that the doctors might be at some risk as the negotiations dragged on and political and military tension increased. Souphanouvong promised to send instructions to his local commanders to ensure that the doctors would be able to continue their work unmolested.

The military situation was indeed the cause of growing concern in April and May as Phoumi made one last desperate attempt to involve the US military on the ground in Laos. After the fiasco of January, Phoumi's troops had reoccupied Nam Tha. Against the advice of USMAAG he now built up the garrison at Nam Tha to a strength of 5000 troops, flown in via an airstrip at the nearby village of Muong Sing close to the Chinese border. Sorties were then made into Pathet Lao territory with the clear intention of provoking retaliation. At first there was no response, as Souphanouvong was aware from the reaction to the incidents in January how sensitive Nam Tha was internationally. But further provocative sallies led to a resumption of Pathet Lao mortaring. About the same time Pathet Lao troops occupied Muong Sing to prevent use of its airstrip to reinforce Nam Tha. Phoumi announced that Muong Sing had been attacked by Chinese troops, and this predictably caused panic in Nam Tha. Some 2000 of its garrison surrendered to the Pathet Lao and the remaining 3000 fled south-west to Ban Houei Sai, a small town on the Mekong, across the river from Thailand, whence they were airlifted back to Vientiane. Phoumi was hoping that the Pathet Lao would follow up and occupy Ban Houei Sai, since any appearance of Pathet Lao soldiers on their borders would seriously alarm the Thais and probably lead to the resumption of Sarit's support for Phoumi. But the Pathet Lao were well aware of the danger and made no such move. To reassure Sarit after the abandonment of Ban Houei Sai the Americans moved 1000 marines already in Thailand closer to the Mekong, and sent a further 4000 troops who began to arrive on 16 May. There were also small token assignments of troops to Thailand from Australia, New Zealand and Britain (which was to cause me some trouble later). This ensured that Sarit gave no further support to Phoumi, whose last gamble thus failed. He could resist the combined pressures on him no longer. The government in Vientiane sent a message to Souvanna Phouma agreeing to the proposed composition of his coalition government. Souvanna Phouma returned to the Plain of Jars and called for a meeting of the three princes there to finalize the agreement, setting a deadline date of 16 June, after which he would return to Paris. It really looked as if the long-drawn-out crisis was about to be resolved.

Unfortunately I was not to be around when this happened, as unexpected events were to remove me from the scene for some time.

9

An Involuntary
Tour of the South

The adventure began for me with a dramatic cliché — a stone thrown at a window. It was Sunday night 27 May and, unusually for a Sunday, we had been giving a party, a buffet supper, for some visitors from London. All the guests had gone but we lingered a while, as hosts and hostesses do, to discuss how well the party had gone. Just as we were going to bed there was a rattle at the window, which might have been the wind or a gecko; but a second rattle confirmed that someone was trying to attract our attention. I looked down and saw Colonel John Isaac. He had been at our party and on returning home had found a message, passed through French military channels, stating that doctors Colin Prentice and Tony Bryceson, together with their Lao male nurse, a young man called Sian, had been captured by the Pathet Lao near Thateng, a village on the Plateau Bolovens in the south of Laos.

As we learned later Colin and Tony, who normally worked separately from their bases in Saravane and Thateng respectively, had joined forces at Thateng for a weekend prior to coming to Vientiane to proceed on local leave. On Saturday 26 May they were making a final tour of the villages in the area, fortunately leaving Jane Prentice behind in Thateng, and were holding a clinic in a village they had not previously visited, Ban Kok la Kang, about 15 kilometres north-east of Thateng. While they were with their Land Rover surrounded as usual by villagers clamouring for medicines they suddenly found Sten guns thrust at them by a small group of Pathet Lao. After a time they were told that they could continue with their work, but soon a larger band came into the village and an order was given to arrest them. They were tied up tightly along with their male nurse Sian, and at this moment thought they were going to be shot. In a little while a further group came into the village headed by their leader Sithone Komma-dom, riding a horse and looking, so the doctors said, like the personification of death, with peaked military cap, enormous black sunglasses and stern features which did not move or turn in their direction as he passed by.

Sithone did not speak to them until the following day, when he accused them of being American spies — 'Why have you got cameras, maps and compasses?' When they explained that they were Colombo Plan doctors doing humanitarian and non-political work for the villagers he said that even so they had no right to work in 'liberated areas' without documents signed by Prince Souvanna Phouma and Prince Souphanouvong. He would only release them if he got a letter from the two princes to that effect, and this might take one or two months to arrive. When they suggested that the embassy might be able to obtain such a letter more quickly, he agreed that the doctors could write to the Ambassador asking him to obtain such a letter and prom-ising that anyone bringing the letter would not be molested. The doctors' letter was written, in English, on 28 May and reached Jane Prentice at Thateng the same evening. Meanwhile the doctors and Sian were moved with their Land Rover, mainly by night, to Ban Phone, a large village captured by the Pathet Lao some two months earlier, and their most important post to the west of the Sekong river, a major tributary of the Mekong which had hitherto marked the west-ern boundary of Pathet Lao territory in that area. They arrived at Ban Phone late on 29 May. The Land Rover was abandoned here and on the following day they were taken away on foot towards the Sekong.

When the news was reported to John Addis on the Monday morning 28 May, he immediately sent a telegram to Prince Souphanouvong, through Prince Souvanna Phouma, reminding him of his previous assurance and asking him to investigate and order the release of the medical team. A further telegram with more details was sent to the two princes on 29 May. On the same morning David Campbell and Major 'Spots' Leaphard were sent down to the south to find out what they could and if possible to make contact with the doctors. David returned the same day bringing with him Jane Prentice and the letter from the doctors asking for a letter from the two princes.

On John's instructions I had already arranged to go up to the Plain of Jars to see the two princes on the following day, 30 May. When I arrived at Khang Khay I immediately broached the question of the doctors and Souvanna Phouma said it was a matter for his brother. I gave the two princes a list of the embassy's requirements: a letter signed by both, giving approval to the work of the doctors and instructions for their release together with their nurse Sian; a *laissez-passer* for their future work; a *laissez-passer* for myself to carry the letter to Sithone; and a telegram from Souphanouvong through his own channels confirming the release instructions. Souphanouvong's immediate response was that no letter was necessary: *'J'ai déjà câblé.'* When I asked him how long his cable might take to arrive he said three or four days (on later indications a serious underestimate). I suggested that I could get a letter to Sithone more quickly myself and said that in view of what the doctors had said in their letter this seemed to very desirable. I also said that there was now a substantial press corps in Vientiane, including correspondents from the main British papers, and that it would be difficult to explain the embassy's inaction if we just sat back and waited for what might be a week or more when we had the means to get the message through more quickly. Souphanou-vong was reluctant but after further discussion, in which I was supported by Souvanna Phouma, he agreed to see what he could do. He refused, however, to give a *laissez-passer* for me, saying that he could not take responsibility for my safety. I made it clear that I would if necessary go looking for the doctors, adding something pompous about my duty as HM Consul to do everything possible to protect British subjects.

We then had lunch, at which we were joined by Quinim, and talked about current military and political problems, notably the breaches of the cease-fire in Nam Tha and the continuing delaying tactics by Boun Oum and Phoumi (they had just gone off on a visit to Manila). Souphanouvong then went off *'pour régler votre affaire'*. I waited with Souvanna Phouma long past the time when I should have left to catch the return plane. Souphanouvong at last came rushing in with a letter hand-written by himself in Lao on a plain piece of paper, signed by him and stamped with a Neo Lao Hak Sat (the political party of the Pathet Lao) stamp. It was countersigned in my presence by Souvanna Phouma. It was not a very generous letter. It said briefly that, if the two doctors and the Lao nurse had been captured by any Pathet Lao troops for entering liberated zones without permission, then Souphanouvong agreed that they should be released along with their personal effects. But it seemed perfectly adequate for my purposes and I took it gratefully and dashed off to catch my plane back to Vientiane.

My hope was that I would travel down to the Plateau Bolovens, deliver the message from the two princes and return either the same evening or the next day with the doctors. Allowing for a little extra delay, I prepared for an absence of two or three nights and, lacking a suitably sized weekend bag, used Beth's red vinyl tennis bag to pack pyjamas and spare shirts, underwear and socks. A later report in the press that I had gone off into the jungle with a tennis bag provoked some amused comment in the Foreign Office about my optimism in hoping to arrange a game of tennis with the Pathet Lao.

On the next morning (31 May) I left home at about 7.00 a.m. for the airport on the far side of Vientiane. On the way into town, enjoying the cool freshness of the tropical early morning, I stopped to talk to Malcolm Morris, who was returning on foot from a very early game of badminton. He wished me luck, neither of us suspecting that it would be some considerable time before we would meet again. From the airport I flew down to Saravane in a USMAAG plane and from there was taken in an American helicopter to Thateng where I arrived about 1.00 p.m. I had hoped that Sithone and the doctors would not be too far away from Thateng and that Spots would have managed to establish some kind of channel through which the letter could be sent. Spots had written a letter to Sithone but had been unable to find a villager courageous enough to leave Thateng with it.

Moreover the latest news was that the doctors' Land Rover had been seen in Ban Phone, 37 kilometres to the east and that the doctors had been led away further east. This report stated that they were being taken to Chavane, deep in the heart of Pathet Lao territory in the mountains east of the Sekong.

This news posed a dilemma. I could have plausibly justified a decision to return to Vientiane, report that I had been unable to deliver the message and accept that we must leave it to Souphanou-vong to arrange for the release of the doctors. Instead I decided that Spots and I must go after the Pathet Lao and that, since I judged that time was of the essence, there was no time, with the means of communication at our disposal, to consult the Ambassador. There were three reasons for this decision. First of all I thought that the British press and the doctors' families would have reacted badly if I had not made every effort to deliver the message, and the reputation of the Foreign Office would have suffered accordingly. Secondly, and this was the reason for the urgency, I was alarmed by the report that the doctors were being taken to Chavane. According to some reports I had recently seen, Chavane was the secret headquarters of the Pathet Lao in the south, seething with troops including two battalions of Viet Minh and with an airstrip where a steady stream of Russian planes brought in supplies from North Vietnam. I feared that if the doctors were taken there and saw these military installations the Pathet Lao and Viet Minh would be even more reluctant to release them. So I was anxious to catch up with them before they got anywhere near Chavane.

The third reason was personal and at least partly subconscious. Going after the Pathet Lao would certainly involve risk: at the first encounter they might well shoot first and ask questions later. But this element of risk made me more determined to go, not out of gung-ho bravado but out of fear — fear that I would be considered a coward, or would think myself a coward, if I decided to turn back. I suspect that many acts deemed courageous are undertaken because fear of being thought afraid outweighs fear of physical danger or even death. Another subconscious factor was that the high morale in the embassy included a certain degree of recklessness appropriate to the frontier town atmosphere of Vientiane and expressed in such ways as David

Wilson's search for the Pathet Lao, the refusal of the wives to leave before the battle and our collective willingness, even eagerness, to undertake the hazard of flying to the Plain of Jars. Certainly, Spots would have been astonished if I had decided to turn back. Accordingly with the aid of the local civilian and military authorities we commandeered a jeep from a reluctant Chinese merchant, with Spots signing a paper stating that he took full responsibility.

Before leaving we had lunch with a nice Swiss missionary couple with whom Jane Prentice had been staying. They told us that they had had little success in converting the local animist population to Christianity; their main work was looking after groups of lepers who, as in many third-world countries, were driven out into the jungle as soon as their condition was discovered and who would eventually have died of starvation without the support of the missionaries. As I had brought only the town shoes I was wearing (not even tennis shoes) they kindly lent me a pair of canvas jungle boots of about my size, for which I was most grateful. Then at 3.00 p.m. we set off in the jeep down the road to Ban Phone — the beginning of a journey that would take us, mainly on foot, over a substantial area of south-eastern Laos.

The jeep was old and decrepit and we had an uncomfortable passage as we drove as fast as we dared down the narrow, rocky, uneven road, which went mainly downhill from the top of the rounded plateau towards the Sekong river. After we had driven a certain distance we expected as we turned each corner to be stopped by a Pathet Lao patrol. But we went on and on without meeting anyone except the occasional peasant walking along the road. From time to time we passed villages, which seemed deserted except for an occasional woman clutching a child and hurrying away from us. The overcast sky seemed to heighten the atmosphere of fear and tension. Turning a corner we suddenly came upon a small gully or ravine, about five metres deep, traversed by a simple wooden bridge. Unfortunately the bridge had been burned by the Pathet Lao, probably by the group that had captured the doctors, having first taken the Land Rover across. The cross-planks had disappeared but the two thick main struts had survived, badly charred but otherwise apparently sound. If the bridge had been totally destroyed that would have been the end of our mission, since the gully was too deep and steep for the jeep to cross, and if we had continued on foot there would have been no hope of catching up with the Pathet Lao in time. But by chance the width between the two struts was the same as the width between the wheels of the jeep, and the struts themselves were an inch or two wider than the jeep's tyres. So I took the wheel and, with Spots beckoning me on, drove slowly and carefully over the struts, very conscious of the five-metre drop below me, and eventually made it to the other side.

After we had driven about 30 kilometres we eventually came to a village where Pathet Lao soldiers stepped out into the road and waved us to stop. And now my virtue in learning Lao was rewarded, as from this time we did not meet anyone who spoke French. We got out of the jeep and I explained in Lao my mission and said that I had a letter from Souphanouvong. The leader asked to see this (the conversation was pretty basic school primer stuff — 'Where is the letter?' 'Here is the letter'). He then took it away to study while a small group of other soldiers crowded round us in a friendly fashion exchanging such small talk as my Lao permitted. After a while the leader came back with the letter and another note he had written giving us clearance to go on to Ban Phone. He warned us that when we got there we would see a stop sign; we must not move beyond there or we would be shot. As the jeep was difficult to start they gave us a push and we went off amid friendly laughter and cheers.

Within ten minutes we reached Ban Phone and, as advised, halted at a stop sign just outside the village. We waited for five or ten minutes, then shouted to attract attention but to no avail. We therefore got out of the jeep and walked into the village where we saw several shop-keepers, but still no sign of Pathet Lao. I sent Spots back to bring the jeep and just as he reappeared a group of Pathet Lao soldiers came running down the street having been warned by the villagers of our arrival. They were agitated, clearly astonished at our presence, angry and slightly frightened. They surrounded us with menacing gestures from their weapons and shouted questions at us: 'Who were we, what were we doing here and (repeatedly) how many were we?' I replied that there were only two of us bringing a letter for the release of the doctors, but this time the production of the letter did not have the desired effect. Instead the leader, a rather bullying type called Xieng Chan, marched up and down, shouting at us and gesticulating. I did not fully understand him, but he seemed to be saying that the letter from Prince Souphanouvong was of no importance, we had no right to come into their zone without proper authority: there were liberal references to Phoumi-Boun Oum and the Americans. I kept repeating my original statement and waited for reason to prevail, but instead to our dismay we saw ropes being brought. We were tied fairly loosely round the neck and the upper arms and led off up the street to the house of the village headman, along with our luggage, which they unpacked and examined. They were particularly interested in a small slide viewer and several colour slides I had taken of the two princes at the Plain of Jars, which I had brought along in the hope that they would help to establish my authenticity.

It was now getting dark, and we were offered some rice and venison stew — they had just shot a deer. Various soldiers came up to inspect us and one of them, asking belligerently if we were Americans, took away my watch. He became more friendly when I said we were English, and asked me to teach him some English words. We went through various parts of the body and articles of clothing, but he had a lot of difficulty with the word 'watch'. Lao syllables usually consist of a consonant and a vowel and an occasional final consonant, but a double final consonant does not exist. I tried to get him to say two Lao words together, 'wat' (temple) and 'chao' (prince), dropping the final 'ao', but progress was slow. He then asked me to translate 'You give me your watch'. I said firmly in both Lao and English 'I do not give you my watch,' but he kept it all the same.

Later I explained to Xieng Chan how we had received the doctors' message in Vientiane and how I had gone up to Khang Khay the previous day and got the letter from the two princes. He listened carefully but did not comment. We then tried to sleep, but on bare boards and with no blanket or pillow I found this impossible, although a comfortable rumble from my side indicated that Spots, as an old Malayan campaigner, did not find the conditions exceptional. During the night I overheard Xieng Chan reading aloud to himself a letter he was writing to Sithone, which seemed to be a factual account of what I had said. This was dispatched by runner and in the early hours a message came back. Before dawn we were roused and told that we would be taken to a village 11 kilometres away, where we would find the doctors and Sithone.

It was still dark when we set off with guards with rifles holding our ropes and two additional guards armed with Sten guns. The thought of a dawn shooting fleetingly crossed my mind, arousing feelings of resignation and fatalism as with the shelling during the battle of Vientiane. Apart from wondering whether I would be offered, and would refuse, the traditional eye bandage, my thoughts were on the lines of: 'Well, if they're going to shoot me there's nothing I can do about it', 'You bloody fool, you have only yourself to blame; you could easily have thought up a reason for turning back' and 'I'm only 38 but I've had a good life, so I can't grumble'. However, such depressing thoughts were dispelled when the dawn light revealed four porters carrying our baggage. In the cool of the morning it was a most pleasant walk, first across rice fields with the rising sun reflected in the water and then up and down wooded hills with pleasant views in all directions. On the way we sighted a deer and one of the porters borrowed a rifle, but his stalking was clumsy and he scared the animal away. Eventually we came out on top of a steep ridge overlooking the Sekong and walked down it to a village on the edge of the river where we stopped in a small hut on stilts and were offered a meal of rice and rather revolting fish stew, which we could not eat. Even the pleasant spectacle of the attractive bare-breasted young lady who brought us the food crawling on her knees (not out of respect but because the roof of the hut was too low to permit standing) did not revive our appetite. After a rest we were put in boats — we had rather a sinking feeling when we realized that we were being taken across the Sekong — and paddled downstream about four kilometres. We then left the boats on the far side, walked a few hundred metres along the river bank and then turned inland where we immediately came to a village and were taken into a hut where we saw, sleeping on the floor, two rather unshaven doctors together with Sian and Rex, Tony Bryceson's red setter dog.

The doctors were, in their own word, 'thunderstruck' to see us as they thought that it would take at least a fortnight for the embassy to obtain and deliver the letter. They were delighted when I said that I had brought the letter, although a little alarmed that we were roped. They pointed out Sithone sitting on the veranda of a hut opposite and watching us impassively. We saw our luggage being carefully searched in another hut and then Sithone went across to see what the search revealed. He then went back to his hut and after some time came to see us.

I was rather apprehensive of this first encounter with Sithone, an almost legendary figure whose whole life from boyhood had been spent either in fighting Western intruders or in prison, so that he was unlikely to be predisposed in our favour. However, his appearance created a favourable impression. He had a natural air of authority, a stern but handsome face, direct eyes and a most attractive smile. Here, we felt, was a natural leader of men, with whom (as Field Marshal Montgomery had recently said of Mao Tse Tung) one would have been glad to go into the jungle. Our confidence was soon shattered. When I referred to the letter I had brought he immediately said that the letter was a forgery written by the embassy in Vientiane. He had known Souphanouvong for 20 years and the signature on the letter was certainly not his. The letter was not on official paper, it was not typewritten, it had no number, it was not addressed to him and it did not have the proper official stamps of the two princes (nearly all of this was, of course, true). In the ensuing argument, in which I was greatly assisted by the two doctors, who had acquired a good command of colloquial Lao, and occasionally by Sian, interpreting through French, Sithone refused to budge. I recited in circumstantial detail my visit to the two princes, whom I knew well, and said that it was fantastic to think that I would come into Pathet Lao territory with a forged letter. I tried to explain the concept of diplomatic immunity — *Khon satann tut chap bo dai*, literally 'People of the ambassador's house capture not can'. His reply was simple but devastating: '*Dai*' (Yes I can), '*Dai lèw*' (I have already done it), the more so as the vowel of the word '*lèw*' (meaning completed action) is one of the ugliest sounds in any language, a multiple diphthong starting with a very open French 'è' and finishing with 'oo', rather like, but worse than, Eliza Doolittle's cry of 'aooow', which so appalled Professor Higgins in *Pygmalion*. I went on to say that, apart from the question of diplomatic immunity and his own promise that the bearer of a letter would not be molested, it was outrageous to arrest British people, who were not involved in the war in Laos and were doing their utmost to help to form a coalition government and bring about peace. His reply was that Laos was in a state of war and that one had to take sides. We were clearly on the other side because our government recognized Phoumi-Boun Oum (spoken always as one word in the mouths of the Pathet Lao) and not Souvanna Phouma and because we were helping the Americans by putting aeroplanes and (according to Radio Pathet Lao) 2000 troops in Thailand. Unfortunately it was true that some British troops, though far fewer than 2000, had been sent to Thailand as a gesture of SEATO solidarity to reassure Sarit.

All the obvious arguments having failed to move Sithone, we asked whether a further letter in the correct form — official paper, typewritten — would effect our release. He agreed that it would and said that I could write a letter to this effect, in Lao, to the Ambassador and that he himself would write a letter. With the assistance of Sian I accordingly wrote a short letter stating the facts, and after a considerable time Sithone produced a letter, which contained the idea that, if the Ambassador could not get the second letter, he should do everything possible to promote the formation of a coalition government, after which we would be released. Believing that he would sign this I agreed. He then took away the two letters along with Sian and after a further long delay produced a letter that was a combination of his and my drafts for my signature. We read this with great care and, although I did not understand every phrase (Sian's French was not of interpreter standard), it seemed to contain nothing too objectionable apart from the statement that we had been captured because the letter I had brought was a forgery. I said that I could not sign such a statement unless the words '*chao vao va*' (they say that) were inserted after 'because'. Sithone accepted this amendment and so I agreed to the letter as it seemed to be the only way of informing the Ambassador of our situation, and knowing that it would be obvious that at least substantial portions of the letter had not been drafted by myself. I copied out the letter in Lao in my own handwriting, to the astonishment of our guards, many of whom could not read or write even in Lao, and signed it. This whole process took about 36 hours and the letter was dispatched by a runner to Thateng on the morning of 3 June.

Meanwhile Spots and I had been searched shortly after our arrival. My Laotian currency, to the value of about £15 or $35, was removed, but careful note was taken of the amount. I was told that the money would be kept by our guards, who would use it to buy extra food if we wished, that accounts would be kept and any balance restored to me when I was released. This promise was kept and after a month, during which we bought about sixteen chickens, three small pigs and considerable quantities of fruit (most of it shared with our guards) an amount equivalent to £5 was restored to me. I was asked why I was not wearing a watch and said that one of the soldiers had taken it. They asked me the make of the watch and on the following morning it was produced for my inspection. I was told that it would be restored to me when I was freed and this promise again was kept. Spots had brought with him currency to the value of £65, but he skilfully concealed this along with a gold watch when he was searched and managed to retain it throughout our captivity.

The village where we found ourselves, Ban Navar Kang, was in fact deserted, abandoned some time before on the orders of Phoumist troops who told the residents to build a new village on the west side of the Sekong. People from the new village did, however, come across the river to provide food. During this time we were quite loosely and not painfully roped, with the end of the rope, about two metres long, either tied to the wall of the hut or in the hands of a soldier when we went outside the hut. In the hut with us there were always four to six well-armed and alert guards, of whom one was always awake throughout the night. As there was no furniture in the deserted village our food was placed on the floor, the sticky rice on a banana leaf and the soup, either fish stew or vegetable soup with bits of chicken bone in it, poured into troughs made of bamboo cut lengthwise. In these conditions I at first found the food inedible and I developed violent headaches, in effect withdrawal symptoms resulting from the absence of basic foods such as potatoes, bread, coffee, beer and wine to which my body had become accustomed or mildly addicted. But after two days I had adjusted myself to the diet and even looked forward with appetite to the next meal. The highlight of each day for us was a swim in the fast flowing Sekong; we went two at a time watched carefully by three or four guards with their weapons ready.

My knowledge of Lao now began to improve rapidly as I learned the words for domestic matters, including the body's natural functions, which had not been the subject of any of my lessons with Mr Pheng. When I needed to 'go to the lavatory' one of the guards would untie the end of the rope and lead me out, rather like someone taking the dog out last thing at night before locking up. For purposes of defecation I would be taken to an area carpeted with a spinach-like plant with large soft leaves, which served admirably as lavatory paper. However, on the first occasion when I squatted down I was alarmed by loud grunts and snufflings immediately behind me, coming from village pigs waiting to gobble up the result of my efforts as soon as I had finished. This regular experience should have made us wary of eating the occasional pig that was offered to us, but when you are hungry such considerations are forgotten and we never hesitated a moment. Not surprisingly, when I returned to Vientiane I was found to be full of worms which, however, quickly succumbed to medication.

Our guards, though still suspicious and wary, were not unfriendly and were happy to accommodate our wishes, as when we asked if the British prisoners could take exercise in the form of an evening 'constitutional' or stroll around the village. As it would have been wasteful of manpower to allocate a soldier to hold the rope of each of us on our stroll, one unfortunate guard was assigned to accompany us holding the four ropes in his hand. Following sheepishly behind us as we walked slowly along discussing matters of great moment and high philosophy like dons strolling around an Oxbridge quadrangle, he resembled someone driving a coach and four and no doubt felt as foolish as he looked.

With us in the hut were two other Lao prisoners captured by Sithone in his sweep beyond Ban Phone. One was a cheerful rogue who had been working in some minor capacity for the Americans. He stayed with us throughout our captivity and cooked most of our meals, not too badly. The other was a slimy customer who, as a soldier in the Royal Laotian Army, had apparently behaved very badly in the area, being involved in the burning of villages and the taking of women. To save his skin he tried to maintain that he was a

deserter and also informed on various villagers whom he accused of
hiding arms and provisions. He was led out frequently for questioning
and one day he was led out and did not return. We were told later
that he had been shot, after a sort of people's court at which persons
from the villages where he had operated had been asked to vote on
whether he deserved to die.

Sithone had with him in the village some 20 to 25 soldiers, probably
some of his best troops, in reasonably respectable though often
patched uniform of the familiar faded khaki with a variety of head
gear of which the most common was the bus conductor type peaked
cap. They were well armed, about a third of them with automatic
weapons they obviously knew how to handle. Every morning at dawn
we were awakened by the drumming sound of feet stamping the
ground as they did a quarter of an hour's physical training to music
and commands broadcast over Radio Pathet Lao, but apart from that
there was no form of military training. There were regular arrivals
and departures of messengers and from time to time patrols would be
sent out. The general impression was of an efficient guerrilla headquarters.

All the time we were with Sithone he used to come and see us at
least once a day to see how we were getting on and to chat with us.
No doubt he found us a stimulating change from his usual companions. Our talks were usually friendly, even when they got onto
political subjects. Only on one occasion did he become violently angry
during a heated argument with Colin, with Sian acting as interpreter
through French, which ended when Sian, quaking with fear, refused
to translate what Colin was saying lest it provoke Sithone further. In
our discussions we lost no opportunity to point out how mistaken he
was about British policy in Laos and he often smilingly accepted our
arguments, although in the end he usually came back to our non-
recognition of Souvanna Phouma's government and the British
military force in Thailand. When we warned him of the dangers of the
Viet Minh taking over Laos he replied: 'All my life I have been
fighting against people wanting to take over my country, first the
French and now the Americans; if the Vietnamese try to take over
Laos, I will fight them too.' He did not enjoy fighting: '*Bo yak kam,
ma bo yan kam*' ('I don't want war but I don't fear war'); all he

wanted was peaceful independence for his country. In our presence he often gave orders that we should be well treated, and on the whole we were glad that we were with someone of his authority. His deputy, a captain named Sivit, who said he had been a member of Kong Lae's original battalion, was a thoroughly nasty piece of work, a boastful little man who claimed to have been to Peking and Moscow and was almost certainly a communist. He had told the doctors that if they had fallen into his hands he would have shot them straight away. In the early days he also told people in the villages that we passed through that we were Americans.

While we were at Ban Navar Kang, Sian was led out for about an hour each day for indoctrination, either by Sithone or Sivit. He was criticized for working with foreigners and told that that while we might be released one day he would never be released. He would be sent to Xieng Khouang for political training for six months and if that was satisfactory he would go to Moscow to be trained as a doctor. When he said that he would prefer to return to his wife and family he was told that he must forget his family and that his country was more important. As for his wife, there were plenty of other women in Laos. The young man stood up to this treatment very well. He was, of course, immediately subjected to intensive counter-indoctrination as soon as he returned to our hut and he told us that he did not believe anything that he was told. (Later, at Ban Tok, he was separated from us and forbidden to speak to us, but after we left Sithone he rejoined our party and the attempts at indoctrination were not resumed.)

The second day after our capture was 2 June, the day on which the Queen's Birthday was officially celebrated that year. We told Sithone that we wished to celebrate our national day and asked for some whisky from the supply of four bottles that Spots had brought, with the vague idea that they might be useful for bribery. He allowed us only a quarter of a bottle but this was enough for each of us to drink the health of Her Majesty. However, our attempt at singing 'God Save the Queen' was immediately interrupted by alarmed cries of '*kalàm*' (taboo) from our guards. Apparently singing inside houses was taboo because it would disturb the *phis* (pronounced *pee*) or spirits who live in the rafters. But the *phis* did not seem to object to the various party games we then played to the amusement of our guards who, as good

Laotians, recognized and respected a *boun*, one of the festivals that play so large a part in their lives.

My own enjoyment of the *boun* was somewhat marred by worries about what was happening at the embassy's official Queen's Birthday Party back in Vientiane. National day receptions are sadly a major and time-consuming feature of diplomatic life, and some ambassadors from smaller countries, especially in larger posts, seem to regard it as their main function to show the flag by hosting an impressive reception and attending all the other national day receptions. Fortunately in Vientiane there were only a dozen or so embassies, but even so there was an element of competition as to who would provide the best reception. A previous British ambassador, who attached perhaps excessive importance to the pompous aspects of diplomatic life, ordered my predecessor, a very good pianist, to recruit the best possible band to play 'God Save the Queen' at the Queen's Birthday Party. The best musicians were Filipinos playing in the nightclubs, and so over a period of time my predecessor was seen every night sitting in the corner of a different nightclub sipping a whisky and staring fixedly at the band, arousing speculation as to the state of his marriage. He eventually settled on the band of the Vieng Ratray who assured him that they knew the British national anthem, an assurance he unfortunately accepted without verification. The upshot was that when the toast of Her Majesty the Queen was proposed the band burst into 'Colonel Bogey', which is a fine rousing march but, apart from not being the national anthem, has some unofficial and rather rude words known to anyone who had served in the British army.

I was back in England at the time of the 1961 Queen's Birthday Party, and do not know whether there was a band then. For the 1962 party John Addis had asked me to arrange the music, and through the Foreign Ministry I was offered the Vientiane police band, which consisted only of two trumpets, an alto saxophone, a baritone saxophone and drums. They admitted that they did not know 'God Save the Queen' and did not have the music for it. I therefore wrote out an arrangement for the instruments of the band and held several rehearsals with them. Progress was painfully slow as, like many third-world musicians, they played mainly by ear and were very poor readers of music, so that I had to teach it to them note by note. At the time I disappeared to the south I still needed at least two more rehearsals, in the absence of which I feared there might be a small disaster. My fears were justified. At the party they struggled somehow through the first three lines of the anthem. But in the middle, when the trumpets play a rising scale up to the fourth line ('Send her victorious'), the trumpets fizzled out halfway up the scale and the band fell into an embarrassed silence. So perhaps the *phis* were expressing their disapproval in Vientiane as well.

After we had been at Ban Navar Kang for four days Sithone said that he could stay no longer at this deserted village but must move on to a large populated village where he had work to do. We did not like the idea of going further away from Thateng but his motive for moving seemed perfectly reasonable. On 5 June we set off eastwards, each of us roped to a guard, with our escort of about 20 soldiers and Sithone on his horse. From now on we carried our own luggage. Before we left, Sithone inspected us like a good regimental officer and saw that I was carrying my tennis bag by my side. He said that this would unbalance me and cause me problems on the march; a rope was brought so that I could sling the bag over my shoulders, which was much more comfortable. We walked for some six kilometres across fairly flat and open country with trees spaced fairly widely as in a rubber plantation, and across three sizeable streams through which we had to wade almost up to our waists. This short walk soon exposed the poor fit of the jungle boots I had borrowed from the Swiss missionary. I developed blisters on my feet, which were to cause me pain and discomfort to some degree during each of the many miles we were to walk in the jungle.

After two hours we came to the small and poor-looking village of Ban Katak, where we stopped the night. The following morning we got up at dawn to continue the march. We waited for several hours ready to go, wondering what the delay was. Eventually we were told that Sithone's horse had run away while being saddled and had gone back to the previous village. It was not recovered until late in the afternoon when it was too late to start our march. Meanwhile we had spent a boring day enlivened only by the sight of a lovely young woman engaged in weaving on the veranda of a hut across the road from us. From before Ban Phone we had been in the country of the

Alak tribe who, like the other Kha tribes, share many features with the long-house people in Borneo, including the lack of covering for the upper part of the female body. The young woman in question had particularly well-formed breasts, which undulated enticingly as she moved her body backwards and forwards over the loom. I am afraid I was the one who dubbed her 'Bosom the Weaver'.

The following morning, 7 June, we set off and began climbing steadily. After about four kilometres we came to another deserted village. It was apparently quite common for villages to be abandoned, either because of sickness or the activities of unfriendly spirits; also the practice of 'slash-and-burn' rice cultivation in the hilly areas meant that every few years it was necessary to move as the soil became exhausted. This particular deserted village had the bonus of a huge mango tree in the centre and the ground underneath it was covered with hundreds of mangoes in various stages of ripeness. The whole party, including our guards and ourselves, abandoning our ropes, immediately scattered to gather mangoes, which we ate during a brief halt.

After this 'mango break' we moved on to an inhabited village where we had our mid-morning meal and a longer halt. We then climbed more steeply over a fairly high ridge. The tracks became narrow and difficult, slippery and stony, and leeches began to bother us. They were black and about the size of a large caterpillar. Alerted to our approach by the vibrations caused by our steps they would rise up on their hind legs, as it were, and weave about hoping to latch on to a passing boot. When they did they would immediately start arching upwards, trying to get inside the boot from the top in order to plug in to the flesh of the foot. I therefore would walk with my head down watching for the many leeches that climbed on to my boot and knocking them off with a stick cut from a tree, which served me as a walking stick. No leech penetrated my defences, but Spots was not so lucky. His well-worn jungle boots had holes in the canvas through which one or more leeches crawled each day. At the end of the day's journey, when he took off his boots his socks would be soaked in blood and several leeches would fall out, now fat and bloated like black slugs. More seriously some of the leech bites became infected and did not clear up until after we were released.

16. *(above)* The That Luang Festival – the King and Queen of Laos arrive at the Festival.

17. Water festival and Wat Phou: *(above)* Pirogue race at the Water festival, July 1960 *(below)* Beth on an elephant at Wat Phou, February 1962.

18. *(above)* Lao dancing – dancers with orchestra of Khènes.
19. *(below)* Released from the jungle – Tony, Spots, the author and Colin at Thateng, 28 June 1962.

20. *(above)* Back in Vientiane – the ex-prisoners, including Sian with Jane Prentice and Beth, at the airport.
21. *(opposite above)* The Three Princes finally agree.
22. *(opposite below)* In uniform in Luang Prabang – the author with Donald Hopson.

I think that it was on this stretch of track that our guards told us to keep carefully to the path, as there were mantraps on the side of the track. These proved to be pits two or three feet deep, skilfully concealed with brushwood and vegetation and containing wickedly sharp bamboo spikes pointing upwards and coated, they said, with poison. They were intended as a defence against Phoumi-Boun Oum and the Americans, the idea being that as enemy troops approached a concealed Pathet Lao outpost would open fire, causing the enemy to scatter, fall into the pits and cut their feet on the poisoned spikes. With this warning we naturally stuck closely to the track. But Rex, who unlike us was not on a lead, kept leaving the path to explore into the jungle, as dogs do, and several times fell into a pit. His paws were cut, not too seriously, by the bamboo spikes but the wounds healed quickly so we assumed that rain had washed off the poison or greatly reduced its efficacy. The guards also told us that in certain places there were crossbows that fired bolts on a fixed line when activated by a tripwire. I imagined that such primitive devices had been used by Sithone's father during his 25-year long guerrilla campaign against the French.

On the other side of the ridge we descended fairly steeply and then walked along the side of a fertile valley, which was obviously the site of the big village that Sithone was seeking. As we approached the village a messenger was sent ahead and Sithone himself trotted forward on his horse to lead the party in. From the middle of the column we heard rifle shots and then cheers sounding rather like 'Ah-noh, noh, noh'. We then came in view of the village and saw the whole population, perhaps 80 men, women and children, lined up along the side of the path shaking hands with each soldier as they approached and every now and then bursting into cheers. It was a stirring scene, the warrior chieftain returning home after a successful expedition with his captives in tow.

This large village was called Ban Tok (meaning 'linked') and in fact consisted of three Alak villages. The Alak people build their houses in a circle and when the circle is completed the only way the village can expand is to begin another circle. We lodged in a house in the original centre circle. One of the other circles was built on the top of a cliff and some of the houses perched precariously on the very edge of the cliff.

We had our evening meal of rice and soup and after dark settled down as usual to try to sleep. Our guards then told us that we must accompany them to a political meeting that was being held that evening. We were rather apprehensive that our presence there might be exploited by Sithone, but felt on the whole that the experience would be interesting and therefore did not object. In fact Sithone behaved perfectly correctly and did not make any reference to us at any time during the meeting. In the dark we walked down a slope, waded through a shallow stream and came to an open space underneath the overhanging cliff, which had been prepared for the meeting. The villagers were all seated on benches, which formed a hollow square, at one end of which was a table and chair for Sithone with, behind him, a bamboo arch and a small photograph of Prince Souphanouvong. The scene was most dramatic, with a log fire in the middle of the square casting a flickering light on the impassive faces of the villagers and above us the silhouettes of the huts of the other village, outlined starkly against a starlit sky.

As we approached the square with Sithone in his best uniform leading us, we were greeted with the now familiar three cheers. We were seated on a bench at the side of the square and, after Sithone had seen that we were properly guarded and secured, the meeting began. His deputy, Sivit, made a brief introductory statement and then Sithone rose and stepped forward into the firelight to make a speech. He spoke well in circumstances of considerable difficulty. His audience remained impassive and showed no signs of enthusiasm during his speech. There were constant distractions: someone stepping forward to put more wood on the fire, dogs chasing around his feet, children crying. And a constant and uninspiring background to his speech was the bubbling of the tribal pipes — bassoon-size bamboo tubes containing water at the bottom and a small pipe with a tobacco bowl set into the side below the water level; when the tobacco is lit the mouth is applied to the open top of the bamboo tube and the tobacco smoke sucked in through the water on the same principle as the Turkish hookah. These were smoked by the whole population, male and female down to quite small children. After introductory remarks about the support given to the soldiers by the villagers, Sithone gave what was in effect a current affairs talk on the political situation. He referred to Phoumi-Boun Oum's constant sabotage of the political negotiations, the wicked activities of the Americans who wanted to wage war in Laos and restore colonialism, assisted by Chiang Kai-shek, the Vietnamese and Thais and also by the British with their aircraft and troops in Thailand. His peroration, accompanied by clumsy gestures, spoke of the necessity for continuous struggle to achieve a united, peaceful and independent Laos. There was very little ideological jargon; it was the speech of an anti-colonial nationalist rather than a communist. When he finished he received the conventional three cheers, after which there were several speeches of no importance by local headmen. Finally everyone joined in a *lamvong*, the graceful Laotian dance in which Sithone participated with obvious reluctance and many embarrassed side glances at us.

This was the only event of any significance at Ban Tok where we were to stay five days. It was the most agreeable prison that one could imagine, the finest tribal village the doctors had ever seen and probably the most beautiful of its kind in southern Laos, set in a wide fertile valley and surrounded by wooded hills and mountains. As we bathed every day in a rushing mountain stream we thought how lucky we would regard ourselves if we were there on a camping holiday. The only drawback was the food, as chicken pest and some disease of pigs in the village had greatly reduced the supply of meat. The villagers therefore refused to sell us any chickens or pigs and the Pathet Lao were not prepared to coerce them. On the positive side the 'red' mountain rice, still retaining part of the husk after being pounded in a mortar, was more nutritious and tastier than the sticky rice of the Mekong and Sekong valleys. There were also plenty of pineapples and mangoes, although even they began to get a bit monotonous.

By now I had got to know the doctors pretty well, having previously met them only briefly during their visits to Vientiane. Colin and Tony had met as medical students at Cambridge and had become friends, perhaps because of the attraction of opposites. Colin had been a golden boy at school, head prefect and academically brilliant and had taken a first-class degree at Cambridge. He was a natural leader, self-confident with a touch of arrogance and at times impetuous, as when he pushed Sithone almost too far in argument, but definitely a good person to have on your side. By contrast, Tony was quieter, thoughtful, reflective and caring, his qualities usefully complementing those of the more flamboyant Colin. It was of course a great comfort to have the doctors with us since, once we had survived the first encounter with the Pathet Lao, the greatest risk was of succumbing to some tropical ailment. If we had caught a nasty disease we would have been in trouble, as the doctors' stock of drugs had been confiscated when they were captured. Fortunately they had managed to conceal a small quantity of anti-malarial chloroquin, as there were always mosquitoes around and we had of course no mosquito nets. Apart from ensuring that we took our weekly dose of chloroquin, the doctors insisted that our drinking water should be boiled. But they assured us that there was little risk of dysentery or cholera, which are essentially urban diseases, the result of insanitary conditions in overcrowded towns. At first sight our own conditions were not very sanitary. The huts where we lived were built on stilts and the floors were often made of bamboo poles; and it was the general habit (which we adopted) while eating inside the hut to dispose of inedible items such as chicken bones by dropping them through gaps in the floor. But there was a very efficient sanitary system provided by chickens, pigs and dogs scavenging underneath the floor and, as we have seen, the pigs' omnivorous diet made a sewage system unnecessary.

The village people were also personally very clean. Wherever, as at Ban Tok, there was a river or stream nearby everyone would take a daily bath in the late afternoon, with different times allocated to men and women. The Lao, like other oriental people, are very modest about their bodies and when we went down to the stream for our daily bathe Sian and the guards who accompanied us and also bathed always covered their private parts with one hand. Our failure to do likewise surprised and shocked them. One afternoon, as we were disporting ourselves in the stream in our usual state of nature, we heard suppressed feminine giggles from behind some bushes on the banks of the stream. Our guards must have told the young women of the village about our shocking behaviour and invited them to see for themselves. But they did not stay long. Colin, who by now had a respectable beard, emerged like Neptune from the waves, this time with one hand strategically placed and the other pointing sternly at the girls as he admonished them severely for their immodest behaviour. They scurried away shamefaced and head down, and did not appear again.

Life in these aboriginal villages had changed little since the Stone Age. The only sign of modern technology was the weaponry carried by our guards. There was no wheeled transport of any kind, not even bicycles, or any animal transport apart from Sithone's horse, probably the only one in the whole of the Kha country. Buffaloes were not used to carry loads; firewood and other burdens were carried on the backs of men or, more usually, women. There was of course no electricity or gas, not even any alternative form of artificial light, no oil lamps or even candles. After dark the only light came from the dying flames or embers of the fire used for cooking. So activity began at dawn and ended at nightfall when everyone went to bed. We were awakened by the crowing of a cock (for years afterwards if I was staying in the countryside and was woken by a cock crowing, I would for a few seconds imagine that I was back in the Laotian jungle) followed by a thumping sound as the women pounded rice in a large mortar for the day's two meals.

The houses where we lived in the Alak country were well constructed and attractive to look at and, like the larger long houses of Borneo, which they resembled, were raised on stilts. The framework consisted of three or more triple uprights of solid timber with large sturdy crossbeams; both uprights and crossbeams were decorated with paintings or carvings, usually geometric or floral. The roofs were excellently thatched with rice straw, which seemed to be completely weatherproof. Inside, however, they were totally lacking in domestic comforts. There were no beds, so we slept on the floor using our boots as pillows. There were no chairs or tables, no plates, knives, forks or spoons, so we squatted on the floor to eat off banana leaves with our fingers until the enterprising young Sian carved spoons for us from bamboo. Chimneys had not been invented, so smoke from the cooking fire billowed around the room before exiting through the open space that served as a door. Long, sooty cobwebs hung from the rafters since, in order to avoid disturbing the *phis*, it was *kalàm* to clean the rafters or the inside walls above a height of about one metre. Apart from living in the rafters of individual houses, the *phis* also had a *phi*-house, like a large doll's house on stilts, in the centre of the village. Scattered around the *phi*-house were a number of buffalo posts, sturdy pieces of timber projecting about two metres above ground, to one of which a water buffalo would be tied on ceremonial occasions for ritual slaughter to propitiate the *phis*. There would follow a feasting orgy, with the villagers drinking rice wine and gorging themselves on the buffalo meat, which, in the absence of any method of salting or smoking to preserve it, had to be eaten up within a day or two. Afterwards the buffalo skull would be hung up on the interior wall of one of the huts. The age of the hut could be roughly calculated by the number of buffalo skulls. As Ban Tok was a long-established village most of the huts, including our own, had a fine display of skulls at about head height around all four interior walls. On nights when there was sufficient moon to provide some light through the open door, it was an eerie feeling to wake up and become aware of the row of ghostly soot-blackened buffalo skulls peering down, and one was glad of the company of fellow prisoners and guards.

Except at the first uninhabited village we were always lodged in a hut alongside the family that lived there. In Ban Tok the family consisted of a couple with two children, the youngest aged two or three still being suckled by his mother, and an elderly grandfather. The hut, built on stilts, comprised an open veranda at the front, a small enclosed room at the back where the grandfather slept and a square central room which served as living room, dining room, kitchen and bedroom for the rest of the family and any visitors, in this case six prisoners and four to six guards. The room was big enough for all prisoners and guards to sleep, fairly closely packed, on one side while the family slept on the other side. By now the prison regime had been relaxed. At first the ends of our ropes were tied to the rafters and the guards would untie them when we needed to go out and retie them when they brought us back. By the time we got to Ban Tok we ourselves would untie the rope and hand it to the guard, and then retie it to the rafter when we came back. After a few days the guards no longer bothered to tie the ropes to the rafters or hold the end when we went out, so we would walk about with the rope still around the chest and upper arms but with the end tucked into our pocket. However, they would not allow us to get rid of the ropes entirely. While the ropes would never at any stage have been a serious impediment if we had tried to escape, they seemed to be important as a symbol of our status as prisoners.

Our guards were illiterate young peasants, some of them little more than boys, who had little idea of what was going on in the outside world and, with rare exceptions such as Sivit, even less idea of what communism meant. They had by now lost their wariness of us and had become quite friendly. Our exotic presence added an unusual interest to their normally humdrum lives. It also carried an extra bonus in that they shared any extra food that was bought for us with my money to supplement the basic rice diet. Except at Ban Tok we were usually able to buy a small scrawny chicken which was chopped up into small pieces and placed in a cooking pot, bones, beak, claws and all, with water and a green spinach-like vegetable with large soft leaves (yes, the same one) to make a soup. Divided among the six prisoners, the guards and the family with whom we were sharing, this provided each of us with a few small pieces of bone with a bit of meat attached. We left the beak and claws to be crunched contentedly by the normally protein-starved guards.

Throughout our captivity we spent a great deal of time discussing our prospects of release. I had been worried by Sithone's talk of releasing us after the coalition government was formed. After the frustrations of the past year I had acquired a great respect for Phoumi's skilful delaying tactics and rated the chances of an early agreement as pretty low. I feared that if we were not released before 16 June, Souvanna Phouma's deadline date, we might be detained indefinitely. Sithone had a radio receiver with him and we listened with great interest to the news from Xieng Khouang and Vientiane. To our delight and my astonishment the news of the Three Princes' meetings was good. Sithone was obviously pleased and told us that if the government were formed he would ask for a helicopter to take himself and possibly us to Xieng Khouang. This prospect was not unwelcome. However, he went on to say that if he could not get a helicopter he might have to march to Tchepone (200 kilometres to the north) and then into North Vietnam and to Hanoi by railway and from there to Xieng Khouang by air, taking us with him. This idea naturally cast us into profound gloom. He also told us that he had sent a message

about us to the *Khoueng* (province) by which we gathered he meant
the Pathet Lao civil administrative centre some way to the east.

On 11 June a representative of the Khoueng arrived at Ban Tok, but
we were not told what message he brought. On the same evening we
learned that agreement had been reached at Xieng Khouang on the
composition of the coalition government. I therefore suggested to
Sithone that he should now release us to Thateng in accordance with
his previous promise. He said that this was not possible and that on
the next day we would be taken to the Khoueng, which was some
distance further inland. We protested vigorously but to no avail, and
we parted on very bad terms.

On 12 June we set off with a party of six or seven guards under
Sivit. We were a little apprehensive as to how he would treat us, but
in fact he was very genial throughout the journey; and by now our
ropes were finally abandoned. In his attitude there was an element of
fawning. He had realized by now that we were VIPs (Very Important
Prisoners). He had a highly fantastic imagination and was overheard
telling his comrades that I was an important member of the British
government and a personal friend of President Diem of South
Vietnam, and that if the South Vietnamese could discover where I
was, they would send eight battalions of parachutists to rescue me!

We climbed steeply northwards out of the Ban Tok valley and then
descended into another valley where we turned eastwards and after a
short day's march of about 11 kilometres stopped the night at a small
village whose name we did not find out. (Each day we tried to
estimate and memorize the length and direction of our march and the
topography to help us retrace our steps if ever an escape became
necessary.) At this stage we were told that we were being taken to
Chavane, the town that had acquired for us an almost mystic quality
from its reputation as the secret headquarters of the Pathet Lao. Next
morning we continued eastwards climbing slowly up the valley
through varied scenery, sometimes bamboo forests, sometimes marshy
grass. On the way we experienced the first rainstorm of the monsoon
season, which begins in June in Laos; waterproof capes were quickly
produced and we continued walking with our heads wet but our
bodies reasonably dry. After eight kilometres we fed and rested at Ban
Taleng, which was the last of the Alak villages we were to see. We

then turned south and began walking along a long ridge, which was to mark our path for the rest of our journey inland. The view on all sides was magnificent. On our right, to the west, the wooded hills and valleys through which we had travelled sloped down to the Sekong beyond which rose the dark blue-grey mass of the Plateau Bolovens. To our left, ridge after ridge of hills rose to an impressive range of mountains, which we were told marked the frontier with Vietnam. The highest mountain of all had two peaks separated by a ridge several hundred metres long. This mountain we kept in view from different angles as we marched over 30 kilometres first south and then south-east.

Because of its proximity to the Vietnamese frontier we speculated that this north–south track might be part of the famous Ho Chi Minh Trail along which supplies and soldiers were passed from North Vietnam through Laos into South Vietnam. But there was no sign that the track was being used for this purpose; and indeed at several points trees had been felled across the track to prevent any vehicle traffic. Nor during the considerable time we spent in the area, during which we conversed freely with our guards and the village people, did we hear the hint of a rumour that Viet Minh troops and supplies were passing through. However, as we were at a latitude some way south of the 17th parallel dividing North from South Vietnam, it seemed more likely that at that time the Trail would turn east into South Vietnam some distance to the north of us. Later, as the war in South Vietnam intensified, the Trail became more extensive, with several branches running right down to the southern frontier of Laos and even into Cambodia before turning east into South Vietnam.

The next village we came to, Ban Katrou, marked our arrival in the country of the Tallieng tribe of the Kha people. We stopped here for a short time and bought a small pig to take with us to Chavane, which we could see on the top of a hill in the distance and where we were due to spend the night. But just as we left the village we met a tribesman who told us that we could not go to Chavane. It was *kalàm*; in order to propitiate the spirits at the time of rice planting no one could enter or leave the village for three days. This was both frustrating and extremely funny, given that the place was supposed to be the secret headquarters of the Pathet Lao in the south. Up to now we had thought that the Khoueng was also in Chavane, and we had visions of negotiating with the Khoueng over the village wall, with the Khoueng not allowed to come out and ourselves not allowed to go in. However, we were now told that the Khoueng was some distance beyond Chavane.

We therefore ate our pig and stayed the night at Ban Katrou. By now we were high enough for the nights to be quite cold, and we were each issued with a grey blanket, indistinguishable from standard British army issue. On the next morning we covered the six kilometres to Chavane. We found that in fact the whole village was not *kalàm*, only certain houses, because of sickness (nothing to do with the rice planting). We were therefore allowed to enter the mystic city and rest awhile. We found what was, in effect, nothing more than a large Tallieng village, or two villages joined together in a long oval giving the impression of a main street — but no shops, no school, no dispensary, no troops of any kind and certainly no Viet Minh. The former French military post the Pathet Lao had captured was pointed out to us, but it was no longer in use. However, our guides told us with obvious pride that there was an airstrip and that we would shortly see it. We set off again after our rest and within about two kilometres came to the airstrip, which was set on the flat back of the ridge along which we were walking. We gazed in astonishment as our guides proudly pointed it out to us. The strip and the whole field were completely covered with a forest of sharp bamboo spikes, making the field unusable for aircraft and hazardous for parachute drops. The strip was about 600 or 700 metres long and no doubt it would not have taken long to clear away the bamboo spikes and make it usable again; but it certainly had not been used for some time. It seemed therefore that the secret reports picturing Chavane as a major base were either Pathet Lao disinformation or more probably part of Phoumi's campaign to exaggerate the Pathet Lao threat and Viet Minh presence in order to alarm the Americans.

From Chavane the ridge turned south-east and we walked along a good laterite track which had obviously been motorable not very long ago and which we were told led to South Vietnam. After about 15 kilometres we stopped for our afternoon meal and were told that the Khoueng was not very far away. In the late afternoon we were taken another two kilometres to the village of Ban Dak Dung where we spent the night. Here Sivit left us and went on to the Khoueng taking our original luggage with him.

On the following morning, Friday 15 June, we got up early and we were told that we were to be taken to the Khoueng. We therefore used our last razor blade to make ourselves moderately respectable. We walked two kilometres in a south-westerly direction, coming suddenly into an area of open pasture and woodland, reminiscent of the South Downs, and close by we turned into a village called Ban Tia Kad. We were shown into a hut and told that shortly the Khoueng would come to see us.

We waited impatiently all morning for the representatives of the Khoueng to appear but as nothing happened we lay sunbathing in the centre of the village. Around noon two little men came unobtrusively into the village, one of them stern-faced and dressed in the usual faded khaki, and the other more smiling in drab blue shirt and trousers of North Vietnamese origin. The only notable thing about them was that they were not carrying weapons and in fact we hardly paid any attention to them. They sat in a hut watching us and eventually called Sian over to them by name. After a time they asked the rest of us to join them and said they were the representatives of the Khoueng. The stern-faced one said that he hoped that we would not think ill of the Pathet Lao for what had happened and that the soldiers had treated us well. If they had treated us at all badly it would only be because they did not fully understand the situation. The other one, whose name turned out to be Boun Kong, spoke on similar lines and explained that Sithone as a military commander had not the right to release prisoners. This was the function of the civil administration, that is the Khoueng, and in the case of such important prisoners as ourselves this could only be done on the orders of the two princes. They had instructions to ask us certain questions, the answers to which they would send to Xieng Khouang, after which we would probably be released. As regards our possessions, those that had arrived with us would be returned. If we gave them a full list of the things that had been taken away from us they would do their best to return these also but they could not promise.

The whole tone was very conciliatory and we replied appropriately saying that we had in fact been well treated. We stressed the importance of our being released as quickly as possible as we all had important work to do. It was then about three o'clock in the afternoon and the two men said that they would start asking us questions on the following day. We said we were quite ready to answer questions immediately and eventually persuaded them to begin straightaway. They started with me and I braced myself for a series of penetrating questions about embassy work and British policy. To my astonishment they began with a series of innocuous bureaucratic questions — name, age, date and place of birth, occupation, father's name, mother's maiden name. They then asked which places I had visited in Laos and the nature of my work in the embassy; but they seemed satisfied with my reply that as the Ambassador's deputy I dealt with all work at the embassy. They then passed to Colin Prentice and in addition to the bureaucratic questions asked him more closely about his work. What was the Colombo Plan? Which government had asked for them to be sent to Laos? Were they really doctors or were they also acting as agents for the Americans? Why did they need a compass and maps? However, they accepted without argument the answers he gave and the questions were not in any way hostile. This whole process, with answers written down laboriously in Lao, took over two hours, and as it was getting dark the questioning was adjourned until the following day. Similar questions were then put to Tony Bryceson and Spots Leaphard, again without any attempt at hostile browbeating. They did not attempt to probe into the nature of the work of an Assistant Military Attaché and accepted Sian's explanation that every ambassador had a military attaché in the same way as the King had a bodyguard. They then asked Sian about the nature of the doctors' work in the villages and asked him whether they did any propaganda or showed films. He said that they did show films but these and any other propaganda were entirely related to hygiene and sanitation.

The afternoon was spent by the two men in laboriously writing out fair copies of our answers. They told us that these would be transmitted by telegraph to the two princes. When we impatiently asked them how long it would take to send these and get an answer they said it would take two or three days. But they later told Sian that they could not understand why we were asking so many questions about their communications, which had nothing to do with us. In fact, they said, the telegraph was five to ten days' walk away. Again this cast us into profound gloom. On the next day, 17 June, it rained all day and the two men from the Khoueng did not move from the village. They left for their office on the morning of 18 June, saying that they would do their best for us and that the order for our release might come in two or three days but on the other hand it might take a fortnight. We therefore reconciled ourselves to a wait of anything up to twenty days.

Ban Tia Kad was not the place we would have chosen for a long stay. Tallieng villages are generally smaller and poorer than those of the Alak people, and Ban Tia Kad was the smallest and poorest we had seen, with limited washing facilities and no kind of fruit to vary our diet. While Alak villages are built in a neat circle, in Tallieng villages the houses are clustered around in a less regular pattern. There is usually no *phi*-house and few or no buffalo posts. The houses themselves are smaller than those of the Alak, more like huts than houses, and practically all the space beneath the roof is occupied by one large room, totally enclosed and used as kitchen, bedroom and living room. In each of the four walls there is an opening, which can be closed by a primitive sliding door suspended from a bamboo rod on the principle of a curtain rod. The thatched roof, instead of leaving the front entrance open, comes down at the same level all round the house including the front and rear, giving the impression of an oval-shaped beehive. This no doubt makes for warmth but it also means that it is difficult for smoke to escape from the cooking fires, in the absence of chimneys. The smoke probably accounts for the prevalence of eye disease among the villagers, but at least it reduces the number of mosquitoes inside the house. In the house we shared with a family in Ban Tia Kad there were only a few buffalo skulls, placed just inside the entrance rather than in the body of the house. In the gloomy and smoky interior, with cooking pots hanging from sooty beams and weapons, utensils and containers stacked in corners, it was easy to imagine oneself transported back in time some 2000 years.

As we settled down for a long wait, the problem of occupying our time, always difficult, loomed even larger than usual. The only events of our day were a morning meal of rice and soup about 10.00 a.m., an evening meal of rice and soup about 5.00 p.m. and a walk down a slippery hill, muddy because of the rain, to a spring for our daily wash and laundry. By then we had used up our last razor blade (although Spots insisted on scraping away with a blunt blade) and we had run out of soap so that washing our clothes was an unrewarding process: we could not get them clean but at least we kept them fairly fresh. In our early days of captivity we had no materials at all with which to amuse ourselves and so we played word games, twenty questions and quizzes. On arrival at Ban Tia Kad young Sian, who was reconciling himself to a long stay after our release, said that he wanted to learn English. He borrowed some paper from the soldiers, cut himself a pen out of bamboo, brewed some ink from herbs used by the tribal people to dye their woven blankets and started compiling a Lao–English vocabulary. With the pen and ink and an old medical magazine Colin cut out and marked a pack of playing cards with which we played bridge, and also made a very presentable chess set with paper chess-men which could be inserted into slots in the board. We also played single-wicket cricket, using a buffalo post as the wicket, a bamboo stick as the bat and a piece of charcoal as the ball. After a time we were delighted to see the villagers and soldiers trying to imitate us.

I came to realize that sport and leisure-time activities were inven-tions of relatively wealthy societies and played little or no part in aboriginal life. While we were with Sithone his troops played games of volleyball in which we were invited to join, but it was not a normal village activity. The only 'sport' for the men was occasional hunting, although with their primitive weapons they probably did not have much success: in Ban Tia Kad there was a moment of hilarity when one of the Pathet Lao guards borrowed a crossbow and tried to stalk a chicken for the pot, but failed to hit it in several attempts from a range of only a few metres. Even the children did not appear to play games, their main occupation being looking after smaller children. They were utterly delighted when Colin made them some paper aero-planes, probably the first toys they had ever had. So the introduction of a form of cricket was quite an innovation. I cherish the hope that they continued to play after we left and that in 100 years' time some anthropologist will write a learned treatise speculating quite erro-neously on the origins of this curious ritual.

Music likewise seemed to play no part in daily life, at least in the Tallieng villages. There was no sign of musical instruments and they never sang. I suppose there must have been music at the big meeting at Ban Tok when Sithone led the *lam vong* dance, but I do not recall what form it took (perhaps an ancient hand-wound gramophone?). My only clear recollection of music was I think in Ban Tok when a very young guard, probably not more than 16, and a Lao rather than a Kha, amused himself by playing the *khène* the double-banked five-note Pan pipes, and a homemade five-stringed ukelele. Noting my interest he smilingly invited me to play each instrument in turn, which I was able to do as they are both extremely simple. I then suggested that he should play a tune on the *khène* while I improvised an accompaniment on the ukelele. Since both were tuned to the same pentatonic scale, whatever I played was bound to fit in and so we had what amounted to a primitive jam session.

Despite the low density of the human population, we saw very little wild life apart from one or two deer sighted during our marches. Once we heard a troop of gibbons whooping in the distance, but we never saw any monkeys of any kind. Bird life was also scarce, but flocks of brightly-coloured parakeets would occasionally erupt screaming from the trees and once we saw a brilliant scarlet bee-eater chasing its black mate. We were told that there were larger animals in the forest, such as the gaur, the huge wild cattle that reach a height of two metres, and even some tigers. We never came across any of these, but once at Ban Tia Kad when I had gone alone to the spring to wash I had the strongest feeling that I was being watched by some creature in the surrounding bushes. I completed my ablutions as quickly as possible without obvious haste and walked slowly away until I was close enough to the village to risk running.

One constant occupation throughout our captivity was the discussion of our escape plans in which Spots Leaphard showed a very fertile and practical imagination. The basic idea was that, if we could somehow manage to get a good start on our guards, we should travel by night and as far as possible retrace our steps until we came to a westward-flowing stream which would lead us down to the Sekong; we would then try and construct a raft and float downstream into Cambodia, which was not too far away. In the early days when we were near friendly territory, escape was not really a feasible proposition. We were roped and our guards were well armed and vigilant, and it would have been very difficult to get away without being shot. After we left Ban Tok our ropes were gradually abandoned, and our professional soldier guards were replaced by hillbilly home guards who did not bother to watch us very closely. They no doubt calculated that, while we might have been able to get away from the village where we were, it would have been extremely difficult for us to cross some 100 kilometres of hostile jungle country without maps and compasses and without food. And they were almost certainly right, especially as we were in the monsoon season, and cloud was likely to obscure the sun and stars on which we would have to rely for orientation. However, we all agreed that escape plans, while being kept constantly up to date, should be held in reserve unless some unforeseen turn of events led to the prolongation of our imprisonment.

Having mentally prepared ourselves for a long wait, it was an agreeable surprise when only five days later, on the morning of 23 June, Boun Kong came into the village followed by some men bearing our luggage containers. This was obviously the moment of release and Rex, sensing our jubilation, pranced around wagging his tail and licking our faces. Boun Kong called us over and explained that there were three problems: our liberation, the return of our property and the question of responsibility for the incident. As regards the first he gave us a letter signed by himself and giving authority for our release which, contrary to what we had feared, also included Sian. He said that police guards would accompany us as far as Ban Phone where we would be handed over to other guards; and that all military posts *en route* had been informed of our release. As regards our property he handed us back the contents of our cases, which by then had dwindled very considerably. I had lost two shirts, the trousers of a suit, the jacket of my pyjamas and my slides and slide viewer, while the doctors' two expensive cameras had disappeared; but all three watches that had been taken were returned to us. We were told that some of the other articles must be regarded as lost but every effort would be made to find them, especially the two cameras, and return them to Thateng.

Boun Kong then said that the third question would be settled if the doctors signed another document, which purported to be a summary in Lao of the questions put to them and their answers. We read this through carefully and it seemed on the whole to be a reasonably fair summary. It stated that they had been arrested because they did not have the correct papers, that on this occasion they would be released but that they must not enter 'liberated areas' again. When asked whether this meant that the doctors would not be able to continue their work in the villages, Boun Kong said that they could certainly do so if they obtained the proper documents from the new government. The only doubtful part of the paper was the question that asked whether they were really doctors or whether they were not acting as agents of the Americans who were seeking war in Laos. The doctors were supposed to have replied: 'England does not want war. England is the co-chairman of the Geneva conference. It is America who wants war. *Amerika bo chop, bo chop* (no good).' I could not of course have signed a statement containing such a phrase but I decided that in the circumstances there was no harm in the doctors' doing so. It had taken so long to prepare the documents that a suggested amendment might well have meant a further delay of several days. Boun Kong said that there were four copies of this paper: one for us, one for him and one for each of the two princes. To our astonishment he then asked Tony Bryceson to sign only one of these, which he then gave to us, so that he himself took away three unsigned copies! He said that we would leave early next morning. His manner was extremely pleasant and friendly throughout and we parted on very good terms.

That night none of us could sleep. I lay awake composing phrases for my report to the Foreign Office and imagining the tastes of hot coffee and cold beer. Next morning, 24 June, we set off with a small group of 'police' guards (who seemed no different from the ordinary Pathet Lao soldiers) and two guides from the civil administration, who were to stay with us throughout our return journey while the guards were changed at intervals. The senior guide was an intelligent and charming young Lao who had been a student in Vientiane at the time of the Kong Lae coup; he was most friendly and was a great help in resolving various difficulties that arose on the way. In our anxiety to get home quickly we set a cracking pace along the relatively good road to Chavane, with Rex trotting happily beside us. We covered the

18 kilometres to Chavane in two-and-a-quarter hours and altogether on the first day covered 32 kilometres in five-and-a-half hours. This was unwise and we inevitably suffered on the following days. I in particular acquired more blisters and strained leg muscles, which slowed me down considerably. However, with careful nursing and encouragement from the doctors I stumbled painfully along at a slow but steady rate and the distance gradually fell behind us. We returned by the same route as we came and reached Ban Phone, about 80 kilometres away, early on the morning of 27 June.

Here we had hoped to pick up the Land Rover and drive the last stretch to Thateng. But we were met on the edge of the village by Xieng Chan who seemed very angry that we were being released; I got the impression that but for the arguments of our guides he might well have detained us. He told us that we could not take the Land Rover or the jeep in which Spots and I had travelled because they had blocked the road to Thateng by burning bridges and felling trees across the road — this turned out to be quite true. We were glad to get away from this hostile atmosphere, and with a fresh batch of guards we walked round the village and up the road to Thateng. We stopped for a meal at the village where Spots and I had first met the Pathet Lao and here we now found approximately a company of Pathet Lao troops, who were quite friendly. The meal was something special, a large fish resembling a carp which had just been caught and which we were invited to share. Sian cooked it, poaching it in a large pot with some lemon grass and ginger root, which he dug up somewhere, and with the additional spice of hunger it made one of the most memorable dishes I had ever tasted.

After the meal we pressed on up the road, hoping to cover most of the road to Thateng before nightfall. However, when we were within 20 kilometres of Thateng we suddenly turned off to the right and started going northeast instead of west. When we protested, our guards said that they had to hand us over to the group of Pathet Lao in the Thateng area otherwise there was a risk of our being shot by a patrol. After about six kilometres we turned back west in the right direction and stopped the night at Ban Sitou where we were handed over to a new group of guards. In the late afternoon Spots and I walked down to the nearby stream for a wash and, for Spots, a shave.

However, we had inadvertently chosen a time just before the hour allocated to the women for their evening bathe. They duly arrived and, after some hesitation caused by our presence, proceeded to disrobe completely for their ablutions, producing an idyllic scene which would have inspired Gauguin and which caused Spots to cut himself several times with his by now extremely blunt razor.

Next morning we set out early and after two kilometres came to a large village, which seemed to be the headquarters of another company, including many of the doctors' original captors. Most of them were friendly but one or two of the leaders seemed hostile and suspicious, and instead of being allowed to proceed we were taken to a hut in the village and told to stay there. After a while we were told that we might have to stay at least a day and a night because a Phoumi patrol was rumoured to be in the vicinity and there might be a battle. This was a bitter blow at the last moment but fortunately after several hours this highly unlikely rumour was dispelled. Our guides told us that what had really happened was that the hostile leaders had not wanted to let us go and had queried the orders to release us; and it had taken our guides some time to persuade them that the orders came from the highest Pathet Lao authority.

We now set out on the last lap, going at a good speed and allowing our guards only the minimum halt at villages. Eventually, within 13 kilometres of Thateng our guides turned off the main road and took us to the village of Ban Lik Nyay, apparently the last village in Pathet Lao territory. Here they handed us over to a villager and took their leave from us, with expressions of mutual esteem — they really had looked after us very well. The village guide took us to the next village, which was neutral territory. Another guide from the neutral village then took us into government-controlled territory to the large village of Ban Kapeu where the doctors were well known, having held a clinic there almost every week for the best part of a year. Here they received a heart-warming reception, all the more remarkable because Laotians are usually undemonstrative. The villagers, men, women and children, all came out to smile and express their delight at the doctors' return and to bring their choicest food, including coconuts, mangoes and pineapples. They also offered us two porters to carry the bags we had hitherto carried on our own shoulders. With our bags slung over a bamboo pole the porters forged ahead at a great rate. We trudged wearily behind and eventually arrived footsore but happy in Thateng at 5.00 p.m. on the evening of 28 June, four weeks almost to the minute since Spots and I had been made prisoners. During our captivity we had covered some 210 kilometres on foot, 130 of them in the five days since the order for our release came through.

The kind Swiss missionaries gave us a warm welcome, took us into their home and asked us what we would like to drink. When I mentioned my dream of cold beer they apologized for the lack of anything cold but thought that they had a bottle of beer in the pantry. A bottle was produced, the size, shape and colour of a beer bottle, though lacking a label, and the amber liquid which was poured out looked like beer, though lacking any froth. But even flat beer was a welcome thought at the time, so I took a good swig and immediately spat it out. It was vinegar. So I had to content myself with coffee, a taste that was also sorely missed in the jungle.

Next morning I shaved off my two weeks' beard, which was not very becoming, having reached the stage only of what would later be considered fashionable designer stubble. But Colin preserved his more luxuriant four weeks' beard for the admiration of Jane. Later in the morning an American helicopter came to transport all of us, including Sian and Rex, to Saravane where we transferred to a small USMAAG aircraft, which took us to Vientiane. There was a large crowd at the airport to welcome us, with John Addis and the whole of the British Embassy and community, numerous other diplomats and Lao officials, a substantial contingent of the British and other foreign press and several television cameras which homed in to close range as Colin and I joyfully embraced our wives. This was undoubtedly one of the happiest moments of my life. In the late afternoon we gave a press conference, which was in essence a brief summary of this chapter, including the episode of the Kha villagers imitating our primitive cricket. Next day the front page of the *Daily Express* bore the headline 'CRICKET AND KISSES END JUNGLE TERROR'.

10

Success at Last

We found that until the day of our release nobody in Vientiane had any idea of our whereabouts or state of health. Apparently my hand-written letter in Lao had been intercepted by local authorities in Thateng or Saravane who had transcribed it on to a typewriter and sent the typed version to Vientiane where it was received on 6 June. But as it lacked my signature there were doubts as to its authenticity. It was more than two weeks later before the original turned up in Vientiane. As it was signed by me and my Lao teacher Mr Pheng recognized my Lao handwriting, it was obviously genuine, but by then it was more than three weeks out of date.

As was to be expected, John Addis had been in frequent contact with Prince Souphanouvong who assured him that he was in touch with our captors, that we were well and that his orders to release us would be carried out, but it would take time because of slow com-munications and the monsoon weather. John believed him and so did Beth, who was perhaps less worried than she might have been in another country because of her faith in the gentle nature of the Lao people. But John had great difficulty in restraining the British press correspondents, who could not understand why it was taking so long and were calling for some dramatic action from the British govern-ment. These calls were repeated in the leading British newspapers and in parliamentary questions in the House of Commons (Harold Wilson) and the Lords. It was largely to appease the media and

Parliament that the Foreign Secretary Lord Home sent a message on 21 June to Souvanna Phouma appealing to him to intervene to speed up our release. But by the time it was received Boun Kong was already on his way to Ban Tia Kad with the final orders for our release.

Poor communications and the distances to be travelled on foot were certainly the main reasons for the delay. As I was able to see for myself Sithone did not have a radio transmitter, only an ordinary portable transistor receiver. The Khoueng, which presumably did have a transmitter and was the channel for messages from Souphanouvong, seemed to be located at least two days' march beyond Chavane, which was several days' march away from Sithone during the early days of our captivity. But I suspect that there was an additional delay because Sithone, on receiving the orders to release us, probably in the first week of June, may have queried them and suggested that we should continue to be held as hostages as a means of pressure to hasten the formation of the coalition government; it would then take at least another week for him to receive the order confirming that we should be released without conditions. There may have been an element of face-saving in this, with Sithone seeking to justify what he must have quickly realized was his mistake in taking us prisoner.

I spent the day after our return dictating the reports that provided the essence of the last chapter (minus the bare breasts and some other details). In due course I received various complimentary messages from the Foreign Office and also the Queen and President Kennedy who had been shown my reports. But the first letter I received from the Foreign Office was from the Establishment and Organization Department, which dealt with allowances. It ran something as follows: 'Dear Mr Brown, I see from press reports that you had to buy some food during your captivity. I trust that you will not be claiming subsistence allowance for this, since during this time you were still receiving your foreign allowance, *less of course 15 per cent for your absence from your post*' (my italics). I replied: Dear Mr X, Until I received your letter I had not thought of claiming subsistence allowance. But since you brought up the subject I think I am entitled to it and have instructed the accountant to pay me £10 in respect of the 16 chickens, 3 pigs and numerous mangoes and pineapples which I bought.' I heard nothing more, but was left wondering at the mentality of someone whose first thought on reading of my release from captivity was to ensure that I did not claim subsistence and that my foreign allowance was cut 'because of my absence from my post'.

However, Malcolm Morris capped my story of government parsimony with an example from Australia. During the war an Australian soldier was captured by the Japanese in Singapore, and while he was a prisoner his wife back in Australia received his full army pay. When news came that he had died in prison camp on, say, 16 May 1943, she received only her widow's pension from that date. After the war, Japanese records showed that he had in fact died on 15 May, whereupon the Army Pay Department wrote to the widow to ask her to refund the difference between full pay and widow's pension for one day.

The very first message received after my release was a telegram proposing that I should return home immediately to recover from my ordeal, after which I would be transferred to another post. I replied that I did not need to recover as I was fitter than ever, having lost 20 pounds weight from a regime of plain food, no alcohol and plenty of walking. I had no desire to leave Laos and I thought that the additional knowledge of the Pathet Lao that I had acquired would be useful in the coming months. The Foreign Office reluctantly acquiesced but insisted that I take some local leave. This was irritating as we were in the monsoon season and I had no desire to spend money on a holiday in either Hong Kong or Bangkok, the obvious places for local leave, in the pouring rain. So I offered to go to Singapore on an official paid journey to report to the Joint Intelligence Committee (Far East) on my experiences, after which I would take a week's holiday there. This was agreed, but the holiday was disappointing. I spent most of it in bed with all the symptoms of malaria — high fever with alternating sweating and shivering. We had of course been bitten by mosquitoes in the jungle, especially in one village on the walk home where there were literally clouds of mosquitoes in our hut; and although we had taken chloroquin while in the jungle, I had foolishly forgotten to continue taking the tablets for the prescribed three weeks afterwards, since there was no malaria in Vientiane and we were not in the habit of taking the drugs. There was likewise no malaria in Singapore, and the army doctor diagnosed flu and prescribed aspirin, which did not do much good. It was only while passing through Bangkok on the way back to Vientiane that malaria was diagnosed and effectively treated so that it never returned.

During my time in the jungle Catherine Pestell, a bright young Second Secretary from Bangkok, had been sent to help out during my absence. She stayed with Beth at our house and they became great friends, having discovered that they had both been to St Hilda's College at Oxford, though not at the same time. I had already met her in the Foreign Office when she was desk officer for France during the 1958 Algeria crisis and I was dealing with North Africa. I now got to know her better as she stayed on for a few weeks, partly to cover my absence on 'holiday' in Singapore. She coped very well with the work, and with her warm, outgoing personality quickly became popular with the embassy staff and diplomatic colleagues, so we were all sorry when she had to return to Bangkok.

Catherine certainly had plenty to do, since the month of June saw the culmination of all our efforts over the previous 18 months, when agreement was finally reached, by the Three Princes' meeting in the Plain of Jars, on the composition of the government of national unity. This was in the form suggested by John Addis nine months earlier, with 11 ministers from the centre (including four 'Vientiane neutralists') and four each from the right wing and the Pathet Lao. Souvanna Phouma was Prime Minister and Minister of Defence, with his loyal henchman Pheng Phongsavan as Minister of the Interior and the left-wing Quinim Pholsena as Foreign Minister. Souphanouvong was Deputy Prime Minister and Minister of the Economy and the Plan, with Phoumi Vongvichit as Minister of Information. General Phoumi (Nosavan) was Deputy Prime Minister and Minister of Finance. The new government took the oath and formally entered into office on 23 June, the day we set off from Ban Tia Kok on the long walk to freedom. Souvanna Phouma left next day for Paris for his daughter's wedding (to a French *vicomte* as I recall) followed by a visit to Geneva for the signature of the Final Act of the conference endorsing the agreement reached in the Plain of Jars. So when we returned to Vientiane from the jungle Souphanouvong, as the senior by age of the two deputies, was acting as Prime Minister.

John Addis now left us. The Foreign Office had planned that he should leave in late May for a new assignment — a year's sabbatical at Harvard University to study the problem of the frontier between India and China, where there had recently been a number of armed clashes. But as the negotiations in Laos seemed to be at a critical final stage it was sensibly decided that he should stay on until agreement was reached. By the time this happened I was a prisoner in southern Laos and it was necessary (partly for reasons of public relations) that he should stay until I was released. So he departed at the beginning of July, having had the satisfaction of seeing the conclusion of the settlement to which he had contributed perhaps more than anyone else; and he was also fortunate in not staying around while the settlement gradually disintegrated.

The new Ambassador, Donald Hopson, arrived on 3 July. With his upright carriage, aquiline features and military moustache he looked every bit the typical British ambassador or senior military officer. He had in fact a fine military record during the war, having joined the Territorial Army before 1939. He served in several campaigns and won the DSO in Normandy where he was wounded. His wife Denise, who did not come out until some months later, had served with the French resistance movement and had met Donald when she was a nurse in the hospital where he was recovering from his wounds. She brought with her their 12-year-old daughter and an attractive *au pair* called Pamela Peak, who had recently won a beauty contest as Miss St Tropez.

A week or so after his arrival Donald Hopson flew up to Luang Prabang with the diplomatic staff of the embassy (those with the rank of Third Secretary and above) to present his credentials to the King. The Air Attaché at Bangkok, Joe Holmes, who was also accredited to Laos, flew us up in his twin-engineered Pioneer, which was reassuringly a short takeoff and landing (STOL) aircraft. Reassurance was necessary as the journey was somewhat hazardous. There were apparently no navigational aids at the Luang Prabang airfield and so the attaché was planning to navigate visually by following the Mekong all the way upstream from Vientiane using, we were a little alarmed to see, a small-scale map of Indo-China in lieu of a chart. In fine weather there would have been no problem, but it was the monsoon season and the whole country was covered in cloud. We flew under the cloud, which was quite high when we set out. But as we went north the clouds became lower and lower, forcing the aircraft down into the river valley. Towards the end we were flying just above the river between the steep sides of the valley, rather like driving a car along a winding country road between high hedges. It was a relief to arrive safely at Luang Prabang.

This was my first visit to Luang Prabang, which must be one of the most beautiful, exotic and peaceful places in the world, the nearest thing to Shangri-La that I can imagine. The city, little more than a large village in size, is built on a small peninsula formed by the confluence of the Mekong and a small tributary, the Nam Khan, at a point where the forest-clad sides of the valley rise steeply to mountain ranges behind. There were few buildings other than the royal palace and a large number of Buddhist temples, and the population consisted mainly of Buddhist monks in their saffron-coloured robes. There were hardly any cars, and people either walked or rode in a *samlor*, the bicycle-propelled rickshaw that was also a principal form of transport in Vientiane. In the centre of the otherwise flat peninsula was a small conical hill surmounted by a Buddhist temple with silvery wind chimes and a huge drum about five metres in diametre. This was beaten every evening at sunset. The sound frequency was so low that one did not so much hear the note as feel the vibration, which seemed to make the whole valley tremble as the sun sank behind the mountains to the west — truly a magical place, which happily managed to survive the upheavals of the next 25 years more or less unchanged.

The credentials ceremony, the first I ever attended, followed a pattern that is fairly standard throughout the world, but the setting of the royal palace and the costumes of the king and his courtiers were more colourful and exotic than usual. Wearing our uniforms, we were driven to the palace in limousines escorted by police motorcycle outriders with flashing blue lights and screaming sirens to warn the non-existent other traffic to keep out of the way. Outside the palace we were greeted by an honour guard of soldiers in white jackets and red trousers. We then entered the palace and, leaving our spiked helmets in an antechamber, filed into the throne room where the King and his entourage were already assembled. All were dressed in high-collared white coats and silk sarongs tucked between the legs. The King wore the red and yellow sash of the Order of the Million Elephants and the White Parasol and also stood out because of his height. At over six feet he towered above most other Laotians (Souvanna Phouma in private used to refer to him, half enviously and half disparagingly, as 'Longshanks'). Donald Hopson advanced to within a few paces of the King, bowed, made a short speech in French extolling the excellent relations between our two countries, and then handed over his credentials, essentially a letter signed by the Queen addressed to 'our good brother the King of Laos' and commending the virtues of her trusty and well-beloved servant Donald Hopson as her Ambassador to the Kingdom. Two courtiers then approached the King, each bearing a *baci* bowl of hand-beaten pure silver. The King placed the credentials in one bowl and from the other took his spectacles and the text of his reply, which he read out to us. Donald then presented his staff to the King, starting with me, and stayed for a short conversation before we all withdrew to partake of a *champagne d'honneur* with the royal household.

The night before, while we were staying at the only hotel, Donald Hopson had organized a rehearsal of our movements at the ceremony, with each of us in turn advancing to within the correct distance of the person playing the role of the King before bowing and shaking his hand. He was particularly insistent that we should execute correctly the court bow as practised at the Court of St James's. In the presence of British royalty male courtiers stand at attention and, instead of bowing from the waist, simply drop the chin onto the chest, while keeping the body upright. Donald watched us closely as we practised this rather unnatural action, criticizing any tendency to drop the shoulders as the head nodded forward. Barrie Gane, the young Third Secretary, performed impeccably and was singled out for special praise. Later in the bar Barrie was proudly showing off his newly acquired skill but finally nodded so vigorously that he dislocated his neck. Fortunately this painful conditon righted itself during the night and next day the ceremony passed off smoothly, though it was noted that Barrie's neck movement was distinctly more cautious than it had been the night before.

Strict protocol requires that a newly arrived ambassador should not attend any official functions until he has presented his credentials. But the Laotians were as relaxed about protocol as they were about most matters. So on the day after his arrival I accompanied Donald to the American Fourth of July reception where I was able to introduce him to Souphanouvong. The Prince was very friendly, reminding me that he had advised me not to go into the jungle but admitting that his people had made a mistake — 'C'était une erreur des miens'. It is highly unusual for a politician, and almost unheard of for a communist, to admit a mistake, and this is one reason why I believed that Souphanouvong was not a communist. Another reason was the retention of his princely title; a committed communist would surely have renounced his title and wanted to be addressed as 'comrade'.

During the remainder of my time in Laos I met Souphanouvong a number of times, and each occasion increased my respect, and indeed liking, for him. The first occasion was an official one. The embassy had put in a formal note to the Ministry of Foreign Affairs, listing with values the items that had been taken from the doctors, Spots and me and requesting the return of the items or financial compensation. The main items were the doctors two cameras valued at £95 each; and various items of clothing brought the total to something like £240. The note had been sent as a matter of formal procedure and we never expected to see either the articles or monetary compensation. But some weeks later I was summoned to Souphanouvong's office in the Ministry of the Economy where he handed over without comment the equivalent of £240 in Laotian currency. I could not imagine that the NLHS central committee would have agreed to this payment and I concluded that he had paid the money out of his own pocket.

In August 1962 the New York Woodwind Quintet came to Laos under the State Department's cultural programme. The clarinettist David Glazer had become a good friend of ours when we were in New York, and he together with the flautist Sam Barron stayed with us at the MIC Site. One of their recitals was at the American Ambassador's residence, preceded by a reception at which I introduced the members of the quintet to Souphanouvong and acted as interpreter for them. They politely asked whether the Prince had any particular requests for them to play, not expecting him to know anything of their rather specialized repertoire. He thought for a moment and said:

'Do they know the Woodwind Quintet in the form of a Chôro by Villa-Lobos?' Astonished, they replied: 'Yes, we know it, but how on earth does he know it?' A few months later the recently arrived head of USAID, the American aid mission, invited us to a dinner in honour of Souphanouvong. Our host was of recent Greek origin, spoke modern Greek and had a good knowledge of classical Greek. He had heard of Souphanouvong's reputation as a brilliant classical scholar in his youth, was somewhat sceptical and proposed to put him to the test. He had copied out some lines of Homer on to a piece of paper, making three deliberate mistakes, and left the paper on a side table. Souphanouvong came in, his eyes darting round the room in his customary manner, taking everything in, including the piece of paper. He picked it up, read it rapidly and exclaimed: 'Ah yes, Homer. But you have made three mistakes, there, there and there.' Such displays of cultural erudition, in which there was certainly an element of showing off, would have been impressive in anyone whose higher education had been in the field of engineering. They were astonishing in a middle-aged prince of a remote Asian country whose adult life had been mostly spent in political conflict and guerrilla warfare in mountainous jungle far removed from the world of concert halls and libraries.

During our remaining time in Laos we also got to know Prince Souvanna Phouma very well, mainly because of his passion for bridge. Whenever he accepted an invitation to dinner it was expected that bridge would be organized after the meal; and he regularly invited senior bridge-playing diplomats to dinner and bridge at the prime ministerial residence. I was an average player and Beth was a good player (I write in the past tense as we hardly ever play nowadays) and she became his favourite partner, so we were always included in these bridge evenings. I recall one occasion when the King's birthday was being celebrated with a late evening garden party at the royal palace in Vientiane, starting at 9.00 p.m. *Le tout Vientiane* was present in all its finery, the Lao ladies in their finest silks and the men in national dress, with the diplomats in white tie or uniform with *décorations pendantes*, and the King in his court dress presiding on a throne on the terrace of the palace. The party seemed set to go on into the small hours, but around 11.00 p.m. Souvanna Phouma came up to us and said: 'How about some bridge?' We naturally agreed and after we had recruited five more to make up two tables he went up to the King, made his respectful *wai* and begged leave to withdraw to deal with pressing matters of state. The rest of us sneaked away to join him at his residence where we played bridge until 3.00 a.m.

I was too junior to return Souvanna Phouma's hospitality but once I succeeded in inviting him by mistake. I had become very friendly with his private secretary La Norindr, whose wife, a German tennis teaching professional, used to engage in lengthy battles with Beth on the tennis court. So when La was appointed ambassador in Paris I organized a farewell lunch for him (his wife was already in Europe) and invited several middle-ranking diplomats and Lao officials. There was never any question of inviting Prince Souvanna Phouma, but I thought it might be nice to invite his son Prince Mankra, a young officer of the Laotian Air Force who was at the time living with his father in the prime minister's residence, which was also his office. In view of his princely status I thought I should write a personal letter of invitation rather than send a card. I accordingly wrote a letter beginning 'Altesse' and explaining the reason for the lunch, and enclosed it in an envelope addressed to 'Prince Mankra Souvanna Phouma' at the prime minister's office (*Présidence du Conseil des Ministres*). Next day I received a reply on the official notepaper of the prime minister accepting my invitation and signed 'Souvanna Phouma'. I could hardly tell the prime minister that I had not intended to invite him, so I had to upgrade my guest list; our delighted cook also upgraded his menu (listed in his little black book under '*Très Grand Dîner — Premier Ministre*') and produced a superb meal with a main dish of rabbit in aspic served in a dish decorated with small candles. It was of course essential to invite my own Ambassador. Fortunately Donald Hopson also played bridge, so when lunch was over and the Prince proposed some bridge he stayed on to make up the four while Beth emerged from the bedroom where she had taken refuge from the men-only gathering.

There were no official residences for the deputy prime ministers, and Prince Souphanouvong also lived at the *Présidence du Conseil*. Despite their political differences, the two half-brothers were very close: I recall Souvanna Phouma once putting his arm around

Souphanouvong's shoulder and receiving from him a look of pure affection. When Souvanna Phouma began hosting his bridge parties Souphanouvong, though not a bridge player, would always be present. He would have dinner with us and afterwards sit by the corner of one of the bridge tables, taking everything in with his quick, darting eyes and occasionally asking questions to elucidate some point of bidding or play. After two or three such evenings he began to play himself, not too badly. And when Souvanna Pouma went off to Paris for a few weeks Souphanouvong took over not only as Acting Prime Minister but also as host for dinner and bridge with exclusively Western, including American, diplomats. I became more and more convinced that he was, as Falaize would say, '*récupérable*' from the Western point of view, or at least would have been a few years earlier if the Americans had given their full backing to the Vientiane Agreements of 1957. But by 1962 it was probably already too late as developments in Vietnam, and consequent greater Viet Minh interest in Laos, meant that he was no longer a free agent.

The summer of 1962 saw the usual turnaround in the diplomatic community. Shortly after John Addis left Winthrop Brown also departed. He had been in Laos only two years, but his identification with Phoumi and his sustained opposition to Souvanna Phouma made him unsuitable as American Ambassador to the government of National Unity. He was a fine man who had been plunged into a major crisis a few weeks after his arrival and compelled to carry out a policy I believe went against his better judgement and his conscience. His successor was Leonard Unger, an able and agreeable career diplomat who had been counsellor in Bangkok and who was accompanied by his charming wife and attractive teenage daughter Debbie. All three of them joined the Mekong Singers and in due course Debbie became engaged to, and I believe subsequently married, our handsome, violin-playing bass singer, Duncan Mackintosh from Shell. In the Australian Embassy Don Kingsmill left and was replaced by another young third secretary Jeremy Hearder, possessed of a puppy-like eagerness and a delightful wife Kay, who was a doctor. Other changes in the diplomatic corps included the establishment of embassies by the communist Chinese and the North Vietnamese; in consequence, the Chinese Nationalists closed their embassy and the

South Vietnamese withdrew their diplomatic staff, without formally closing their mission.

The summer of 1962 also saw the departure of Og and Sally Thomas. British Council staff usually work more closely with the local people than diplomats, who spend most of their time dealing with government ministers and officials, and the Thomases had many Lao friends. A number of these gave the Thomases a farewell party or *baci* at which woollen threads were tied round their wrists to bring them good luck; and as you were not supposed to remove these until they disintegrated of their own accord, by the time they left their forearms were almost weighed down by scores of these goodwill tokens. We gave a farewell party at which the Mekong Singers sang various songs under Og's direction for the last time. I then took over the baton to conduct the madrigal 'Adieu sweet Amaryllis', substituting Og and Sally for Amaryllis, which made for quite an emotional end to the evening. In the absence of any competition I now became the choir's conductor, which was a new experience for me. It turned out to be quite hard work as most of the choir, like the police band, could not read music and so, whenever we tackled new music, I had to teach the different parts note by note. But it was also very agreeable as after Og's training and the arrival of some good new voices the choir was now in good shape.

After the successful conclusion of the international efforts to restore peace to Laos, one might have expected the pressure of work at the embassy to slacken. On the contrary it increased, at least for me personally. It soon became evident that the Laotians would need a great deal of help to make the Geneva Agreement work. The government did set up tripartite commissions on such matters as observance of the cease-fire, the withdrawal of foreign troops and the integration of the armed forces and the administration; but owing to the inadequacy of the civil service and continuing mutual suspicions very little progress was made. So in October 1962 the four Western ambassadors set up working parties of their deputies to consider each of these problems and draft proposals or plans that might help solve them. Within the British Embassy this considerable extra task fell on me as number two to the Ambassador.

There was also the need to support the pitifully weak Laotian

23. *(above)* Presenting credentials at Luang Prabang – the author is presented to the King.

24. *(above)* Diplomatic parties – the author introduces Donald Hopson to Prince Souphanouvong at the US Embassy, 4 July 1962.

25. *(above)* Music in Vientiane – Duncan Mackintosh, Jean-Pierre and the author on bass clarinet.

economy. The Americans had hitherto shouldered this burden by direct subsidies to the Laotian budget amounting to over $40 million a year. They now turned to the French and us and suggested, not unreasonably, that as we had played such a major role in negotiating the settlement, had in effect pushed a reluctant USA into accepting it, we should pick up part of the cheque. They proposed that we and the French should join them in financing a programme of essential Laotian imports estimated at $20 million a year, of which our share might be £2 million ($5.6 million), in addition to our development aid, which included capital projects as well as technical assistance. The appalled British Treasury offered £100,000, which was the figure the aid department of the FO (then known as the Department of Technical Co-operation) was already considering for development aid for 1963. This was clearly inadequate, and after tripartite talks in Paris in October, at which the French offered a total of $8 million a year, including $5 million for the import programme, the Treasury reluctantly agreed to a contribution of £3 million ($8.4 million) to the import programme, spread over three years. In addition we offered £1.35 million ($3.78 million) in development aid, spread over five years. John Addis's active diplomacy had turned out to be rather expensive for the British taxpayer, though it was to be good news for some of our less efficient industries.

The Treasury had insisted not only that the British contribution should be tied to British exports, which was the usual policy for most aid donors, but also that it should be spent as far as possible on products from industries that had surplus capacity. In other words our aid should act as a form of subsidy for ailing, uncompetitive branches of our industry. Our steel industry, which was then in a state of decline, was a major candidate and we were instructed to press hard for the inclusion of various steel products on the list of goods for which we were willing to pay. I recall that the Board of Trade was particularly insistent that we should include large non-mobile cranes to the value of £100,000, despite the fact that Laos as a landlocked country had no port and no possible use for fixed cranes. Another difficulty was that the French, and to a less extent the Americans, also wanted to use their aid as a dumping ground for surplus and unwanted goods, which were often the same as those on our list. In consequence we were faced with some hard bargaining in negotiations with the other donors and the Laotian government in drawing up the list of essential imports and our respective responsibility for them. Although I had no previous experience of commercial or aid work the bulk of this extra task again fell on me. David Campbell, who normally dealt with our small existing aid programme, was at the time on home leave, but in any case he was too junior to handle fairly high-level negotiations with the French and Americans, both of whom had sizeable aid missions already in place.

The major problem in setting up the aid programme was trying to ensure that the aid did in fact benefit Laos and not just a handful of corrupt government ministers and businessmen. The example of the US aid programme, where many millions of dollars had produced little visible result, was ever before us. (It was, I think, an American aid official who suggested that the name of the country should be changed from 'Land of a Million Elephants and the White Parasol' to 'Land of the White Elephant and a Million Parasites'.) And subsequently the establishment of a black market in the Laotian currency, the kip, had increased the possibilities and temptations of corruption. The basic system was that a Laotian importer wishing to import goods from the approved list would place an order with a supplier from, say, the USA and deposit the kip equivalent of the dollar cost, at the official rate of exchange, with the Laotian Treasury. With an official rate of 80 kip to the dollar he would deposit eight million kip for goods costing $100,000. The US Treasury would then pay the US exporter in dollars, against proof of delivery. In a normal situation, bills of lading would be sufficient proof of delivery. But, with most goods shipped by sea via Bangkok, it would be possible for the Laotian importer to sell the goods in Bangkok for Thai baht, a hard currency convertible with the dollar. This hard currency could then be used to buy Laotian kip on the black market at a rate of, say, 160 to the dollar, yielding a sum of 16 million kip and a 100 per cent profit for the (non-)importer on his original investment; and of course nothing to show in Laos for the $100,000 of aid money. So it was necessary to inspect goods on their arrival in Laos before the dollars were released. Even this was not enough as Vientiane, the main point of entry, was just across the Mekong from Thailand so that goods, once inspected, could easily be re-exported across the river to be sold for hard currency. It was quite a challenge to devise a system that was proof against at least the most likely frauds, but agreement was finally reached with the Laotian government at the beginning of 1963. By then Tim Everard, who had been dealing with the problem at the Foreign Office end, had been sent out to the embassy to get the programme off the ground. Cheerful and extrovert, he was a recent late entrant into the Diplomatic Service, having spent the previous ten years as a banker in Africa, finishing up as manager of Barclays Bank in Kinshasa during the alarming events in the Congo in the early 1960s. In temperament and experience he was ideally suited to his new job, and although Laos must have seemed a quiet, safe backwater after the Congo he fitted in happily with our small community. He became a lifelong friend and later served as my deputy in Nigeria.

The Foreign Office has often been criticized for relying on generalists, or 'gifted amateurs', rather than specialists. The Americans make much greater use of specialists, but they can afford to, as the staffs of their embassies are usually several times larger than those of their British counterparts, just as the State Department employs many more people than the Foreign Office. In a small post like the British Embassy in Laos there was no room for specialization and officers had to be prepared to turn their hands to anything. Thus in September 1962 I was given another extra task for which I had no specialist qualifications — an investigation into the finances of the International Control Commission. Under the agreement setting up the Commission the three members India, Canada and Poland were to pay the salaries and allowances of their delegations, which in the case of the Indians included the administrative staff and accountants. The other expenses — like accommodation, local staff, transport, communications — known as common pool expenses, were to be paid in equal shares by the five great powers, the USA, USSR, UK, France and China. But so far the payment record of the Big Five had been unsatisfactory with even the best payers, which included ourselves, being usually many months in arrears. This placed a heavy burden on the Indians who had to make all the payments in the first instance, and they understandably wanted payment in advance. Our Treasury and the other finance ministries preferred to reimburse actual expenditure, but as accounts were presented a year late this would have left the Indians badly out of pocket. We in the UK had offered to pay periodically in advance if the Indians supplied estimates of expected expenditure in a form acceptable to us, but so far the Indians had not been able to do this. In order to resolve the problem the British and Soviet embassies in Vientiane were ordered to carry out an investigation of the ICC finances on the ground and report to the Geneva co-chairmen. I was appointed on the British side while the Soviet Embassy nominated a First Secretary Mr Kuznetsov.

I approached this task with some trepidation for several reasons. Although quite good with figures, I had no special training or experience in finance and accounting, other than the supervising of our small embassy account. I was therefore apprehensive about working with a Russian who was likely, I thought, to be much better qualified. At the height of the Cold War the West tended to exaggerate the strength of the Soviet enemy and Soviet diplomats were all assumed to be brilliant, ruthless and cunning. I was therefore worried that Mr Kuznetsov would run rings round me and use the investigation to curb the activities of the ICC that the Russians did not like; or at least would be suspicious, stubborn and uncooperative, making it very difficult to reach agreement. My fears were supported by my experience in the UN where I had admired the debating skill of the Russian delegates, who would brilliantly argue a weak case and ruthlessly expose any weakness in their opponents' case. But these delegates were the élite of their corps; Mr Kuznetsov was no doubt more typical of their run-of-the-mill diplomats, and my fears proved to be quite unfounded. He was a charming man but very badly briefed. No doubt as a result of the excessive centralization of the Soviet system and the stultifying effect of a harsh discipline imposed by fear, Mr Kuznetsov never put forward a constructive idea or indeed a proposal of any kind; and far from seeking to impose a *nyet* on my own proposals he was quite happy to agree to everything I suggested.

A more substantial concern was the effect the investigation might have on our relations with the Indian delegation and my personal relations with the chairman Avtar Singh. He was understandably upset by the implication of lack of confidence in the ability of the Indians to run the administration of the ICC efficiently and economically. Also, knowing our Treasury, I feared that they would instruct me to press for lots of nit-picking economies, which would further irritate the Indians and make agreement more difficult.

However, as Napoleon said, the most important quality needed by a general is luck, and the same applies to diplomats. I was lucky at the outset of the investigation, when the Indian accountants submitted their estimated expenditure for the next year, amounting to some $5.5 million. The largest item was $1.5 million for hire of aircraft, specifically one elderly Dakota (DC3) and two smaller six-seater planes. I immediately queried this, as I did not need to be an expert to know that for $1.5 million you could buy several Dakotas outright, instead of hiring one for a year. It turned out that the correct figure was $150,000, and the reason for the error, which I worked out later, is of some interest. Traditionally when dealing with large sums of money the Indians talk not of millions but of lakhs of rupees, the lakh being 100,000. Thus 150,000 would be one-and-a-half lakhs, expressed in figures as 1,50,000; and it is easy to see how this could be transcribed as 1,500,000. At any rate I was able at one stroke to reduce the estimates by R1,350,000 or nearly 25 per cent.

This lucky coup immediately established my authority with the experts in the British Treasury, who had failed to pick up this mistake, and also with the Indians, who could hardly complain of an investigation when they had committed such a gross error. I was now in the driving seat and, although much detailed work remained to be done, the way was now clear for a solution. The Treasury had agreed to make quarterly payments in advance, but wanted these to be on the basis of quarterly estimates. I persuaded them that quarterly estimates in addition to annual estimates would add unreasonably to the burden on the Indian accountants, so it was agreed that quarterly advance payments would be made of a quarter of the annual estimates. The major remaining problem was that in several attempts the Indian accountants had failed to produce estimates in a form acceptable to the treasuries of the paying nations. In the end I had to prepare the whole estimates myself, incorporating some additional minor economies, and get them agreed by the Indians. I then wrote a seven-page report to the co-chairmen, which Kuznetsov happily co-signed as a joint report, without demur and without amendment.

On top of all this extra work we had a visit from the Foreign Office inspectors in November 1962. The inspectors, who are ordinary diplomats in mid-career (I was given this assignment a decade later) visit posts every three years or so to assess the allowances, fix staffing levels and generally check that the work is being carried out efficiently and in accordance with instructions. An inspection is always a major event for an embassy and especially for the Head of Chancery, who has to organize the preparation for the visit, including the compilation of local cost of living figures and various statistics, such as the number of telegrams, which indicated the size of the workload. Fortunately by the time the inspectors arrived my investigation of the ICC finances had just been completed, but the aid and political work remained heavy. The inspectors found that the aid work was more complicated and difficult than they had supposed. They recommended that I should concentrate solely on the aid work and that someone from Bangkok should be attached to us to help out with my political and administrative work. We asked for Catherine Pestell, who had been such a success on her previous visit, but Bangkok did not feel able to spare her and instead sent a young Third Secretary Julian Hartland-Swann who, though lacking in experience, fitted in very well. In any case the arrival of Tim Everard in January relieved me of much of the detailed aid work and allowed me to resume my involvement in the political work during my remaining few months in Laos.

A few days after the inspectors left we had a visit from Malcolm MacDonald, the British co-chairman of the Geneva conference. I might have said something earlier about this remarkable man, whom I came to admire greatly. He was arguably the outstanding British diplomat of the postwar period; in fact, in terms of the number of top-level posts he held, it is doubtful whether any British diplomat of any period could equal him. He had the advantage of starting at the top. The son of Ramsay MacDonald, the first Labour prime minister, he entered Parliament as a young man in support of his father's National Labour Party. In 1935, at the age of 33, he became the youngest Cabinet minister since William Pitt the Younger when he was appointed Secretary of State for the Dominions in Baldwin's National government. There were mutterings of nepotism, but he was a more than capable minister and he retained his post in Neville

Chamberlain's government from 1937 until 1940, when Churchill appointed him Minister of Health in his first wartime coalition government. But Malcolm, remaining loyal to his father's memory and to the National Labour Party, which had dwindled to a handful of members, lacked a strong political base and was regarded as expendable when Churchill needed to reshuffle his government early in 1941. In compensation he was offered the post of high commissioner in Canada. Having entered diplomacy by this unorthodox route he was to remain in it and perform outstanding work over the next 30 years.

After the war, when he was still in his early forties, Malcolm was appointed Governor-General of Malaya and Singapore. Two years later, in 1948, he became the first Commissioner-General for Southeast Asia with his headquarters at Phoenix Park in Singapore. In this capacity he travelled widely in the region and got to know all the leading personalities of the different countries including Laos. He also found time to write two books, on the Angkor Wat temples in Cambodia and on the people of the long houses in Borneo. In 1955 he handed over to Rob Scott and was appointed High Commissioner to India, our most important overseas post in the Commonwealth. I first met him in 1959 when he came from New Delhi to Singapore for the annual Eden Hall conference (named after the commissioner-general's residence) of all the British ambassadors, high commissioners and colonial governors in East and Southeast Asia, from Pakistan to Japan. At first sight he was an unimpressive figure, short and slightly built, with an otherwise handsome face marred by protruding teeth. But his unassuming, modest manner and quiet charm, his sly sense of humour and high intelligence soon won people over, and he seemed to be particularly popular with the ladies. After all his years in Malaya and Singapore he knew everyone who mattered in the city, including Han Suyin, the glamorous authoress of A Many-Splendoured Thing and other romantic, semi-autobiographical novels. During the conference he was staying with Rob Scott at Eden Hall. Rob subsequently told me that one afternoon he and his wife were having tea when Malcolm marched in with Han Suyin and continued through to his bedroom, announcing: 'Dr Han is just going to give me a massage.'

His posting to India came to an end just when the Geneva conference on Laos was convened and, with his unrivalled experience of Southeast Asia, he was the obvious candidate for the job of co-chairman. Afterwards he was to become Governor and then Governor-General of Kenya during the transition to independence, when he established a close friendship with Kenyatta, at whose request he made the unusual move from Governor-General to High Commissioner when Kenya became a republic. In the latter half of the 1960s, when Rhodesia became a major problem, he was appointed Special Representative of the British government in Africa and travelled around the continent seeking support for and understanding of British policies. This was his last official post, but after retirement he remained active in Africa and Asia as, *inter alia*, President of Voluntary Service Overseas and the Royal Commonwealth Society, in which capacity he visited and stayed with me in Tanzania and Nigeria.

After the Geneva conference ended, Malcolm was *en disponibilité* before taking up his post as Governor of Kenya the following year. In late 1962, as explained in the next chapter, things were not going too well in Laos and Souvanna Phouma was talking increasingly of throwing in his hand. If he had done so the settlement would have collapsed and civil war would have resumed. So it was agreed that Malcolm should come out to Vientiane in early December to report on the situation and try to bolster Souvanna Phouma's morale. At a dinner party given for him by Donald Hopson and attended by Souvanna Phouma I was able to observe the great man's diplomatic technique, which on this occasion, at least, could be described in one word — flattery. He was clearly aware of Disraeli's dictum: 'Everyone likes flattery, and when it comes to royalty you should lay it on with a trowel.' Souvanna Phouma counted as minor royalty, so he got the full treatment. After small talk during the serving of the meal Malcolm launched into fulsome praise of Souvanna's patriotism, his statesmanship, his great services to his country, his sacrifices without thought of personal gain and his indispensability to the success of the Geneva settlement and the preservation of peace. While much of what he said was true, the terms in which it was couched were, to our reserved British ears, embarrassingly over the top. But Souvanna, not in the least embarrassed, lapped it all up and by the end of the evening was positively purring. Whether or not his threat to resign was genuine, he now assured us of his firm determination to stay on to see the task through.

11

Things Fall Apart

Unfortunately, as Malcolm MacDonald reported to the Foreign Office, Souvanna Phouma 'was not the man he was'. Although he was only 62, the long years of political conflict and high responsibility in difficult circumstances had taken their toll and sapped his energy. A typical representative of his country, he had his share of the indolence which was a national characteristic. His strengths, only slightly exagerted by Malcolm, were his statesmanlike vision of where the interests of his country lay, his international reputation as the consistent champion of a policy of neutrality and peace, and the now general realization that there was no one else in Laos who had any chance of keeping the reluctant coalition together. But even at his best he was not strong on dynamic leadership or the detailed administration needed to ensure that policy decisions were carried out.

Souvanna's frequent absences in Europe did not help. For two whole months before the agreement was reached in June he was in France, having gone there for medical reasons and decided to stay away until Phoumi had agreed to his proposals for the coalition government. Then immediately after the new government took office on 23 June he took off again to Paris for his daughter's wedding and stayed away for six weeks. And having returned to Vientiane in early August, he flew the next day to Luang Prabang to attend the wedding of the Crown Prince, thus giving the impression that the wedding was the main reason for the timing of his return. Again Souvanna was a typical Lao in his respect for religious and family festivals. But his prolonged absence at this crucial period, when more than ever strong leadership was required, was certainly a factor in the steady deterioration of the situation. In the Plain of Jars, Kong Lae and the neutralist troops who were Souvanna's main power base were left almost leaderless at a time when they were coming under growing pressure from the Pathet Lao. Assisted by some left-wing sympathizers among Kong Lae's troops, notably his deputy Colonel Heuaneh, and with the trump card of control of the distribution of supplies, which now came almost solely from Hanoi, the Pathet Lao worked effect-tively to encourage defections and to undermine the authority of Kong Lae and Souvanna Phouma. In the political field, it became increasingly apparent that two leading neutralist ministers, Quinim Pholsena and Khamsouk Keola, had sold out to the Pathet Lao; and little or no progress was made in building up an effective Neutralist Party to fight the elections which, as part of the Geneva settlement, were due to take place in the near future.

In Vientiane the neutralist and Pathet Lao ministers were not allowed to take over their ministries until after Souvanna returned. Phoumi then negotiated the handover of the ministries in return for Pathet Lao agreement to the setting-up of checkpoints in their area to control the departure of Viet Minh troops; and the handover took place at the end of August. Meanwhile three committees of the three parties had been set up to supervise the cease-fire and to organize the integration of the civil administration and the armed forces. But for some time the only progress made was in the withdrawal of foreign troops, which was required to be completed within three months of the signature of the Geneva Agreement. The US military mission, consisting of over 1000 Americans and Filipinos, duly left before 7 October, but their departure was not matched by the withdrawal of Viet Minh troops, believed to number several thousand. The Pathet Lao at first maintained that there were no Viet Minh in their area, but after strong pressure they grudgingly allowed the ICC to count out a mere 45 departing Viet Minh at the checkpoints that had been established. The Agreement also required the ending of the Russian airlift to the Plain of Jars and the American airlift to the Meo hilltop outposts within Pathet Lao territory. Kong Lae's troops, which had relied on the Russian airlift for both civilian and military supplies, were now left at the mercy of the Pathet Lao, who were able to continue to receive supplies by road from North Vietnam. The Americans, with the agreement of Souvanna Phouma, continued with a 'humanitarian' airlift to the Meos with food and non-military supplies, an ostensible breach of the Agreement, which the Pathet Lao exploited as an excuse for their non-compliance.

As Donald Hopson reported to the Foreign Office, Souvanna Phouma's government sat in Vientiane but did not govern. The country remained effectively partitioned. The Pathet Lao, controlling most of the country, showed no sign of accepting that central government orders applied to their territory and refused access to central government agents or the ICC wishing to investigate breaches of the cease-fire. This intransigence contrasted with Souphanouvong's apparent eagerness to make the settlement work, but there were increasing signs that he was no longer in control. The hardline communists Kaysone and Nouhak seemed to be dominant. Whereas Souphanouvong was, I believe, a true nationalist whose aim was to establish a genuinely independent Laos not under the domination of any foreign power, whether France, the USA or North Vietnam, Kaysone and Nouhak saw themselves as part of a wider Indo-Chinese communist movement and took their orders from Hanoi. With the conflict in South Vietnam intensifying it was ever more important for North Vietnam that the Pathet Lao should retain control of the eastern provinces of Laos. In retrospect it can now be seen that there was never any serious chance that the Pathet Lao would agree to submit to the authority of the government and integrate their administration and armed forces.

In Vientiane the installation of the coalition government seemed to make remarkably little difference. In many respects Phoumi still seemed to be in charge. It soon transpired that he had chosen well in accepting the post of Minister of Finance. This enabled him to ensure that the right-wing troops were regularly paid, while funds were withheld from the neutralists and the Pathet Lao, who were given only enough to pay the expenses of their ministers, officials and guards in Vientiane. Although Phoumi no longer held a military command and Souvanna Phouma was titular Minister of Defence, in practice the right-wing generals and colonels still took their orders from Phoumi. Astonishingly, Colonel Siho was left in charge of 'the Coordination' and used his security police to intimidate neutralist ministers and to discourage any switch of political support from Phoumi to Souvanna Phouma. Bodyguards of the neutralist ministers were beaten up, and on one occasion two officers of Souvanna Phouma's staff were arrested on their return from Khang Khay. And in November 1962, when a new Soviet Ambassador arrived at Vientiane airport, he was detained and harassed by the security police and not released for 48 hours.

In private conversation Phoumi made it clear that he regarded the Geneva Agreement as merely a temporary setback to his plans. Convinced, rightly as it turned out, that the Pathet Lao would not relinquish control of their territory, he concentrated on retaining the essentials of power in his own hands against the day when partition would be accepted as the only realistic solution. At the same time he continued to do everything possible to undermine and discredit Souvanna Phouma so that Phoumi would be left as the sole credible anti-communist worthy of American support.

In this policy he continued to receive encouragement from unrepentant elements of the CIA and the American military, both in Vientiane and in Washington, whose acceptance of the Geneva arrangements was at best half-hearted. I saw evidence of this in the committee of deputy ambassadors set up to consider plans for the demobilization and integration of the three armed forces. Our meetings, which were also attended by the military attachés of the four Western embassies, usually began with a military situation report presented by the American attaché. This would mention any recent breaches of the cease-fire and describe the present disposition of 'government' troops and 'enemy' forces, which included the neutralists as well as the Pathet Lao. I had to point out gently that, now that there was a coalition government and that we were working for the integration of the forces, none of the three elements could be regarded as the enemy. This thought seemed to take the attaché by surprise, but the word 'enemy' disappeared from the briefings, if not from the thinking of the American military. Similarly, their idea of demobilization and integration was that most of the Pathet Lao and neutralist troops should be demobilized and that the integrated army should be firmly based on the somewhat reduced right-wing forces with only a few token troops from the other two factions. They hated the idea of forming new units from elements of all three forces, having an exaggerated fear that the Pathet Lao soldiers, mostly illiterate hill peasants, would subvert the other troops and convert them to communism. The only plan consistent with the agreed policy of supporting the neutralist-dominated coalition and strengthening the authority of Souvanna Phouma would have been to base a new integrated army on a strengthened neutralist centre, incorporating greatly reduced numbers of right-wing and left-wing troops. Not surprisingly such a solution was anathema to the American military, who had no faith in the ability of the neutralist soldiers to stand up to the Pathet Lao (the proven inability of Phoumi's troops to resist the Pathet Lao was conveniently overlooked).

In these circumstances virtually no progress was made on the military questions, despite the urgent need for demobilization for economic as well as political reasons. Phoumi's army alone, amounting to some 60,000 men, was far larger than the country could support and, with the addition of 11,000 neutralist and an estimated 14,000 Pathet Lao troops, amounted to an intolerable burden on the economy. Of course large-scale demobilization would have created serious problems of reintegrating the soldiers into civilian life, with very few salaried jobs available; and there would have been a risk that some would turn to armed banditry. But these questions remained academic in the absence of any political will to demobilize. At the end of November, under pressure from the Western embassies, the three leaders did agree to the formation of a single army of 30,000 (still far more than the country needed or could afford) drawn equally from the three factions. Phoumi did demobilize some troops, but this still left him with well over 50,000; the neutralists, who had suffered wastage on the Plain of Jars, hardly exceeded 10,000 in any case; and there was no sign of any demobilization by the Pathet Lao.

Progress in integrating the civilian administration was equally slow. A high point was reached after seven months when the three leaders agreed in February 1963 that all civilian authorities would receive instructions from, and report to, government ministers in Vientiane;

that civil air flights would be permitted to all provincial centres; that the 'counterfeit' currency issued by the neutralists and Pathet Lao for use in their areas should be exchanged for government currency at par; and that a mixed police force should be established in Vientiane. But whether the Pathet Lao would have permitted access to their zone, or whether Colonel Siho would have tamely relinquished control of Vientiane to a mixed police force was never put to the test as within a few weeks the whole edifice began to fall apart.

For the foreign community little seemed to change after the Geneva Agreement. Hopes that one might now be free to travel all over the country were dashed by the Pathet Lao's refusal to admit outsiders to their zone. A number of former ministers who had been familiar figures on the cocktail circuit, such as Khamphan Panya, Nouphat and Sisouk na Champassac, were sent abroad as ambassadors to make room for the new ministers from the centre and the left wing. The latter were less sociable than their predecessors and I have no clear recollection of any of them except for Prince Souphanouvong and the new foreign minister Quinim Pholsena, whom we had got to know in Vientiane in 1960 and later in the Plain of Jars. Quinim was perhaps the most able and energetic of the 'neutralist' ministers but also the most disloyal to Souvanna Phouma. His somewhat foxy appearance accurately reflected his untrustworthy nature and there was growing evidence that he was completely committed to the left-wing cause. In the Plain of Jars especially he intrigued with his henchman Colonel Deuane to undermine Kong Lae and therefore Souvanna Phouma.

There was the usual turnover in the diplomatic community. In addition to the new Soviet Ambassador Afanassiev, who was so badly treated at the airport on his arrival, there was a new Indian Ambassador Bikram Shah, an aristocrat from northern India, and a new Thai Ambassador, a charming man who had been a very good badminton player in his youth and joined us frequently on our court at the MIC site. The most exotic new faces at receptions were the senior staff of the newly opened Chinese Embassy, but they did not add much to the gaiety of nations. With China poised between the disastrous Great Leap Forward and the appalling Cultural Revolution, diplomatic life abroad was much safer and more agreeable than life at home, and not to be risked by the slightest indiscretion. They always stood in pairs or larger groups to avoid any danger of being suborned by the wicked imperialists; and although a number of them spoke reasonable French they were not very communicative even when a common language was established. One of the few people who could make contact with them was Beth who, as mentioned earlier, had continued to take lessons in Chinese and could by now converse quite fluently in Mandarin. Given the rare opportunity of speaking to a foreigner in their own language, the Chinese diplomats relaxed and became quite friendly, even smiling occasionally.

In the British Embassy the euphoria we shared at the conclusion of the Geneva Agreement slowly faded. While morale and spirits remained high, we were no longer uplifted by the missionary zeal with which we had pursued the Holy Grail of a peaceful, neutral and united Laos. The task of making the agreement work on the ground was less glamorous and newsworthy, and the role of foreign diplomats was less clear cut. Having worked so hard to bring the settlement about, we were desperately anxious for it to succeed, and our disappointment was accordingly greater as hopes foundered against the intransigence of the Pathet Lao and the right wing. Donald Hopson, coming new to the situation with a fresh mind and energy, did everything he could in the diplomatic field to encourage support for and commitment to Souvanna Phouma; and the new American Ambassador Len Unger appeared to be entirely loyal to what was now official US government policy. However, it gradually emerged that American policy was to support the neutralists only provided that this did not involve weakening the right wing — a proviso that fatally undermined the chances of success. And back in Washington the State Department's old doubts about Souvanna Phouma re-emerged. With the growing US involvement in Vietnam, Laos was seen more and more as an aspect of Vietnam, where the mistake of treating a political problem by military means was being repeated. In view of the Pentagon/CIA concern to retain Phoumi's army as a bulwark against a communist takeover, the US government failed to give the whole-hearted support to Souvanna Phouma that was essential if the settlement was to succeed.

Amid the gathering gloom, social life and recreation in Vientiane remained very agreeable. There was the pleasure of watching the burgeoning romance between Duncan Mackintoch and Debbie Unger and, more surprisingly, the developing relationship between our former Miss St Tropez, Pamela Peak, and Spots Leaphard, nearly 30 years her senior but still vigorous and handsome. Of course in those relatively chaste days the word relationship did not have the connotations it had acquired by the 1990s. As my old college chum Philip Larkin told us in his poem *Annus Mirabilis*

> 'Sexual intercourse began
> In nineteen sixty-three
> (Which was rather late for me)'

and this was only 1962. Whatever the precise state of the relationship, it seemed unlikely, because of the great difference in age, that anything permanent would come of it; but it is nice to record that when Spots was posted to Belize after Laos, Pamela visited him there.

One could always watch the glamorous Madame Laigret and other attractive ladies, mainly but not exclusively French, water-skiing on the Mekong (I had a go at water-skiing myself but gave up after two undignified failed attempts to stand up in the water). Occasionally there were reminders that water-skiing can be a dangerous sport: one of the Laotians we knew best, the Director of Protocol Ouday Souvannavong, was devastated when his younger brother was drowned or strangled, or both, when the towrope became entangled around his neck. But more often there were lighter moments. On one occasion Donald Hopson went out to water-ski with David and Philippa Campbell, taking his official chauffeur to steer the motorboat. The Mekong was flowing fast, and at one stage Donald threw out an anchor to hold the boat in position. This was unwise, as when the anchor rope tightened the force of the current capsized the boat, plunging them all into the water. Worried that his driver might not be able to swim, Donald called out to him '*Jean, connaissez-vous nager?*' Jean replied '*Oui*', '*je le sais*,' thus managing with four well-chosen monosyllables both to reassure his employer and correct his French.

There was a steady round of receptions, dinners and dancing, either to traditional Lao orchestras or to efficient Filipino dance bands, from whom I occasionally borrowed a saxophone to improvise a solo. And for a lucky few there were the pleasures of bridge with Souvanna Phouma and/or Souphanouvong. There were several tennis tournaments, but I have a clear recollection of only one of them, which was I think the national championship. Although I always entered the singles, I never had any realistic hopes of advancing beyond the semifinals, as the best Lao and Vietnamese players, like their French teachers, played mainly singles and, on the slow concrete courts, had a consistency off the ground that I could not match. Doubles was another matter, as we British play far more doubles than the French or their pupils, and I could hold my own with any of them. On this occasion I had acquired as my partner a Vietnamese who was one of the best doubles players, and I had high hopes of success. We progressed with little difficulty to the final where we met the holders, who were also the two top Laotian singles players. I had a good day, playing just about as well as I could. But my partner played really badly, making mistake after mistake and sometimes missing the ball completely. It was all very embarrassing, but to my surprise every time he missed a shot the sizeable crowd shouted with laughter. I had heard that oriental people tend to titter or laugh to cover up their embarrassment, but there was an element of gleeful delight in the laughter, which was inconsistent with this explanation. After the match, which of course we lost very quickly, my partner departed immediately, averting his eyes from mine. I asked a Laotian friend why the crowd had laughed so cruelly. He explained that somehow they all knew that my partner had smoked a couple of pipes of opium before the match, and so he was probably seeing two or three balls at a time and only occasionally hitting the right one.

Music continued as usual, with occasional evenings of chamber music and regular choir practices, usually on Sunday mornings. We again prepared a programme of Christmas carols but we decided that rather than repeat the bibulous tour of the embassies we would give a concert at one of them (the French, I think) to which all would be invited. We were also asked by Tony Beamish to record the concert for broadcasting by Radio Laos. We assembled in a recording studio lined with acoustic tiles, which completely deadened any resonance. Unable to hear any echo of their voices the singers quickly lost confidence and pitch. The playback sounded awful and we finished almost two tones lower than we started. So we abandoned the studio and Len Unger invited us back to his residence while I fetched my personal tape recorder. As we started to sing, the rich resonance from the bare polished floor brought delighted smiles all round. The choir sang at its best and with the delectable Danielle announcing the carols in her beautifully modulated French the programme was a great success.

It was still possible to travel to the Plain of Jars on the weekly ICC flight. The extra workload I was carrying meant that I could not get away from Vientiane, and I was never to see the Plain of Jars again. But Donald Hopson and other members of the embassy went from time to time and reported a steady deterioration of the neutralist position there. The joint neutralist/Pathet Lao military command continued to function at Khang Khay but, although Kong Lae's paratroops outnumbered the Pathet Lao forces in the immediate vicinity, the Pathet Lao were the dominant partner thanks to their control of supplies from Hanoi, including ammunition for the paratroopers' Russian weapons. In the absence of Souvanna Phouma and the other neutralist political leaders in Vientiane, the young general Kong Lae lacked the authority to stand up to the constant Pathet Lao pressure, and had difficulty in maintaining the unity of his own forces. In November 1962 quarrelling broke out in Khang Khay between troops loyal to Souvanna Phouma led by Colonel Ketsana, Kong Lae's able and sensible Chief of Staff, and the left-wingers led by Quinim's protégé Colonel Deuane, who now openly took the side of the Pathet Lao. In December, with the Pathet Lao starving Kong Lae of the most basic supplies, Souvanna Phouma asked the Americans to airlift supplies to the Plain of Jars for the neutralists; but this stopped when an American aircraft was shot down over the Plain, apparently by Deuane's men on the orders of the Pathet Lao commander, General Singkapo. A visit by the two princely brothers at the end of December effected a reconciliation between Deuane and Kong Lae, but this did not last long.

In mid-January 1963 the two princes paid another visit to Khang Khay, this time accompanied by Donald Hopson and the Indian Ambassador Bikram Shah and their wives. Donald reported that it was a happy visit with the two brothers still getting on well together. Souvanna insisted on getting the cards out for a game of bridge in which Souphanouvong joined. At one stage they were interrupted by a tearful young lady, apparently Kong Lae's wife No. 3, a pretty Chinese woman from Hanoi who showed Souvanna a letter she had intercepted from his wife in Sam Neua. Souvanna explained that Kong Lae also had a wife in Savannakhet and another in Luang Prabang. His peripatetic soldier's life was obviously hard but it had provided opportunities and consolations of which he had taken full advantage.

In the second week of February we received another high-level visitor, Lord Selkirk, who at the end of 1959 had succeeded Rob Scott as Commissioner-General for Southeast Asia, to which he had added the position of High Commissioner in Singapore, which had just become self-governing. Rob, as a Foreign Office man, had not found it easy to impose his authority on high commissioners and governors appointed by the Commonwealth Relations Office and the Colonial Office respectively; he had accordingly recommended that his replacement should be a politician. Lord Selkirk was a Conservative politician who had been First Lord of the Admiralty in Macmillan's government. Unlike his predecessors he had no previous experience of Southeast Asia and, although he worked hard to overcome this handicap, he inevitably brought less to the job than they did; and the post was abolished after he left. On this occasion in Vientiane he had talks with the King and the leaders of the three factions. On 11 February the King, accompanied by Souvanna and Quinim as Foreign Minister, departed on a royal tour taking in Moscow, Zurich and Washington. On the same day Lord Selkirk and Donald Hopson flew up to the Plain of Jars in response to a charming invitation addressed to Donald in English by Captain Kong Lae (as he still styled himself, despite his promotion to General):

Dear Mr Ambassador,
   It is giving me a great privilege as well as a great honour to acknowledge you that I have received your telegram for the last 24 hours. Availing of this opportunity, permit me, Your Excellency, to extend my healthy thanks to you for your new visit announcement to me.

With a great pleasure, I am always ready to greet and welcome you, your Colonel Isaac, your First Secretary Brown and
your Commissioner-General Lord Selkierd. Your Excellency,
this is my third time and opportunity as well to meet you; and
also this is my first time to meet your Lord Selkierd on next
Monday, the 11th of February 1963.

I commanded all my anti-aircraft gunners to be aware of your
Lord Selkierd's plane. I can guarantee you that nothing will
happen neither to your Lord Selkierd nor to his plane.

Now the weather in Xieng Khouang is splendidly pleasant but
it is little windy. I surely hope that your Lord Selkierd will like
it. If your Lord Selkierd has much time or wants to stay longer
there I shall bring him and his followers to visit Xieng Khouang
and other interesting places.

Please accept, Excellency, the assurances of my deep consider-
ation and esteem.

(sgd) Captain Kongle

In Khang Khay, Kong Lae entertained the visitors to lunch at his
house with Colonel Ketsana and General Singkapo. In a private
meeting Kong Lae complained bitterly of the behaviour of the Pathet
Lao, Quinim and the North Vietnamese in starving him of supplies,
and of Phoumi in denying him money for paying his soldiers. But
otherwise he seemed to be in good spirits and the visitors returned to
Vientiane the same day worried about the situation, but with no sense
of impending disaster.

Disaster struck the very next day when they learned that Colonel
Ketsana, with whom they had lunched the previous day, had been
shot dead, apparently by one of Deuane's dissident neutralist soldiers.
It was believed that the assassination had been planned beforehand by
Quinim to take place after he and Souvanna had departed with the
King, so as to put maximum pressure on Kong Lae's loyal troops
while Souvanna was away. There was immediate talk of reprisals
against the Deuane faction, but Souvanna, on learning of the assassination in Moscow, sent instructions to calm things down. Nevertheless
the situation in the Plain of Jars remained tense. In March one of

Kong Lae's battalion commanders defected to Deuane with 100 paratroopers. Deuane hijacked a convoy from Hanoi destined specifically for Kong Lae. A left-wing neutralist director of education at Xieng Khouang was shot dead, allegedly because of family connections with Quinim. And, under increasing pressure from the Pathet Lao, Kong Lae abandoned the joint headquarters at Khang Khay and moved to a camp adjacent to the airstrip on the Plain of Jars. Here he adopted a defensive position against future Pathet Lao attacks and over the next few months began to collaborate with the right-wing Meo guerrillas and with Phoumist troops in the near vicinity.

Against this unhappy background Beth and I were packing up to return home at the end of a four-year stint in Southeast Asia. In addition to the usual round of diplomatic farewell parties, Souvanna arranged a final bridge evening and the tennis club organized a fare-well mixed doubles tournament for us. We reached the final where we met the formidable combination of Madame La Norindr, the German professional, and a tall, handsome, young Lao called Pan Bouaket, who was an athletic and powerful doubles player. We had a close and enjoyable match, but quite correctly the sentiment of the occasion was not carried to the point of allowing us to win.

Almost our last engagement was a farewell concert of chamber and vocal music, which we gave in the elegant main reception room of the newly opened Lan Xang Hotel. (There was also a fine dining room, but shortly before the opening it was realized that the architect had forgotten to provide a kitchen, so for some months meals were pre-pared in a makeshift hut behind the hotel.) I did not keep a pro-gramme, but I recall that Beth and I played a clarinet/piano version of the Mozart Clarinet Quintet and the Mekong Singers sang a number of songs including my own favourite, a beautiful arrangement for four voices of 'Drink to me only with thine eyes'. The choir sang like angels, and when they sang 'Drink to me only' a second time as the final encore I had the wonderful feeling that I could slow down or speed up the tempo at will and they would follow me like one voice. *Le tout Vientiane* filled the hall and in the front row the two Deputy Prime Ministers, Prince Souphanouvong and General Phoumi, sat side by side. It was probably the last time they attended a function together.

On 1 April when we were leaving the embassy for the airport we discovered that our cholera injections, essential for entry into Thailand, were a few weeks out of date. The resourceful Fred Kempson took our international health certificates, scrawled an indecipherable signature in the next available space and stamped it with an embassy date stamp, which fortunately satisfied the Thai health authorities. At the airport the Mekong Singers serenaded us for the last time and we climbed the ladder into the Air Laos Dakota with tears in our eyes.

There was an extra reason for tears: we had just heard that Quinim had that morning been shot dead. The immediate thought was that this must be the work of Colonel Siho's thugs. But this theory was soon dispelled by the confession of the assassin, a corporal of the neutralist paratroops who had been assigned as bodyguard to Quinim and had been awaiting his opportunity to avenge the death of his former commander Colonel Ketsana. These assassinations were particularly shocking in that they were totally out of keeping with the Laotians' peaceful, Buddhist way of life. They also marked the effective end of the Geneva Agreement. In understandable fear that they would be next on the assassination list, Souphanouvong and Phoumi Vongvichit retreated to Khang Khay and stayed there (although the two Pathet Lao junior ministers remained in Vientiane for a considerable time). Souvanna Phouma continued desperately to try to patch things up with negotiations, meetings and compromises, but the period of coalition government was effectively over.

It was sad to be leaving Laos at a time when the settlement for which we had worked so hard and with such a belief in its rightness appeared to be collapsing. At the same time we left with many happy memories of warm friendship with colleagues in the embassy and elsewhere in the diplomatic corps, friendship strengthened by shared hopes, excitements and dangers and by shared laughter at the occasional absurdities thrown up by the situation. As always, our relations were particularly close with those with whom we had common interests: the musicians and singers, almost exclusively expatriate, with whom we rehearsed and gave concerts, and the tennis players, mainly Laotian, whom we met regularly on the tennis court; while our bridge evenings, and in my case many discussions and

shared meals at the Plain of Jars, developed a special affection for
Souvanna Phouma and, dare I say it, Souphanouvong.

We would miss the country, with its dramatic mountain scenery, the
peaceful villages with houses on stilts, the rice fields and the water
buffaloes, the exotic temples and the saffron-robed monks, and especially the view from our veranda with the majestic Mekong flowing
endlessly by and the spectacular storms and sunsets during the
monsoon season. And we would miss the Laotian people, their charm,
grace and beauty, their smiles and their natural courtesy, even perhaps
their indolence. For those brought up on the Protestant work ethic,
indolence is a pejorative term, but it can have positive aspects. Years
later in Africa, when an expatriate was generalizing in typical fashion
about the laziness of 'the African', a colleague who knew Africa better
than most replied: 'No, the African is not lazy; he just places a high
value on leisure.' The same could be said of 'the Laotian' or at least of
the Laotian male — as in most parts of the world the requirements of
housekeeping, cooking and child rearing left the women with little
leisure. The Laotian male would work hard when necessary, for
example during the planting and harvesting seasons, or when building
a house. But he would see no point in working just for the sake of
working. It was said, and I believe the story is true, that a technical
assistance expert from the Food and Agriculture Organization came
out to Laos to teach a method of intensive rice cultivation with a
higher-yielding plant, which would double the yield from a given plot
of land. The Laotians welcomed the new method and next year
planted half the acreage, thus creating more of the leisure they valued
more than the extra money an increased crop would bring. And who
is to blame them when they made such good use of their leisure time
— in making music, dancing, making love, taking part in family and
religious festivals or simply enjoying the beauties of their natural
environment? Happiness is difficult to define, but I believe that in the
pre-colonial days, or even under the relatively light yoke of French
colonialism before 1939, Laotian village society may have come as
close to a state of idyllic happiness as was possible in our imperfect
world.

Nearly 40 years later I still retain vivid memories of the many
exciting events in which we participated — the Kong Lae coup, the

blockade and the bombs in the garden, the battle of Vientiane, the night when the frog almost swallowed the moon, the visits to the two princes at the Plain of Jars and to the third prince for the Wat Phou festival — and of many happy hours of making music and playing bridge, especially the time when, playing goulash (cards dealt in groups to encourage eccentric distribution) I bid six diamonds, was doubled by Souvanna, redoubled and made seven.

But not surprisingly the most enduring memories are of my time as a prisoner in the remote jungle of southern Laos. As will be apparent from my account, this period of captivity was not nearly as harrowing and disagreeable as one might have expected. It was very different from the experience of some American prisoners, captured in the north while working with the Meos or shot down while airlifting supplies to them, who had been harshly, even brutally treated by the Pathet Lao. We were never treated with deliberate harshness, and the discomforts we suffered arose from the primitive living conditions we shared with our captors and the local village people. The worst feature was the simple fact of being prisoners, the total loss of freedom, the horrible and humiliating feeling of being at the mercy of other human beings who could decide our fate, whether to be shot or released or kept indefinitely in captivity, without our being able to do anything about it. But even at the time this humiliation was outweighed by the interest of seeing a remote part of the country that had not been visited by Europeans for many years; and the fascination of experiencing directly, if only for a few weeks, life as it was in the Stone Age. It is one thing to read about people living in primitive civilizations, to see television documentaries about them, even to visit them as tourists. It is quite another to live among them for a period of time, cut off from contact with the outside world, to share every aspect of their daily lives and to adjust to the total lack of creature comforts and even of items we would have regarded as basic necessities — doors, chimneys, tables, chairs, plates, eating imple- ments, beds, mattresses, pillows, sanitation, soap, the list is very long. The overall impression is of the monotony of their existence, with every day the same, consisting of sleep, work and rest, with little concept of leisure activities or entertainment and with hardly any variation in their daily diet of rice, rice and rice. But they were sufficiently far removed from so-called civilization to be largely unaware of what they were lacking. Living in harmony with their natural environment on which, in the absence of shops or even itinerant traders, they were dependent for all their simple needs, they seemed to be, as far as we could judge, happy or at least content with their lot. Once they got used to the strangers intruding so unexpectedly in their lives, they showed themselves to be basically kind and friendly, like the vast majority of ordinary people all over the world. And so I look back on the episode with feelings not of resentment at my temporary loss of freedom, but rather of gratitude for an educative and rewarding experience.

12

Dream Turns to Nightmare

The image of Laos as a peaceful paradise, which so many Europeans carried away, was perhaps never very accurate. In the eighteenth and nineteenth centuries the country suffered a series of invasions and occupations by Burmese, Siamese and Vietnamese forces, which almost succeeded in destroying its national identity. The period of the French occupation, when the French ruled with a very light hand was probably closest to the image, at least for the Lao of the Mekong valley who would be little affected by the occasional rebellion of peoples in the remote mountains. From the Second World War onwards the tranquil idyll was disturbed successively by the Japanese invasion, the return of the French, various Viet Minh incursions and then the developing civil war. But, apart from the blockade and the battle of 1960, life in Vientiane and the Mekong towns while we were there was little affected by the war. Such fighting as there was took place in the distant mountains and was mainly a matter of noise and rumour with one side, usually the Royal Laotian Army, fleeing at the first sign of danger, so that there were very few casualties. In the villages of the Mekong valley, daily life continued in its unchanging, peaceful, smiling way. And as I saw during my captivity life continued as usual in the areas under Pathet Lao control. Less fortunate were the village people in the areas of contention between the two zones. When the Royal Laotian Army made a sortie into an area previously controlled by the Pathet Lao they would accuse the villagers of helping the Pathet Lao and punish them in various ways, such as seizing their crops and cattle and raping or carrying off their women. When the Pathet Lao returned they would in general behave better, but might arrest or even shoot people who had been particularly friendly with the government troops. It was a miserable existence for people who wanted no more than to be left in peace. But their suffering was as nothing compared with what was to happen over the next 25 years, as developments in Indo-China as a whole turned Laos from an imperfect paradise into something which, with little exaggeration, might be described as a hell on earth.

For a long time after Souphanouvong's move to Khang Khay, Souvanna Phouma refused to abandon hope of restoring the unity of the coalition. The two Pathet Lao junior ministers in fact stayed on in Vientiane for more than a year; and Souvanna kept the two senior ministerial posts open for Souphanouvong and Phoumi Vongvichit. Souphanouvong seemed to share Souvanna's wish to retain at least the façade of the Geneva Agreement and maintained a constant dialogue with his half-brother on ways in which the coalition government might be re-established. For the Pathet Lao the main stumbling block was Colonel Siho and the Coordination, but Phoumi vetoed any suggestion of removing Siho and neutralizing Vientiane. By now the threat from Siho's police was directed mainly against neutralist officers and civil servants and caused a number of them to send their families away from the city or to leave themselves. More neutralists, including two deputy ministers, fled the capital in December 1963 after the commander of Souvanna Phouma's personal guard had been assassinated.

Souvanna still managed to get away to Paris occasionally, once for the marriage of his son Prince Mankra. By now Macmillan had resigned and been replaced by Lord Home, who gave up his peerage and reverted to being plain, or plainer, Sir Alec Douglas-Home in order to become prime minister. Murray Simons, now on the Laos desk in the FO, correctly advised that it would be appropriate for the new prime minister to send a present for the wedding. The Treasury

generously granted £35 for the purpose and Murray set off for
Wedgwoods and came back with a handsome pair of porcelain owls.
These were sent over to No. 10 Downing Street, where Sir Alec
showed himself to be a wise old bird by asking whether the owl was
an auspicious bird in Laos. A hasty call to the Laotian Embassy
produced a very definite answer: the owl was a bird of very ill omen
in Laos. So a pair of colourful jays was substituted and a minor
diplomatic embarrassment was averted. Well done, Sir Alec.

Meanwhile the development of the Ho Chi Minh Trail and
America's deepening commitment to the war in South Vietnam
further reduced the chances of peace in Laos. In April 1964 Souvanna
flew to Peking and Hanoi in an unsuccessful attempt to obtain
Chinese and North Vietnamese support for dissociating Laos from the
war in Vietnam. On his return he held a tripartite summit at Kong
Lae's headquarters on the west of the Plain of Jars. But the Pathet Lao
remained intransigent in refusing access to their zone by government
representatives and the ICC; while Phoumi was equally firm in
rejecting Souphanouvong's proposal to transfer the government to a
neutralized Luang Prabang with a tripartite police force. In despair
Souvanna, on his return to Vientiane on 18 April, announced his
intention to resign. This provoked a right-wing military coup early
next morning when Siho's police and Vientiane garrison troops commanded by General Kouprasith occupied all key points in the capital
and arrested all senior neutralists, including Souvanna himself. The
main aim of the coup was to eliminate the neutralists, but it was also
directed against Phoumi, whose arrogant exercise of power and
personal wealth derived from his control of gambling and opium and
gold smuggling, had aroused the fear and envy of his colleagues. He
was dismissed along with all other ministers, and when the coup
leaders set up a Revolutionary Committee he was the only general not
included.

However, the Revolutionary Committee did not last long in the face
of diplomatic opposition. Within hours of the coup, the ambassadors
of the four Western powers joined with the Soviet Ambassador to
announce continued support for Souvanna Phouma, the refusal of all
contact with the Committee and the suspension of their aid. With the
King also confirming his support for Souvanna, and Kong Lae

threatening to march on Vientiane with his 7000 paratroops, the coup quickly collapsed. A face-saving formula was found; Souvanna was reinstated as prime minister and declared himself head of the combined neutralist and right-wing factions. He also announced the merger of right-wing and neutralist forces under his (dubious) authority as defence minister. Phoumi, shorn of his lucrative illegal rackets, also survived as deputy prime minister but with his authority much reduced; the army no longer took its orders from him.

The neutralist position was already crumbling under the combined pressure of the right and left wing forces. Deuane and his men, calling themselves the Patriotic Neutralists, were now fully integrated with the Pathet Lao troops; and were joined by several hundred more defectors from Kong Lae after the announced amalgamation with the right wing. A few weeks after the failed coup in Vientiane the Pathet Lao, with Viet Minh support, launched a major offensive against Kong Lae and drove his troops completely off the Plain of Jars. However, Kong Lae survived and with his loyal troops, completely re-equipped with US material, retained a separate but hardly independent existence as an appendage to the right-wing forces.

After resuming office Souvanna reshuffled his government to replace disloyal ministers; but he still retained the two Pathet Lao junior ministers and kept open Souphanouvong's and Phoumi Vongvichit's posts. However, the Pathet Lao refused to accept the changes to which they had not agreed, and in June 1964 they formally withdrew from the government of National Union. In consequence the Russians, Chinese and North Vietnamese withdrew their recognition from Souvanna Phouma's government. This marked the final collapse of the Geneva Agreement, though in Vientiane the façade of the agreement was retained, mainly in the person of Souvanna Phouma as the embodiment of Laotian neutrality. The country reverted to the partition that had existed in 1961, with the Pathet Lao occupying virtually all the high ground and the government forces the Mekong valley. But there was a significant political difference as a result of the change in American policy imposed by Kennedy. In 1960/1 the Americans had been supporting an unpopular right-wing military government against a neutralist/left-wing coalition backed by the overwhelming weight of international opinion. From 1963 the

Americans had the full backing of their Western allies and the majority of international opinion in supporting what became a neutralist/right-wing coalition led by Souvanna Phouma; while the blame for the breakdown of the Geneva Agreement was placed firmly on the shoulders of the Pathet Lao and the North Vietnamese. For the Pathet Lao the loss of the respectable 'cover' provided by their alliance with the neutralists and participation in the coalition government was a serious political disadvantage. They also suffered economically as they received none of the substantial Western aid, which was channelled through Vientiane to the areas controlled by the right wing and the neutralists. Worsening living conditions in their zone and patriotic resentment against the growing North Vietnamese domination caused many of them to defect to the government side. However, their military position was not weakened and may indeed have been strengthened as defecting Pathet Lao soldiers were replaced by North Vietnamese.

Souvanna's precarious authority had to survive one more upheaval in Vientiane. At the end of January 1965 Phoumi made a desperate bid to recover power. His former Military Chef de Cabinet Colonel Bounleuth seized Vientiane radio with a battalion and established roadblocks while Khamkhong, a regional commander who supported Phoumi, marched on Vientiane. Siho, now a general, also switched sides again to support his old boss with the combined police forces of the Coordination. However, the bulk of the army remained loyal under General Kouprasith and, helped by the defection of Bounleuth to the government side, defeated the forces of Khamkhong, Siho and Phoumi in two days' fighting; Phoumi and Siho with many of their supporters fled to Thailand. The British Ambassador, now Fred Warner, reported that the departure of the two most hated and feared men in Laos caused a remarkable change in the atmosphere in Vientiane. Siho's National Directorate for Coordination was disbanded and replaced by a civilian police force under the Ministry of Interior. In July National Assembly elections in the areas controlled by Vientiane confirmed Souvanna Phouma as the unchallenged leader, and the new Assembly gave him and his government a massive vote of confidence. Souvanna retained the ministries of foreign affairs and defence, and the key post of minister of finance was given to Sisouk na Champassac, whom I had known well as junior minister for foreign affairs and one of the honorary *première série* at the tennis club. He was an able and energetic man and under his direction the economy began to improve.

With some of its more discordant elements removed, the army was in a better position to carry out its proper task of defending government territory. Kouprasith, the commander of the Vientiane region and the most forceful of the generals, was responsible for further measures to ensure the unity of the government forces. Resistance of the neutralist forces to full integration into the Royal Army ended when Kong Lae was removed from their command late in 1966 and sent off to virtual exile in Paris. The air force commander General Thao Ma, who had been reluctant to accept orders from the army command, was also brought to heel and sent abroad, but only after he had bombed Vientiane in the course of an attempted rebellion. For a short time the army had some success in recovering territory lost to the Pathet Lao. But the generals were more interested in exploiting their opportunities for corrupt enrichment, and the various regional commanders operated as virtual warlords in their regions. The most senior officer, the long-serving chief of staff General Ouane Rattikone (another of my tennis court acquaintances), spent most of his time on his business affairs, especially the illegal opium trade, which he had inherited from Phoumi. This trade, which had become even more lucrative as more American troops were poured into South Vietnam, was the cause of a little 'opium war' in 1967. Former Chinese Nationalist soldiers based in northern Thailand had established a stranglehold on the opium trade in the 'Golden Triangle' (north-east Burma, north Thailand and north Laos) where most of the world's illegal opium was grown. In an attempt to break the stranglehold, a Shan warlord tried to send a consignment of opium from Burma by packhorse to supply General Ouane's opium refineries near Ban Houei Sai. Nationalist Chinese soldiers went into Laos to intercept the caravan, whereupon Ouane bombed both sides and sent in his own troops to seize the opium. This setback to the Chinese gave Ouane a guaranteed direct supply of opium, which, together with opium grown in Laos, made him a principal supplier to the heroin market in South Vietnam.

The defeat of Phoumi's attempted coup lifted a burden from the shoulders of Souvanna Phouma and he seemed a changed man. No longer did he have to balance the interests of Souphanouvong and Phoumi and secure their agreement before making any decision. With no conceivable rival in sight he belied the former American image of him as weak and indecisive and showed himself an autocratic and increasingly intolerant Laotian prince. Attempts by the elected deputies to dictate his choice of ministers and to decide economic policy finally led him to dissolve the Assembly at the end of 1966. The new Assembly was more tractable and he became even more autocratic, often taking important decisions without consulting even the cabinet. In the last resort he was dependent on the support of the King and the army, but his confidence came from the knowledge that there was no feasible alternative to him, especially for the Americans, who needed him as a respectable front for their increasingly dubious activities.

In fact by the mid-1960s neither Souvanna Phouma nor any other Laotian could be said to be in control of the destinies of Laos. As the war in Vietnam escalated, the conflict in Laos became increasingly important to both the North Vietnamese and the Americans, not for its own sake but for the contribution it could make to the outcome in South Vietnam. The main area of contention was the Ho Chi Minh Trail, a combination of roads and tracks developed from North Vietnam through eastern and south-eastern Laos into South Vietnam, which was of vital importance to the North Vietnamese for the channelling of equipment, supplies and reinforcements to the insurgents in the south. The other key area was the Plain of Jars, which was dangerously close to North Vietnam and a potential base for American infiltration or military invasion. The North Vietnamese therefore increasingly took control of the eastern part of Laos and the Plain of Jars area, reducing the Pathet Lao to a mere appendage in the wider struggle for Indo-China.

On the other side the Americans believed that it was only the constant flow of weapons and men along the Trail that prevented them from defeating the Vietcong, and it was a major aim of their strategy to deny its use to the enemy. But they were also keen to maintain pressure on the Plain of Jars, to compel the North Vietnamese to divert troops and material from the main struggle in South

Vietnam. In the south-east the American efforts to close the Trail relied entirely on air bombing on a massive scale. Elsewhere, and especially in the Plain of Jars area, the fighting was mainly a matter of ground forces, with initially at least only limited air support on the Lao government side. The role of the Royal Laotian Army was mainly defensive, to retain control of the western half of the country. From time to time it made sorties to recover territory from the Pathet Lao, usually in the rainy season when the Pathet Lao, lacking air transport, were at a disadvantage. These sorties were usually followed by effecttive Pathet Lao counterattacks in the dry season, when the dried-out roads restored their mobility. In general these military engagements were on a minor scale, with not many casualties. The most serious fighting took place around the Plain of Jars in what became known as the 'secret war', involving the 'secret army' of Meo guerrillas financed and directed by the CIA. The Meo, who were commanded by a General Vang Pao, had originally been armed in order to defend their villages against being taken over by the Pathet Lao. But as the fighting developed they were used increasingly in offensive operations against the Pathet Lao and the North Vietnamese, at a heavy cost to the Meo in casualties and many thousands of refugees when the inevitable counterattacks came.

While directing these major military operations in a supposedly neutral country, the Americans were able to maintain a cover of legality by proclaiming that they were assisting the legitimate neutralist government of Laos as established by the Geneva Agreement. For this they needed the cooperation of Souvanna Phouma, which he gave when he came to realize the extent to which the Pathet Lao relied on North Vietnam and the growing number of Vietnamese troops in Laos. His sense of betrayal by the Pathet Lao and his desire to protect his country from communism and the traditional Vietnamese enemy led him, as early as 1964, to authorize what were euphemistically called 'armed reconnaissance' flights over northern Laos, with the face-saving proviso that they would be used only against Vietnamese targets. The bombing in the north started with Royal Laotian Air Force T-28 fighter-bombers but soon escalated with the use of T-28s with Laotian markings flown out of Thailand with Thai and American pilots and then US jet aircraft based in

Thailand. The bombing of the Ho Chi Minh Trail, which started in 1965 using US navy and air force jets rather than T-28s, was authorized by Souvanna with the proviso that there would be no public announcement. Within a year this task was being carried out on a daily basis by huge B-52 bombers flying out of Guam in the Pacific more than 2000 miles away. The whole military operation was coordinated at the US military base at Udorn in Thailand, under the direction and control of the US ambassador in Vientiane. In the mid-1960s the ambassador was Bill Sullivan, an outstanding diplomat whom I had met and liked when he was fulfilling a more normal diplomatic role as assistant to Harriman in his efforts to bring about the 1962 settlement.

In addition to controlling most aspects of the war in Laos, the American embassy was running much of the economy through its aid mission USAID, which set up a parallel administration taking over much of the work of the relevant government departments. Lao ministers and politicians were thus reduced to the position of helpless bystanders while outsiders decided the fate of the kingdom. Denied any important role in the most serious matters affecting their country, they were free to devote even more of their energies to increasing their personal wealth by graft and corruption. Souvanna Phouma, who was never interested in the spoils of office, remained above all this and his relationship with the Americans was never one of subservience: for example, he resisted any suggestions that US ground forces might be deployed in Laos. But as time went on he became more and more a figurehead; and the question arises, why did he stay on when he could so easily have retreated to a dignified and comfortable exile in Paris? The answer is his continued belief in the idea of an independent and neutral Laos of which he was by now almost the sole embodiment. In the face of all the difficulties he continued to hope that when the war in Vietnam was over and foreign troops were withdrawn from Laos he would be able to re-establish a government of national unity dedicated to neutralism in accordance with the Geneva Agreement.

Unfortunately the Vietnam War lasted longer than anyone expected. In 1968 the Vietcong Tet offensive convinced many people in the United States that they could not win the war, and President Johnson initiated peace negotiations, but it would be five years before they reached a conclusion. The immediate effect in Laos was to intensify the war as both sides sought to improve their military situation. More Vietnamese joined the Pathet Lao in attacking the Meo around the Plain of Jars and in capturing the strategic Nam Bak valley east of Luang Prabang from the Royal Laotian Army. In response American bombers obliterated the towns of Sam Neua and Xieng Khouang and the Pathet Lao headquarters at Khang Khay, leaving not a single building standing. The destruction of Xieng Khouang, a former royal capital with many beautiful temples and other buildings of historical and artistic interest, was a particular act of cultural vandalism. With nothing left but piles of rubble it was later decided that it was not feasible to rebuild the town, and the provincial capital was moved to Phongsavan on the Plain of Jars.

In the context of the Vietnamese peace negotiations Johnson ordered a partial halt to the bombing of North Vietnam, whereupon the aircraft so released were redirected against targets in Laos. The bombing of the Ho Chi Minh Trail was stepped up and in northern Laos the bombing became so heavy that the Pathet Lao leaders sought shelter in the extensive limestone caves of Vieng Say, close to the Vietnamese frontier, which were developed and further excavated to create an underground city containing a vast assembly hall to hold 400 people, school rooms, hospital units, canteens and garages as well as sleeping accommodation. With every village a target, villagers in the Plain of Jars area took refuge in the forest where they sheltered in caves and holes in the ground, emerging only at night to tend their crops, at the risk of being blown up by anti-personnel mines which the bombers had scattered liberally over all cultivated land. Even caves were not safe as the American airmen developed the technique of dispatching guided missiles to explode inside the caves. To counter this, walls were built in front of the entrances to caves at Vieng Say and elsewhere, but this was not always effective. In one village called Muang Kham to the north of the Plain of Jars the whole village population used to take refuge in a large limestone cavern, the entrance of which was concealed behind a high stone wall. But the Americans discovered the existence of the cave and in February 1968 dispatched two aircraft with rockets, the first of which demolished the wall and the second exploded deep inside the cave killing all 365 people sheltering there.

The arrival of President Nixon in the White House in 1969 brought no respite, despite the promise to end the Vietnam War. On the contrary the war in Laos was further intensified, both on the ground and in the air, under the direction of a hawkish new US ambassador G. McMurtrie Godley. In response the North Vietnamese increased their own involvement in Laos to an estimated 40,000 troops (not counting those in transit on the Ho Chi Minh Trail) of which 25,000 were needed to maintain and repair the roads and organize supplies and field hospitals. The remainder were allocated to the north to fight alongside the Pathet Lao, mainly against Colonel Vang Pao's Meo guerrillas who now numbered about 40,000. In 1969 fierce fighting in the Plain of Jars, in which the Meos were supported by Thai artillery and, for the first time in the north B-52 bombers, caused heavy casualties, particularly among the Meo, who had to rely increasingly on Thai 'volunteers' to maintain their numbers.

In the south there was a major escalation in 1970 when Cambodia was brought into the war. Prince Sihanouk, who had remained ostensibly neutral but had permitted the North Vietnamese to establish an extension of the Ho Chi Minh Trail in north-eastern Cambodia, was overthrown, probably with CIA help, by General Lon Nol. The general immediately allied himself with the USA and South Vietnam, both of which sent in troops to clear the North Vietnamese from the Cambodian extension of the Trail. The loss of this route increased the importance of the main trail through Laos, and the North Vietnamese moved to consolidate their control of south-eastern Laos, overrunning the Plateau Bolovens and the provincial capitals of Saravane and Attopeu. The bombing of the Trail was now increased to as many as 200 sorties a day, mainly by B-52s operating round the clock. But even this unprecedented onslaught failed to stop the flow of men and equipment into South Vietnam. So early in 1971 an attempt was made to cut the Trail using ground forces. Some 20,000 South Vietnamese troops invaded Laos from just south of the demilitarized zone in the direction of Tchepone. But they did not get very far and within six weeks, after suffering heavy casualties, they were forced to withdraw, leaving the North Vietnamese still in control of the Trail.

While the long-drawn-out negotiations continued in Paris, there was no let-up in the war in Laos. In the north the fighting achieved a new intensity as the Vietnamese deployed tanks and new heavy artillery and more and more Thai 'volunteers' were brought in to make up the terrible losses suffered by Vang Pao's Meo guerrillas. The bombing campaign continued unremittingly, with the whole of eastern Laos now regarded as a legitimate target and American aircrews feeling free to unload any unused bombs at random on their return journey. (One area off limits was the northern province of Phong Saly where the Chinese, whom the Americans did not want to provoke, were still engaged in building roads.) One of the most extraordinary features of this whole campaign was that, with the attention of the world's media and governments concentrated on Vietnam, the Americans were able to conceal the extent of this 'secret war' and their own involvement in it from the world at large and their own people. The bombing of Laos was concealed under the umbrella of bombing raids on North Vietnam, which were announced regularly. Presumably if the massive destruction, the terrible loss of life and the appalling suffering inflicted on a supposedly neutral country had been properly understood, there would have been such an outcry that the US government might have had to revise its policy. But it was not until some years later that the full facts became known.

By the time a cease-fire was declared early in 1973 it is estimated that well over 30,000 of the Meo guerrillas had died, more than 10 per cent of their population. There were huge numbers of refugees, some 170,000 in northern Laos kept alive by American airdrops of food, and many thousands more in areas controlled by the Royal Laotian government. Over the whole Pathet Lao zone more than two million tons of bombs had been dropped, said to be more than the US Air Force dropped during the Second World War in all theatres of operations. With an estimated population of one million in eastern Laos this amounts to two tons of bombs per person, the heaviest bombing per head in the history of warfare. In terms of territory it amounts to an average of 20 tons of bombs per square kilometre, but of course it was much more intensive in areas such as the Plain of Jars, which was reduced to a flattened moonscape of craters with no human habitation in sight. And in all inhabited and cultivable areas were scattered many thousands of unexploded anti-personnel mines which were to cause death and loss of limbs for many years afterwards and still do. Almost all the villages in the Pathet Lao zone, around 3500, were partly or totally destroyed. My own feelings can easily be imagined when years later I became aware of the horrendous scale of the destruction and realized that, among those who saw their homes and crops destroyed, their families and friends killed or mutilated and who spent their time hiding in terror from the daily rain of death from the sky, would be the simple and friendly people with whom the doctors, Spots and I stayed during our month in the jungle — people who had only the vaguest idea of what communism meant and who would have been totally uncomprehending if told that the dealers of death came from a country which was proud to be regarded as the defender of the free world and the champion of democracy.

Because of the remoteness of the areas where most of the fighting and bombing took place, and the disruption of what communications there were, there can be no precision as to the extent of the human loss caused by the ten years of war. Most estimates are in excess of 200,000 killed and 400,000 wounded on both sides, with the bulk of the losses suffered by the hill peoples in the eastern half of the country; while the number of people who were at some time forced from their homes to become refugees was probably not far short of a million. Some hard-faced hawks might have argued that destruction and suffering even on so horrendous a scale were justified to defend the free world and to prevent the first domino, South Vietnam, from falling under communist rule. But the huge military effort failed to achieve its purpose. The most prolonged and destructive air bombing campaign in history failed to stem the flow of supplies and men that sustained the Vietcong rebellion. The most that can be said is that it may have delayed the communist takeover of South Vietnam for a short time. But at what a price.

The ten years 'secret war' also failed to destroy the Pathet Lao or even seriously to weaken it. On the contrary it emerged at the end of the war politically, as well as militarily, stronger than ever. While their North Vietnamese allies increasingly took over the direction of the fighting, the Pathet Lao leaders in their caves and underground shelters concentrated on strengthening their political organization and recruiting new members. In the process the movement gradually changed in character from an anti-colonial nationalist party with communist leanings into something approaching a fully-fledged Marxist communist party. The original political party set up in 1956, the Neo Lao Hak Sat or Lao Patriotic Front (LPF) with Souphanou- vong as president, was indeed a broad front embracing not only most of the minority hill peoples but also patriotic nationalists throughout the country and especially young left-wing students, as well as a small hard core of communists, members of the Indo-Chinese Communist Party. These latter had in 1955 set up within the LPF a small, secret communist party called the Lao People's Party with its leader Kaysone Phomvihan, in typical communist style, occupying the key post of secretary-general. While Souphanouvong and other Pathet Lao/LPF leaders became deputies and ministers, Kaysone remained in the background and so was not one of those arrested in 1959. The incarceration of his main rivals for the leadership helped Kaysone to establish his authority in the political organization. This authority, and the influence of the Lao People's Party within the LPF continued to grow during the ten years of the 'American war'. However, the LPF remained in being until well into the 1970s as a relatively respectable, moderate 'front' (in another sense of the word) for the communist Lao People's Party, which in 1972 changed its name to the Lao People's Revolutionary Party. Unlike the communists in Cambodia, the LPF never set itself up as an alternative government. Its policy statements always mentioned respect for Buddhism and the monarchy along with a return to the Geneva Agreement of 1962 and the re-establishment of the government of National Unity, with of course a much larger role for the Pathet Lao/LPF.

Peace in Laos had to await signature of the Vietnam peace settlement in January 1973. Within a month a cease-fire was agreed in Laos, followed by an agreement on the Restoration of Peace and National Reconciliation. This provided for the withdrawal of foreign troops and the establishment of a Provisional Government of National Union in Vientiane and a National Political Consultative Council, of equal status to the government, in Luang Prabang, both cities to be neutralized by the presence of equal numbers of troops and police from both sides. Elections for a national assembly were to be held 'as soon as possible', followed by the formation of a definitive government. Souvanna Phouma remained prime minister but the

Pathet Lao took six of twelve ministerial portfolios in the government, with the remaining six going to the right wing. The Consultative Council consisted of 42 members, 16 each to the Pathet Lao and the right wing, with the other ten nominated jointly by the two sides. Souphanouvong, instead of resuming as deputy prime minister, left this position to Phoumi Vongvichit, and chose instead to be President of the Consultative Council, which gave him equal status with Souvanna Phouma. For a time the Pathet Lao cooperated well in the government; and the Consultative Council adopted an 18-point programme, drafted mainly by Souphanouvong, which was moderate and liberal in tone, upholding the monarchy and Buddhism, proclaiming democratic rights and freedoms and advocating economic development based on agriculture and forestry within a mixed economy with only limited state intervention.

American military forces and the Thai volunteers in due course withdrew, but there was little sign of withdrawal of North Vietnamese forces, and some 20,000 Chinese construction troops remained in the north. The Pathet Lao had established themselves in Vientiane and Luang Prabang but there was no reciprocal access into their own zone. The withdrawal of American support weakened the ability and will of the right wing to resist Pathet Lao political and military pressure, reinforced by demonstrations of left-wing students and trade unionists. When the Khmer Rouge entered Phnom Penh and the People's Army of Vietnam took over Saigon in the spring of 1975, without any attempt at intervention by the Americans, the collapse of the right in Laos followed soon afterwards. A large May Day demonstration calling for punishment of the leading right-wing families — specifically the Sananikones, the Abhays and the na Champasscs — was followed by the assassination of a brother of Boun Oum. In fear of their lives a number of right-wing ministers, including Sisouk na Champassac, and generals, including Kouprasith and the 'secret army' commander Vang Pao, fled to Thailand, along with thousands of people from the Mekong towns, many of them from the Chinese and Vietnamese trading community. I hope, but do not know, that the latter included our cook Phan Dai and our steward Dao, — if indeed they had not left earlier (quite likely in view of Phan Dai's success in escaping from Hanoi before the communist takeover there).

Accepting the inevitable Souvanna Phouma appointed as acting minister of defence a Pathet Lao general who, with Souvanna's agreement, instructed Royal Lao Army commanders not to resist Pathet Lao troop movements into their area. Souvanna has been criticized for facilitating the Pathet Lao takeover but his motive was to avoid pointless bloodshed: without American support the RLA was in no condition to take on the Pathet Lao forces, and military resistance would have postponed the Pathet Lao victory by only a few days at the most. In the main provincial towns, organized demonstrations against right-wing families and USAID offices were followed by a takeover by Pathet Lao forces: Pakse, Savannakhet, Thakhek and finally Luang Prabang were all 'liberated' by early June. In Vientiane demonstrators occupied the USAID compound and compelled the withdrawal of all USAID personnel. The Americans drastically reduced the size of their embassy and announced the termination of all their aid. The aid gap was to be only partly filled by the Soviet Union and other communist donors.

The Lao People's Revolutionary Party (LPRP), now out in the open, moved to take control of all aspects of the nation's life, political, economic and social. Senior officials were denounced and sometimes brought to trial for corruption. People's Revolutionary Committees were set up throughout the country to impose new controls on prices, property transactions, personal movement and behaviour, eliminating Western practices such as men wearing long hair and women wearing jeans. Thousands of middle-ranking civil servants and Royal Army officers, who had stayed on expecting a Lao-type reconciliation once the fighting was over, were imprisoned for political offences or sent to camps in the remote north on political re-education courses. These courses were accepted willingly, in the belief that they would last only a few weeks or months. But in many cases political re-education turned out to be political imprisonment, and hard labour in the fields, lasting for many years.

Press censorship was introduced and the first steps were taken to set up a one-party state. In November 1975 elections were held for people's administrative committees at the district and provincial levels, but all candidates had to be endorsed by the Lao Patriotic Front. Later in the month, following well-orchestrated demonstrations against the monarchy and Souvanna Phouma's government, a joint meeting of the government and the Consultative Council decided to abolish the monarchy and establish a communist people's republic. The King accepted the position with dignity and on 2 December a secret National Congress of People's Representatives, unelected and with no legitimate constitutional authority, confirmed the abolition of the monarchy and proclaimed the Lao People's Democratic Republic.

The structure of the new republic and of the now all-powerful LPRP followed closely that of Vietnam and the various People's Democratic Republics of eastern Europe. A Supreme People's Assembly was in theory the source of all authority but in practice served as a rubber stamp for the decisions of the Party. Some 45 members of the National Congress were appointed to form an interim People's Assembly, with Souphanouvong as President, pending elections; in fact the first elections for the Assembly were not to be held until over 13 years later. The government, or Council of Ministers, was in theory responsible to the Assembly but in practice was answerable only to the Party. The LPRP was run by a Secretariat, with Kaysone as Secretary-General, and a Central Committee of 21 members, but all important decisions were taken by the seven-member Politburo. The membership and ranking order of the Politburo, which were made public for the first time, indicated clearly where the real power now lay. Kaysone was number one, with Nouhak as number two. Souphanouvong, whose intellect, force of character and great prestige as founder president of the Pathet Lao ought to have merited the number one position, was no higher than number three, with his fellow moderate Phoumi Vongvichit as number four; and significantly these two were the only members of the Politburo who were not also members of the Secretariat. The ascendancy of Kaysone was confirmed when he became prime minister. Souphanouvong, whose ability and popularity made him Kaysone's most dangerous rival, was not even a member of the government; instead he was shunted off to the largely honorific post of President of the Republic (henceforward he dropped his princely title and was addressed as 'Monsieur le Président' rather than 'Altesse').

In the early days at least Souphanouvong still retained considerable influence, which was shown in transitional arrangements which eased the change from monarchy to people's republic. The deposed king was named Counsellor to the President and the Crown Prince was made a member of the Supreme People's Assembly, while Souvanna Phouma, whom one would have expected to retire to France, stayed on as Counsellor to the government. However, early in 1977 some right-wing rebels, including former members of the Meo 'secret army', briefly captured a village near Luang Prabang. Fearing that rebels might seize the ex-King and use him to stir up a general revolt, the government removed the King, Queen and Crown Prince to a re-education work camp at the wartime headquarters of the Pathet Lao at Vieng Say near the Vietnamese frontier. Detained in conditions of considerable hardship and made to work long hours in the fields on inadequate rations, they all died from overwork and undernourishment within the next few years. According to one account the Crown Prince died first, having given his rations to his father in the hope of prolonging his life.

The hill peoples of northern and eastern Laos had suffered terribly during the decade of the 'American War'. It was now the turn of the Lao of the Mekong valley, and especially in the towns, to suffer a less severe, but more prolonged, torment under the harsh regime of the People's Democratic Republic. Their suffering was of course minor compared with the horrors of the murderous Khmer Rouge in Cambodia, which caused the deaths of something like a million people. Not many Laotians were deliberately put to death by the communist government, although a number of generals were shot. But many thousands suffered severe hardship as prisoners in the re-education concentration camps, and a considerable number died as a result. Families were broken up as large numbers fled to Thailand, though later flight became more difficult as government troops and gunboats patrolled the Mekong to prevent escape. In Thailand those who had no relations or friends there to support them lived in miserable conditions in refugee camps. Those who remained in Laos suffered from restrictions of movement, censorship and other controls and were required to attend lengthy political meetings aimed at inculcating communist principles and encouraging the denunciation of those considered disloyal to the regime. They also suffered severe economic hardship as the withdrawal of Western aid and the government's mishandling of the economy led to inflation and a steep decline in living standards.

Kaysone and Nouhak, wishing to introduce a classical Marxist economy as quickly as possible, ignored Marx's advice that there had to be a capitalist phase on the road to communism. Instead they tried to move directly from a peasant agricultural economy to a communist economy, with disastrous results. Private commercial and industrial companies were nationalized along with transport and most retailing. State trading companies and state shops were set up though, as a result of strict import controls imposed to save foreign currency, there were not many goods to sell. Attempts to make farming cooperative were not popular with peasants, who responded by withholding food from the markets. The shortages of food and other supplies were compounded by the inefficiency of government departments and nationalized companies, as nearly all the experienced officials had emigrated or been sent to the re-education camps; while among those who remained, promotions became dependent on party loyalty rather than efficiency.

The virtual collapse of the economy led to the gradual abandonment of Marxist policies. Within a decade market forces were reintroduced into the operation of commerce and finance. Around the same time communist economic policies were being dropped in the Soviet Union and Eastern Europe and even in China and Vietnam. However, as in China and Vietnam (but not the Soviet Union), the economic changes in Laos were not accompanied by political liberalization and at the end of the century the country remained a dictatorial one-party state.

It is beyond the scope of this book to describe in any detail the political events and developments under the Lao People's Democratic Republic. My interest has been mainly to discover what happened to the main actors on the Laotian stage in the early 1960s. In most cases it has not been possible to find out more than the bare facts since the LPRP, like the communist governments of Eastern Europe at the height of the Cold War, imposed the strictest controls on such foreign journalists as were allowed into the country and virtually prohibited social contacts with foreign diplomats. Donald Cape, who was British Ambassador in Vientiane from 1976 to 1978, has told me that his only conversation with Souphanouvong was when he presented his credentials on arrival; and his contacts with other leading figures of the regime were limited to a very few formal official functions where serious conversation was not possible. As the parlous state of the Laotian economy also meant that there was little scope for promoting trade, it is not surprising that it was decided to close the British embassy in 1985. Subsequently successive British ambassadors in Bangkok have been accredited to Laos and they and members of their staff have maintained some contact by occasional visits. Towards the end of the century, with the development of tourism and the encouragement of foreign investment the atmosphere became more relaxed; but by then nearly all the people I had known were dead.

Apart from occasional visits to France to see his family, Souvanna Phouma stayed on in Laos until he died in 1982, when he was given a splendid Buddhist funeral. He was always treated with great respect as an elder statesman and, unlike most ministers and other leading figures of the regime, he was allowed to entertain and be entertained by foreign embassies. But despite the consolation of his bridge parties, he must have been a sad and disappointed man. His lifetime's work devoted to creating a united, neutral and independent Laos had succeeded in achieving only the first aim. Under the communist regime Laos was united for the first time since it was a French colony, perhaps the major achievement of the LPRP. But of course it was not neutral in the terms of the Cold War (though this became of less significance when the Cold War ended). Nor was it any more independent (except in the purely formal sense) than it had ever been, being totally dependent economically on aid from the Soviet bloc which, though much less than previous Western aid, was still substantial, deploying some 2000 aid workers in Laos. For its defence it was equally dependent on Soviet military aid and the continuing presence of as many as 30,000 Vietnamese troops, which were used to suppress attempted rebellions by groups of Meos (now called Hmong) and other opponents of the regime. In consequence Laos slavishly followed the Soviet/Vietnamese line in foreign affairs, especially during the years of the Soviet/Chinese split which was exacerbated by the Vietnamese/Cambodian conflict, with the Soviet Union (and Laos) supporting Vietnam and the Chinese supporting the Pol Pot regime in

Cambodia. The Laotian government's support for the Soviet Union went as far as shutting down China's aid programme and reducing the numbers of the Chinese Embassy staff. Laos's dependence on and subservience to the traditional Vietnamese enemy must have been a particularly bitter pill for Souvanna Phouma to swallow in his last years. And, however understandable his motives were at the time, he must have been burdened by the guilt of having acquiesced in the massive American bombing of his country, though he may never have realized the full extent of the destruction.

I have no means of knowing Souphanouvong's feelings, but the proud prince I knew would likewise have been unhappy at the subordination of his country to Vietnam. Conscious of his high abilities, he must also have resented being sidelined to largely honorific duties as President and being denied an active role in the detailed management of the country's affairs. As with his half-brother, one wonders why he stayed on, lending his name and prestige to the regime, when he must have disapproved of much that was happening. One can only speculate, but a fundamental reason may have been that, having devoted the main part of his life to achieving independence for Laos in alliance with the Vietnamese communists, to resign would have been tantamount to admitting that his life's work had ended in failure. It is possible, even probable, that he became a card-carrying communist, since it is unlikely that he would have been made a member of the Politburo otherwise. I still believe that his prime motivating force was nationalism rather than a doctrinaire belief in communism. But, whether or not he became formally a member of the Party, the massive destruction and suffering caused by American bombing, which he personally witnessed, must have developed strong anti-American feelings which were a major component of communist and pro-communist attitudes in the 1960s and 1970s and which would have inclined him to show solidarity with his overtly communist colleagues. He would also have been affected by the loss of his son, who was abducted near Vieng Say and beaten to death by some of the Meo guerrillas financed and supported by the CIA. Whatever the reasons, he remained as President of the Republic and President of the Lao Patriotic Front, which in 1979 changed its name to the Lao Front for National Reconstruction. In 1986, when he was 74, ill health caused him to step down from active duties and Phoumi Vongvichit was appointed as acting president of both the Republic and the Front. Souphanouvong formally resigned as President of the Front in 1988 but stayed on as a member of the Politburo and as titular President of the Republic until 1991 when the People's Republic for the first time adopted a formal constitution. He died in 1992 and was given a state funeral with full Buddhist rites. His ashes repose under a Buddhist funerary stupa, elaborately decorated and located very close to the That Luang pagoda.

In general the Pathet Lao leadership showed a remarkable longevity. Until almost the end of the century the country was still being directed by the same group who as young men came together originally in the Lao Issara movement to oppose the return of the French in 1946. Kaysone, who as Prime Minister and Secretary-General of the LPRP was effectively dictator, remained a shadowy figure, hardly ever appearing in public, apparently because of an obsessive fear of assassination. Donald Cape, as British Ambassador for two years, never had a private conversation with him and saw him only once at a very large official function. (However, he seems to have relaxed a little in later years as his position became more secure: the last British ambassador Bernard Dobbs recalls a function at which he danced the *lamvong* with an attractive Swedish lady aid officer.) Kaysone retained power in his own hands until the very end; and in the late 1980s he was strong enough to push through the introduction of market forces against the opposition of Nouhak and most of the Old Guard. In 1991, under the new constitution he became President of the Republic, with enhanced powers, in succession to Souphanou-vong. In the same year the Secretariat of the Party, which he had headed, was abolished but he retained control in the newly created post of President of the Party. However, he relinquished the premiership and died a year later, shortly after Souphanouvong.

The new prime minister was someone I have not mentioned before, Khamtay Siphandone, another member of the Lao Issara resistance movement 45 years earlier — he had fought with Sithone Kommadom in the south-east. In 1963, shortly after we left Laos, he was appointed commander of the Pathet Lao army in replacement of General Singkapo, whom I had met and liked in the Plain of Jars but who had been dismissed because he was too friendly with Kong Lae and the neutralists. As commander of the army, later renamed the Lao People's Liberation Army, Khamtay occupied the fifth position in the Politburo, where he worked successfully to strengthen the army's influence and representation in the party's inner circles. In 1991 he took over Souphanouvong's number three slot and also succeeded Kaysone as prime minister. After Kaysone's death Khamtay became President of the Party and number one in the Politburo while retaining the premiership, thus assuming Kaysone's position as the all-powerful leader of the country. Nouhak, whose long service as deputy leader to Kaysone and number two in the Politburo would have given him expectations of succeeding to the leadership, had to content himself with retaining the number two position. Unlike Kaysone, who had been a law student, Nouhak had little education, having earned a living as a truck driver before joining the liberation movement. A dour and forceful character, and a convinced communist, he was put in charge of the economy in the first communist government of 1975. The subsequent collapse of the economy and his reluctance to adapt to the introduction of market forces weakened his influence, and in 1986 he was relieved of his economic responsibilities and became President of the Supreme People's Assembly, a prestigious but relatively powerless position. In 1992, on Kaysone's death, he succeeded to the even more prestigious but no more powerful position of President of the Republic, which he retained until 1998. Khamtay then succeeded him as President of the Republic and, like Kaysone in 1991, relinquished the premiership (to another soldier) while retaining the presidency of the party. Under Khamtay the power and influence of the army further increased, with generals occupying six of the nine places in the extended Politburo.

As for my captor Sithone Kommadom, from the beginnings of the Pathet Lao movement he had occupied a high position, as minister without portfolio in the resistance government of 1950 and as vice-president of the Lao Patriotic Front, reflecting the importance of the hill peoples to the movement. He was also one of only four named as Heroes of the Revolution, the others being Souphanouvong, Kaysone and Faydang. But neither he nor Faydang was a member of the inner circle of the LPRP and they were not elected to the Central Committee, let alone the Politburo. This may have been partly due to their lack of formal education but I would guess also because they were not committed communists — this would fit in with my impression of Sithone. He was, however, appointed to the Supreme People's Assembly in 1975, and when Souphanouvong became President of the Republic Sithone succeeded him as President of the Assembly. When Donald Cape called on him in 1976 they talked about the time when I was his prisoner and he asked Donald to send me his good wishes, which I was happy to reciprocate. He died a year later.

Of the right-wing leaders of the early 1960s, Prince Boun Oum had stayed on as Inspector-General of the Kingdom until 1975 when, after the murder of his brother, he retreated into voluntary exile in France, where he died in 1980. General Phoumi Nosavan remained in Thailand until he died some five years after Boun Oum. His strong-arm henchman Siho, who had also taken refuge in Thailand, disappeared from the scene much earlier. In 1966 he consulted a soothsayer who assured him that it would be safe for him to return to Laos; and he actually informed foreign embassies that he would return on a certain day in June. When he did so, he was promptly arrested and shot a couple of days later 'while trying to escape'. At least that was the official version — according to a story current at the time he was taken up in a helicopter by General Kouprasith and pushed out without a parachute. As for Kouprasith, he retreated to a fortress-like house in St Malo where he lived in constant fear of assassination for two decades before dying of natural causes a few years ago.

The 'little captain' Kong Lae emerged from his French exile briefly in the early 1980s. During the time when Laos was siding with Russia and Vietnam against China over events elsewhere in Indo-China, China accepted a number of Laotian refugees, including some members of the LPRP. The Chinese toyed with the idea of destabilizing the Laotian regime by sending guerrilla bands, recruited from the refugees, into northern Laos; and Kong Lae was invited to help organize these bands. But the Lao refugees quarrelled so much among themselves that the Chinese abandoned the idea. Kong Lae returned to France, where he still lives.

To complete the picture I need to say something about what happened to some of the non-Laotian characters who figured in my account of the early 1960s, starting with John Addis. After leaving Laos in 1962 John, as already mentioned, spent a sabbatical year at Harvard studying the dispute between India and China over the ill-defined frontier between the two countries. His dispassionate conclusions, drawn entirely from open sources, enraged the Indians and were not welcome to the American and British governments: all our diplomatic posts received a circular emphasizing that Mr Addis's views were not shared by his government. His next posting was as ambassador to the Philippines, where his encounter with the armed robber took place. Then, after a spell attached to the Royal College of Defence Studies he achieved his life's ambition and became the first fully-accredited British Ambassador to the Chinese People's Republic (owing to the Hong Kong question and our continued consular representation in Formosa, the Chinese had previously kept our diplomatic relations at the level of chargé d'affaires). He retired in 1974 and took up a fellowship at Nuffield College, Oxford, but sadly he died of leukaemia a few years later.

His successor Donald Hopson did not even reach retiring age. After Laos he was appointed Chargé d'Affaires in Peking, unfortunately when the Cultural Revolution was at its height. On one occasion the infamous Red Guards attacked the embassy and Donald was badly roughed up and almost killed; and this, together with the constant verbal abuse and psychological pressure to which he was subjected, destroyed his self-confidence so that, so I am told, he was never the same person again. Later he became ambassador in Buenos Aires, where he died suddenly at the age of only 58. In fact an unusually high proportion of our small community failed to achieve their allotted span. I have already mentioned Tony Beamish of the BBC. Others were the two doctors Tony Brown and Dick Herniman and the administration officer Fred Kempson. Particularly sad was the case of Oggy Thomas who, after devoting all his adult life to helping the poor of the Third World, was struck down by a wasting disease and died while still in his fifties.

The rest of us have been more fortunate. Our oldest member Trevor Wilson retired from Laos to Cirencester when nearly seventy and lived on for the best part of twenty more years. The others of our group are, at the time of writing, still around, though most have retired from active duty, though not from active life. While I cannot mention them all, it is good to record that Hugh Toye, now in his eighties, is fit and active and preparing a revised edition of his book on Subhas Chandra Bose, though sadly Betty died a short time ago. The two doctors who were my companions in the jungle went on to distinguished medical careers and are still active, Colin Prentice as Professor of Medicine at Leeds University and Tony Bryceson as a senior consultant at University College Hospital in London. The young Lao male nurse Sian was rewarded for his loyalty by being sent on a course in Britain to study nursing and improve his English, and we entertained him in London at that time. Alas we lost touch with him after he went back to Laos and do not know what happened to him.

Perhaps the most remarkable post-Vientiane story is that of the fifth member of our jungle group, Major Clarke 'Spots' Leaphard. Belize, to which he was transferred after Laos, proved to be his last army posting. We lost touch with him thereafter and only heard what happened when an obituary appeared in the *Daily Telegraph* in 1996. On retirement he joined the Save the Children Fund and worked for them in Nigeria during the civil war and in various other trouble spots, such as North Africa, Bangladesh and Nicaragua. From 1973 he worked for the Fund in South East Asia, beginning in Saigon. When the communists took over in 1975 he left Vietnam by bicycle, escaping to Cambodia disguised as a doctor. He was arrested but escaped again and made his way to Singapore. He was the charity's field director in Thailand from 1976 to 1983 when, at the age of 70, he was asked to retire. He then went back to Laos where he continued to work as a volunteer in Save the Children's field office for another 13 years until his death in 1996. The obituary records that when asked, at the age of 80, why he had settled in Laos, he replied, 'What makes you think I have settled down?' It goes on to say: 'Many have said that he was the best field director the fund ever had. He was always able to get things done, sometimes by unconventional means. He was the truest of volunteers, loyal, modest and shy.' I salute his memory and wish, as with so many friends that we have met around the world, that we had kept in touch.

Unlike Spots, I never returned to Laos. The Foreign Office, in its mysterious way, never made use of the experience and linguistic knowledge I had acquired in Southeast Asia. On my return to London I was posted to the Foreign Office department dealing with southern Europe. Then after a short time I became Assistant (deputy head) of the main department dealing with Africa, which was to become the focus of the rest of my career. In due course I was appointed Ambassador to Madagascar, a most delightful island where I found many echoes of Laos, not surprisingly as the first inhabitants of Madagascar came from Indonesia and were racially akin to the pre-Thai population of Laos. After a spell in the Foreign and Commonwealth Office dealing with administrative matters, I was sent to Tanzania as High Commissioner. Then a brief spell at the United Nations in New York in 1978 offered a change of scenery but not of subject matter: I spent nearly all of my time dealing with the problems of southern Africa — Rhodesia, Namibia and apartheid in South Africa — which indeed dominated the political agenda at the UN throughout the 1960s and 1970s. My final posting was as High Commissioner to the sprawling, turbulent, fascinating country of Nigeria where I managed to survive for a record four and a half years, a considerable achievement bearing in mind that my successor and my predecessor but one were both expelled.

Thus while I was in the Service I was never given another Far Eastern posting, from which a return trip to Laos might have been easy to make. By the time I had retired in 1983 I had lost the desire to go back, partly because of all I had read about the grey, austere regime of the People's Republic, but mainly because nearly everyone I knew in the early 1960s would be either dead or in exile. I now think that I was wrong. I should have realized that it would take more than 20 years of communist oppression to destroy the easygoing, graceful charm of the Lao. If I do go back, I may not meet many Lao that I knew. But I am sure that I shall meet many other delightful people. And if I apologize, as I should, for not having returned sooner, they will simply smile and say 'Bo pen nyang'.

13

Ends and Means

This book started out as a personal memoir of the exciting and amusing things that happened to us in Laos while it was the focus of a world crisis. But it seemed to me necessary to describe the political and military situation so that the reader could understand the background against which we worked; and I found it impossible to do so without being critical of American policy. This was not hindsight, as I was equally critical at the time, along with virtually everyone in the British, French and Australian embassies, the Canadian delegation to the ICC and the UN office, as well as the press corps, including nearly all the American journalists. But perhaps I was less discreet than others in voicing the criticism. Murray Simons told me that when visiting the American Embassy he had read upside down on someone's desk a letter describing me as anti-American.

The accusation would have surprised my many American friends — diplomats, musicians, tennis players and others. The USA has always been one of my favourite countries. Having lived in New York for several years and travelled extensively over most of the country, I have come to know and appreciate the warmth, friendliness and generosity of its people and to admire the astonishing beauty of its vast landscapes. Like all British diplomats I have throughout my career worked closely with American colleagues in pursuit of our common aims, and many of them became and remained good friends. Being critical of US policy in Laos did not make me, or the rest of the

British Embassy, anti-American any more than being critical (even more so) of British policy over Suez made me, or the whole of the Foreign Office, anti-British.

Similarly, our disapproval of what we saw as the American obsessive anti-communism did not mean that we were soft on communism. I personally have been anti-communist ever since schoolboy studies of the French Revolution made me mistrust any form of totalitarian rule; and unlike many of my contemporaries in the 1930s and 1940s I was never remotely tempted to join the Communist Party as the best or only way of resisting the rise of fascism. I did not accept the conventional linear projection of political beliefs, with communism on the extreme left at the furthest distance from fascism on the extreme right. In my view the spectrum of beliefs was better represented by a horseshoe, with the extreme right and left closer to each other than either was to the democratic, liberal centre; and communism, certainly as practised in the Soviet Union, seemed to me at least as obnoxious as fascism. So I was as anxious as any member of the CIA or the Pentagon to prevent a communist takeover of Laos. Our difference was not over aims and objectives, but over methods.

In the light of the eventual outcome, can one say, nearly 40 years later, whether we were right to oppose American policy? There can be no definite answer to this question. Diplomacy is an art, not a science, and the rightness or wrongness of policies cannot be subject to experimental, scientific proof. One cannot turn the clock back to 1957 and find out what would have happened if the Americans had supported, rather than sabotaged, the Vientiane Agreements and Souvanna Phouma's policy of conciliation with the Pathet Lao. All one can do is to apply some general principles and the collective judgement of experienced diplomatic observers at the time and subsequently.

When I joined the Foreign Office I was put to work immediately on a desk without any preliminary training. Six months later, a group of recent entrants, including myself, were given a short course of lectures and visits to other government departments. One lecture was on foreign policy, and I recall the lecturer summing up as follows: 'The overriding aim of foreign policy is to avoid war. But if war is unavoidable, you should so conduct your policy that your country enters the war in the most favourable position to pursue it (for

example with the maximum number of allies) and that moral right is
on your side.' On this basis American policy in Laos in the late 1950s
would be found wanting. Instead of avoiding war, their policy of
sabotaging the Vientiane Agreements made civil war inevitable. By the
end of 1960 their traditional Western allies and the bulk of international opinion had turned against them, leaving only Thailand and
South Vietnam on their side. And their behaviour in disregarding
international treaty obligations and working successfully for the
overthrow of legitimately established governments meant that they
had lost the high moral ground.

American fears of communism, both as a military force and a sub-
versive threat, were of course entirely justified, and were shared by
British governments at the time. But the successive shocks of the communist takeover in Czechoslovakia, the collapse of Chiang Kai-Chek,
the explosion of the first Soviet atomic bomb and subsequent reve-
lations of successful communist espionage in the heart of the US and
British governments created a state of paranoia which clouded American judgement in matters of foreign affairs, especially in the Far East.
Thus, in Southeast Asia, policies came to be based on a series of mistaken premises. These errors were compounded by a belief that the
spread of communism, essentially a political problem, could best be
resisted by military force. One might speculate on the extent to which
this view was influenced by Hollywood Western films in which the
hero, played by John Wayne, Gary Cooper, Alan Ladd or Henry
Fonda, emerged victorious not because of the virtues of law and order
which he personified but because he could shoot straighter and faster
than the bad guys. And so many millions of dollars were squandered
on trying to build up Phoumi's ineffectual army when smaller sums
spent on economic development could have been much more effective
in countering the spread of Pathet Lao influence.

One of the mistaken premises was a belief in a monolithic world
communist conspiracy taking its orders from Moscow. There may
have been some basis for this in the early 1950s when the young
Chinese People's Republic might have accepted at least guidance from
the older and more experienced Soviet Union. But after Stalin's death
it was inevitable that the very different national interests of the two
countries would assert themselves and lead to active hostility within a

decade. As for smaller countries the example of Yugoslavia under Tito, rarely mentioned in the context of Southeast Asia, showed that a country could become communist without taking orders from Moscow and without posing any threat to Western interests.

A country that was frequently mentioned in the context of Laos was Czechoslovakia, as an example of the danger of admitting communists inside a democratic government. Thus it became a basic principle of American policy in the late 1950s and early 1960s to exclude the Pathet Lao from the government; and even after President Kennedy announced support for a neutralist government headed by Souvanna Phouma it took some time for it to be accepted that Souvanna's policy of national reconciliation necessarily involved the participation of the Pathet Lao in government. It was not only Americans who believed in the almost magical powers of communists to subvert and take over any government of which they were members. While I was in Laos an expert on communism in the Foreign Office Research Department sent us a paper he had written forecasting that if Souphanouvong and other Pathet Lao members joined the government they would take it over within a year. I replied giving a number of reasons why I did not think that this would happen; and of course it was over a decade before the communists took over, in quite different circumstances. I suggested that while we should not underestimate our enemies it was equally important not to overestimate them. Laos was of course very different from Czechoslovakia; when the awful example was pointed out to him, Souvanna Phouma used to say that Finland was a more relevant comparison.

The second mistaken premise was the domino theory. One might argue that the theory was proved when the communists took over Laos and Cambodia soon after they completed their conquest of South Vietnam. But it is more plausible to argue that Laos and Cambodia succumbed to communism because of American anti-communist policies rather than in spite of them; and that if the USA had supported Souvanna Phouma in Laos and Sihanouk in Cambodia from the outset, instead of undermining them, the countries would have been in a much better position to resist any communist encroachments. In any case, after 1975, when the Pathet Lao and the Khmer Rouge had taken over, there was no sign of any more dominoes falling in the next decade and a half before the international collapse of communism removed the threat.

Anti-communism also clouded the Americans' judgement of the main Laotian personalities. I believe that they were wrong in regarding Souphanouvong as a committed communist working under the direction of Hanoi and Peking for a communist takeover of Laos. He was essentially a nationalist fighting to establish and maintain his country's independence, first from French colonialism and secondly from American imperialism which interfered so blatantly in Laos to impose a regime to its own liking. With his French education and wide culture he was temperamentally more disposed to the West than the East in the ideological struggle. His high intelligence and knowledgeable interest in economic matters also made him well aware that the substantial resources needed to overcome Laos's backwardness and poverty could only come from the West, and principally the USA. While he was in Vientiane in 1962/3 as deputy prime minister I never saw any sign of anti-Americanism. As I have recorded, he accepted invitations from the American Ambassador to receptions on 4 July and during the visit of the New York Woodwind Quintet, and also from other Americans such as the head of USAID. And when in Souvanna's absence he organized bridge parties at the prime minister's residence, he invited Americans along with other Western diplomats, but none from the communist bloc. He was certainly ambitious, and when he was a member of the coalition governments of 1957 and 1962 he would undoubtedly have hoped to succeed his half-brother as prime minister. If he had done so, I believe that he would have asserted Laos's independence and would not have taken orders from Vietnam, China, the Soviet Union or anyone else.

The Americans were equally mistaken in their view of Souvanna Phouma as a weak dilettante, whose policy of neutrality and conciliation with the Pathet Lao would facilitate a communist takeover. Such a view was the inevitable consequence of the Dulles doctrine that 'he that is not with me is against me'. The Americans believed that Souvanna was a weak character because he was pursuing policies they regarded as weak. (I am reminded of the Foreign Office habit, in the reverse situation, of using the word 'robust' to describe a president, prime minister or foreign minister who agrees with and supports

British policy.) Souvanna in fact showed remarkable toughness and tenacity in pursuing his policies over the years in the face of great difficulties and often personal discomfort, when he always had the agreeable alternative of retiring to Paris. He was a proud Laotian patriot who believed, rightly in the opinion of most informed observers, that conciliation and neutrality were the only ways of ensuring Laos's integrity and independence. As I have shown earlier, he had no personal sympathy with communism; and he shared the fear and mistrust most Lao felt towards North Vietnam. When from 1963 onwards it became apparent that the Pathet Lao were sabotaging the Geneva Agreement because they were now controlled by North Vietnam, he became outspokenly critical of the North Vietnamese and supportive of American policy in Vietnam. Paradoxically, after devoting so much effort to removing Souvanna from office and trying to prevent his return, the Americans ended up supporting him for over a decade as the best prime minister from their point of view. But by then it was too late to save Laos.

The most obvious American misjudgement was to regard Kong Lae as a communist or at least a willing tool of the communists. It transpired that there was no evidence for this, merely an assumption that someone who carried out a coup against a right-wing government must be working for the communists. When Graham Parsons came to Vientiane in October 1960 he attended a lunch with the Western ambassadors at which he gave a presentation of American policy and of the assumptions on which it was based. John Addis argued cogently against the policy and asked for the evidence underpinning the assumptions, which included the belief that Kong Lae was a communist. Under close questioning Parsons admitted that they had no evidence and that they were working on the basis of 'hypothesis'. The fallacy of this hypothesis was amply demonstrated over the next few years when Kong Lae in the Plain of Jars maintained his loyalty to Souvanna Phouma and the separate identity of his forces in the face of intense pressure from the Pathet Lao.

Underlying all these mistaken judgements was a failure to understand the nature of anti-colonial nationalism. In the 1950s and 1960s, when most of the colonial territories achieved independence, many of the leaders of the nationalist movements had close links with socialism or communism. The reason was partly that in French universities and British institutions such as the London School of Economics, where many of the nationalist leaders were trained, the general ethos was distinctly left-wing; and partly that socialist and communist parties in France and elsewhere, including the British Labour Party, were sympathetic to the nationalists' demands for independence, whereas conservative parties tended to be less sympathetic if not actively hostile. Most of the nationalists also accepted aid in the form of money and training (and arms when there was a 'liberation struggle') from the Soviet Union, China and other communist states. This is hardly surprising, as there were few other sources of the aid they needed. Virtually all the Western countries were either colonial powers themselves or closely allied to the colonial powers, and therefore hardly likely to provide aid, and especially arms, to liberation movements.

However, accepting aid from the communist powers did not mean that the anti-colonialist leaders became communists. And even those who were sympathetic to communism were likely to suffer a change of heart once they had achieved their goal of independence. Having agitated for so long to get rid of colonial rule, they had no desire to submit to another form of foreign domination and accept orders from the Soviet Union or China. Those who were concerned to promote their country's economic development soon realized that the essential external help was more likely to come from the West than the East, and adjusted their policies accordingly.

Lee Kuan Yew in Singapore was perhaps an extreme example of this tendency. He had been the leading agitator for independence, and he and his People's Action Party, supported by communist-led trade unions, were regarded as dangerously left wing. I was there in 1959 when the PAP won the elections leading to self-government and I recall the colonial establishment's alarm and gloomy view of the future. Yet once full independence was achieved Lee Kuan Yew's true colours were soon revealed. Under the aegis of a generally benevolent dictatorship, he imprisoned communist union leaders and established full-blown capitalism, which together with a strictly enforced social discipline transformed the small island into one of the most prosperous countries in the world.

Conditions in Indo-China were of course very different. Ho Chi Minh was certainly a communist, but people who know Vietnam better than I do have described him as a nationalist first and a communist second. His aim was to recover his country's independence rather than to extend the world communist empire. Though fruitless, it is interesting to speculate on what might have happened if the 1954 Geneva Agreement had been fully implemented and nationwide elections held in Vietnam, leading to the expected victory of the Viet Minh. The American hypothesis would have been that Ho Chi Minh, in obedience to his Russian/Chinese masters and as part of the world communist conspiracy, would have set about subverting and perhaps invading his neighbours Cambodia and Laos. But an alternative and perhaps more plausible hypothesis is that Ho Chi Minh, having achieved his goal in Vietnam, would have concentrated on, and been fully occupied with, the tasks of unifying his country and developing its economy. In other words he would have been more likely to develop into a 'Tito' than a faithful satellite of Moscow or Peking (the latter always improbable in view of ancient fears and hostility between the two countries, which emerged into open warfare only two decades later). He would have had little incentive to expend energy and resources on subverting or conquering his neighbours, especially if Cambodia was in the hands of the neutralist Sihanouk, and Laos was governed by a neutralist-led coalition, including the Pathet Lao. And if, instead of squandering billions of dollars on the vain attempt to shore up the government of South Vietnam, the United States had offered a fraction of the money in economic aid to a united Vietnam, then the risk to the independence of Laos and Cambodia would have been further reduced.

In the actual circumstances of the early 1960s, the question of whether a neutralist-led coalition could ever have survived in Laos even with American support is debatable. The Americans did support Souvanna Phouma's coalition government after the Geneva Agreement of 1962, but by then it was too late. The Ho Chi Minh Trail was already in use and the Pathet Lao dependence on North Vietnam had become so complete that they were compelled to sabotage the Geneva Agreement by refusing access to their zone. The earlier opportunity for a peaceful settlement provided by Kong Lae's coup in

August 1960 may already have been too late — John Addis described
it as the last chance, which unfortunately was not taken. Thanks
partly to John Addis's advocacy but mainly to President Kennedy's
arrival at the White House, American policy did change to one of
support for neutralism. Continuing support for Phoumi by the CIA
and the Pentagon delayed the settlement for 15 more months until the
chances of success for the new policy had disappeared. But at least the
change of policy ensured that the Americans were in a stronger moral
position than they had been at the end of 1960. It also avoided the
disastrous consequences that would have ensued if they had continued
to pursue a military solution into 1961 and 1962, involving the commitment of US troops against the North Vietnamese in conditions
even less favourable than they encountered later in South Vietnam,
with the added risk of intervention by China.

   In retrospect, the last chance for a peaceful settlement in Laos may
have disappeared when the Americans sabotaged the Vientiane Agreements of 1957 and orchestrated the overthrow of Souvanna Phouma
in 1958. The Pathet Lao were then a much weaker force and, perhaps
more important, Souphanouvong was still its undisputed leader. If the
Americans had thrown their full weight behind the coalition and
provided substantial economic, rather than military, aid, then I believe
that Souphanouvong would have worked loyally with his half-brother
to integrate the Pathet Lao fully with the rest of the country. Also, as
an efficient and energetic Minister of the Plan, he could have ensured
that much of the aid was directed to the hitherto neglected hill tribes.
It is possible, even likely, that Kaysone, Nouhak and the tiny group of
dedicated communists within the Pathet Lao would have still tried to
undermine the settlement and work for a communist takeover. But
with the Pathet Lao well represented in the National Assembly and
the government, and with action being taken to improve the situation
of the hill peoples, they would have found little support in the body of
the Pathet Lao movement. In 1957 the coalition government would
have had several years to consolidate the integration of the country
before the renewal of the Vietnam War could begin to threaten the
Laotian peace. And of course if the neutralist solution had worked in
Laos it might have influenced American policy in Vietnam. But this
may be carrying speculation too far.

Returning to reality with a bump I have to temper this critique of American policy by admitting that in the second half of the 1950s the British Embassy in Vientiane and the FO, with some misgivings, went along in general with American policy, although the French did not. Individual views varied. The young Richard Parsons, acting as chargé d'affaires around the time of the Vientiane Agreements, wrote of Souphanouvong in terms that John Addis or I might have employed: 'It is not too sanguine to contemplate the possibility of Souphanouvong emerging as a full-blooded Asian nationalist, almost as independent of Hanoi and Peking as he is of Paris and Washington. He is very different from the usual communist instrument. How far he is a Marxist is controversial. But there is no doubt whatever of his being a prince.' Of Souvanna Phouma he wrote: 'If the State Department are shopping around for an alternative Prime Minister they are making a great mistake. It is impossible to think of any Laotian who could succeed him as Prime Minister with any comparable chance of holding the country together.' But the two ambassadors under whom Richard served took a more orthodox pro-American, anti-communist line. John Addis's predecessor in particular appeared to share the Americans' suspicions of Souvanna Phouma and hostility to Souphanouvong; and in his annual report for 1958, the year in which Souvanna's government was overthrown, he expressed the view that the situation had much improved compared with a year earlier.

So one lesson to be drawn is that the personality, abilities and views of an individual ambassador do matter. One is tempted to wonder what might have happened if John Addis had been sent out to Laos a few years earlier. One can assume that he would have argued forcefully the case for supporting Souvanna Phouma and the Vientiane Agreements. But it is unlikely that such arguments would have had any impact on John Foster Dulles and the almost fanatical anti-communist mood that pervaded Washington in the immediate post-McCarthy years. In these pages I have portrayed Graham Parsons as a true disciple of Dulles. But it is clear from the Foreign Office archives that the US Embassy under Parsons and his successor was regarded as a moderate influence restraining the 'wild men' of the Pentagon, the CIA and even the State Department, which itself was under constant pressure from Congress to maintain a rigid anti-communist line. And before I finish I should pay tribute to my colleagues in the American Embassy, dedicated and capable professionals who remained loyal to their government in the dark days of 1960 but seemed much happier when they lined up with their allies in support of neutralism. It was a pleasure working with them.

Well, it all happened a long time ago, and some people may think that it does not matter now. But it seemed to matter a great deal to us at the time. And it mattered much more to the hundreds of thousands killed or maimed in the bombing and the 'secret war' in Laos, not to mention the far greater casualties of the Vietnam War. Opposition to American policy in Southeast Asia at times appeared to threaten the internal cohesion of the United States itself; while the widespread disapproval the policy aroused in the rest of the world greatly damaged the prestige and influence of the United States and its Western allies, to the advantage of their communist adversaries in the Cold War. It is ironic that a policy aimed at preventing the spread of communism in Southeast Asia (and failing to do so) should have had as one of its results the reinforcing of the communist threat elsewhere in the world. So perhaps there are still lessons to be learned, for the present day and for the future: that even when the end seems to justify the means it is liable to be subverted by them; and that countries that claim to stand for democracy and civilized values need to apply these principles in the conduct of their affairs abroad as well as at home.

Index

Cambodia, 11–14, 18–20, 60, 99,
149, 155, 179, 209, 212, 216,
218–19, 224, 229, 233
Campbell, David, 60, 72, 77, 101,
125, 174
Canada, 19, 83, 175, 179
Cape, Donald, 217, 220, 222
CDNI (Committee for the Defence
of National Interests), 23, 27, 39
Chadbourn, Philip, 37, 91, 119
Champassac, 13, 15, 49; see also
Bassac
Chandler, Patricia, 90, 108
Chavane, 127, 148–50, 157, 162
China, 8, 10, 12; Nationalist, 23–4,
204; People's Republic of, 220,
223, 225, 228
Chinaimo, 59, 65
CIA, 27, 37, 49–50, 81, 86, 96,
116, 119, 185, 188, 206, 209,
219, 227, 234–5
Cooper, Brigadier Stewart, 89
Crosby, Colonel 'Bing', 38, 115
Czechoslovakia, 22, 228–9

Danny, 8–9, 30, 51, 70
Davies, Madeleine, 31, 63, 77
de Gaulle, General, 14
de la Patellière, Colonel Jean, 38
Decoux, Admiral, 14
Deuane, Lieutenant (later Colonel),
187, 191, 193, 202
Dobbs, Bernard, 220
Douglas-Home, Sir Alec, 81, 162,
200
Dulles, John Foster, 18–19, 22, 50,
230, 235

Eckarath, Major, 89
Eisenhower, Dwight, 80

Everard, Timothy, 175, 178

Fa Ngum, 11
Falaize, Pierre, 37, 51, 53, 76,
96–7, 171
Faydang, 16–17, 81, 221
Forsyth, Bill, 38
France, 13–15, 17, 19–20, 32, 34,
39–40, 53, 88, 90, 97, 164, 175,
182, 184, 216, 218, 222, 232
French Embassy, 67, 109

Gane, Barrie, 115, 167
Geneva conference on Indo-China
(1954), 18–19, 23–4, 28, 83,
94
Geneva conference on Laos
(1961–2), 79, 83–4, 94–5, 97,
102, 104, 116, 118, 157, 164,
172, 176, 178, 180, 183, 185,
187–8, 195, 200, 202–3, 206–7,
212, 231, 233
Geoffroy Dechaume, Jean-Pierre,
39, 80
Godley, Ambassador G.
McMurtrie, 209
Gore-Booth, Sir Paul, 110
Granger, Jacqueline, 115

Hammarskjöld, Dag, 26, 48
Han Suyin, 6, 179
Hanoi, 13, 23, 33, 60, 72, 74, 88,
98, 102, 147, 183–4, 191–2, 194,
201, 213, 230, 235
Harriman, Governor Averill, 83,
86, 97, 117, 119, 207
Hartland-Swann, Julian, 178
Herniman, Dr Dick, 34, 56, 68, 93,
223
Hmong, ix, 218; see also Meo